UNFOLDING LIVES

Youth, gender and change

Rachel Thomson

First published in Great Britain in 2011 by

The Policy Press
University of Bristol
Fourth Floor
Beacon House
Queen's Road
Bristol BS8 1QU, UK

Tel +44 (0)117 331 4054
Fax +44 (0)117 331 4093
e-mail tpp-info@bristol.ac.uk
www.policypress.org.uk

North American office:
The Policy Press
c/o International Specialized Books Services (ISBS)
920 NE 58th Avenue, Suite 300
Portland, OR 97213-3786, USA
Tel +1 503 287 3093
Fax +1 503 280 8832
e-mail info@isbs.com

British Library Cataloguing in Publication Data
A catalogue record for this book is available from the British Library.

Library of Congress Cataloging-in-Publication Data
A catalog record for this book has been requested.

ISBN 978 1 84742 902 5 paperback

Cover design by The Policy Press
Front cover: image kindly supplied by Ward Meremans
Printed and bound in Great Britain by Marston Book Services, Oxford

Contents

Preface   iv

Acknowledgements   viii

one   The breadth and depth of youth transitions   1

two   A method-in-practice: constructing longitudinal case histories   13

three   Gender and social change   29

four   Going up! Discipline and opportunism   45

five   Going down? Caught between stasis and mobility   67

six   Coming out: from the closet to stepping stones   89

seven   Acting out: rebellion with a cause   111

eight   Interruption: from explanation to understanding   133

nine   Conversation: reading between the lines   153

ten   Youth, gender and change   171

Appendix: The case history data sets   181

References   183

Index   195

Preface to the paperback edition

I am delighted that this book has made it into paperback and will be more accessible to a wider readership. This paperback edition also provides me with an opportunity for reflection. In the short time since this book was published, and the rather longer period since it was first written, there have been some important changes to the frame within which the work is situated, which I will address briefly in this preface touching on developments within the economy, youth policy and social theory.

The world has changed in a very concrete way, and the lives portrayed in this book, however modest or precarious, begin to look like they may be stories from a relatively 'lucky generation' who benefited from an investment in further and higher education during the years of the New Labour administration in the UK. The credit crunch of 2008 and the subsequent economic recession and change of government are linked to a thorough-going shift in British policy on youth. Perhaps most significantly, the lifting of a cap on student tuition fees and the ending of educational maintenance allowances aimed at helping low income young people stay in education effectively mark a shift away from state support for 'extended dependency' towards a greater reliance on the resources of families and individuals. This is not a response to a rejuvenation of a youth labour market and the view that young people have alternatives to education as a long slow route to independence. Instead it expresses the new official view that supporting young people is no longer a shared 'public' responsibility – a decision which, in the short term, will hit the lower middle classes or 'squeezed middle' hardest first, with what public resources there are aimed at the most disadvantaged – defined in increasingly narrow ways. In comparative terms, the UK has taken a decisive step towards a US model where life-chances are determined primarily by the market and away from a Northern European model in which life-chances are at least mediated by the state, offering all-comers the potential of modest social mobility through ordinary educational achievement. Nevertheless, the neoliberal shift of responsibility for education from the state to families and individuals is a global process, reshaping the local meaning of education as a form of cultural distinction in the process (Jeffrey and McDowell, 2004).

The young lives in this book unfolded during a sustained period of progressive social policy in the UK that involved investment in early years, childcare and youth services. Now we have entered a phase of small government in which inequalities are likely to grow exponentially, with informal and individualised strategies for defending and reproducing privilege undisturbed by progressive strategies for preventing social exclusion (National Equalities Panel, 2010; UK Women's Budget Group, 2010). Youth unemployment would now appear to be the norm of contemporary global capitalism, where the condition of 'waiting' for work, change and adulthood expands as a practical and existential state for young men in both majority and minority worlds (Roberts, 2009; Jeffrey, 2010).

Young women have become the productive subjects of the new world order, the focus of both national and international development strategies, flexible, motivated and socially mobile, regulated in McRobbie's terms by the post-feminist contract where the right to be recognised as female is traded for the right to be treated as a genderless worker (McRobbie, 2007). In this context motherhood operates as a moment of transition that involves profound meanings as well as systematic disenfranchisement, whether that be in the form of social exclusions associated with 'too early' young motherhood, or the economic and social penalties experienced by those who defer maternity for education and career (Thomson et al, 2011).

In theoretical terms the landscape has also shifted since the publication of *Unfolding lives*, with a surge of interest in temporality and the processual. In terms of social policy this has been expressed through the lens of generation, with a particular focus on the historic specificity of the privileges of the baby boomer generation, and a growing realisation of how the welfare state underpins increasingly fragile expectations of what constitutes the stages and sequence of a normal life course. Changes to pension provision, university funding and the care of the elderly are not simply experienced as political changes, but as destabilising our sense of a good or sustainable life. Increasingly we find a consumer model of individual choice superseded by a relational model of interdependency as families seek to balance the competing needs and claims of different generations, seeking collective solutions to individual problems of social mobility and survival (Beckett, 2010; Howker and Malik, 2010; Willetts, 2010).

Within social theory there has also been a shift towards a temporal mode of analysis, with interest in ideas of process, becoming and change that escape the developmentalism of child and adolescent psychology. Often influenced by the philosophy of Deleuze these theoretical tendencies encourage us to think about dynamic processes that are neither contained by ideas of destination – for example the transition to adulthood – nor by the assumption of norms, with repetition and difference no longer understood as mutually exclusive. The new questions are not primarily concerned with tracing 'normal' and 'deviant' pathways but instead involve an empirical tracing of dynamic processes in order to explore what might flow through them. This is also a post-humanist turn in social theory, with people and populations forming assemblages with policies, markets, material culture and virtual landscapes (Wetherell, 2012, forthcoming). Within childhood and youth studies this turn has been associated with a shift in interest from children as 'beings' (associated with the 'new sociology of childhood') towards processes of 'becoming', including new perspectives on the dynamism and effervescence of young people's bodies and relationships as sites of cultural, biological and economic exchange (Coleman, 2009; Jackson, 2010). In gender studies similar processes are in play, associated with a shift away from political questions about 'progress', 'recognition' and 'equity' towards an interest in processes that connect and animate the relationship between material, virtual and embodied phenomena (Grosz, 2005; Ringrose, 2011).

When I began work on *Unfolding lives* I struggled to find theoretical frameworks that allowed me to privilege processes of change in the way demanded by my longitudinal qualitative methodology. My frustrations with the highly static nature of many of the available theoretical tools drove me to read generously and to identify those aspects of familiar tools with the most potential for conceptualising dynamic phenomena. In that sense the book bridges two eras – the late modern theoretical landscape characterised by a dialogue between biographical instability and the remaking of inequalities, and the landscape of post-humanism characterised by a turn to affect, that is also a turn away from the discursive and the biographical. In a recent conversation the US ethnographer of childhood Barrie Thorne explained to me that she was relieved that her landmark book *Gender play* (Thorne, 1993) had taken so long to write, suggesting that she had been unknowingly 'waiting' for post structural theory to arrive in order to make sense of her data. In one sense I feel that I wrote *Unfolding lives* before the Deleuzian turn had fully turn had penetrated my corner of British sociology. On reflection I am glad of that. Certainly, the new theoretical fashions fit well with my data, yet I believe that there are also important losses associated with this recent move – perhaps most importantly in terms of the extent to which sociology can be expected to build bridges between lives as recognisably lived and the arenas of social policy and politics.

What researchers conceptualise as the 'context' of their empirical work is a moveable feast, involving changing policies, theories and technologies and well as the biographies of those involved – researchers and participants. Longitudinal research requires us to take this dynamism as the object of our study, and the qualitative paradigm demands that we take seriously the process through which meanings are made and remade through changing configurations of agents and resources (McLeod and Thomson, 2009). As this book goes into its second edition we are engaging again with the participants of the Inventing Adulthoods study, revisiting those who grew up in Northern Ireland in order to the coincidence of their coming of age and the 'Peace Process' (McGrellis, 2011). Where our sample as a whlole may be characterised retrospectively as 'lucky', these young people appear to fall between generational cohorts – formed by a culture of poltical violence and sectarianism, and struggling to find a place within an environment that seeks to move beyond these legacies. As time passes and we gain perspective on the past, new research questions arise enabling us to look again and re-contextualise a rich and powerful data set. The Inventing Adulthoods study is now available for secondary analysis[1] and we hope that this book will be one of a growing number of commentaries inspired by this rich resource.

Rachel Thomson, London 2011

---

[1] The Inventing Adulthoods data set is deposited at the UK data archive at Essex University. An accessible digital showcase for the archive can be accessed at www.lsbu.ac.uk/inventingadulthoods.

—

References

Beckett, F. (2010) *What did the baby boomers ever do for us?* London: Biteback Books.

Coleman, R. (2009) *The becoming of bodies: Girls, images, experience*, Manchester: Manchester University Press

Grosz, E. (2005) *Time travels: Feminism, nature and power*, Durham, NV: Duke University Press.

Howker, E. and Malik, S. (2010) *Jilted generation: How Britain bankrupted its youth*, London: Icon Books.

Jackson, A.Y. (2010) 'Deleuze and the girl', *International Journal of Qualitative Studies in Education*, vol 23, no 5, pp 579-87.

Jeffrey, C. (2010) *Timepass: Waiting, micropolitics and the Indian middle classes*, Palo Alto, CA: Standford University Press.

Jeffrey, C. and McDowell, L. (2004) 'Youth in a comparative perspective: global change, local lives', *Youth & Society*, vol 36, pp 131-42.

McLeod, J. and Thomson, R. (2009) *Researching social change: Qualitative approaches*, London: Sage.

McGrellis, S. (2011) *Growing up in Northern Ireland: Final report*, York: Joseph Rowntree Foundation.

McRobbie, A. (2007) 'Top girls?: young women and the post-feminist sexual contract', *Cultural Studies*, vol 21, nos 4-5, pp 718–37.

National Equalities Panel (2010) *An anatomy of economic inequality in the UK: Report of the National Equalities Panel*, London: CASE [http://sticerd.lse.ac.uk/dps/case/cr/CASEreport60.pdf]

Ringrose, J. (2011) 'Are you sexy, flirty or a slut? Exploring "sexualisation" and how teen girls perform/negotiate digital sexual identity on social networking sites', in R. Gill and C. Scharff (eds) New femininities: Postfeminism, neoliberalism and identity, Basingstoke: Palgrave.

Roberts, K. (2009) *Youth in transition: Eastern Europe and the West*, Basingstoke: Palgrave.

Thomson, R., Kehily, M.J., Hadfield, L. and Sharpe, S. (2011) *Making modern mothers*, Bristol: The Policy Press.

Thorne, B. (1993) *Gender play: Girls and boys in school*, Piscataway, NJ: Rutgers University Press.

UK Women's Budget Group (2010) *The impact on women of the Coalition's spending review 2010* [http://www.wbg.org.uk/RRB_Reports_4_1653541019.pdf]

Wetherell, M. (2012, forthcoming) *Affecting discourse: Investigating the psychosocial*, London: Sage.

Willetts, D. (2010) *The pinch: How the baby boomers took their children's future – and how they can give it back*, London: Atlantic Books.

Acknowledgements

Thanks to Janet Holland and Rosalind Edwards for long-term support and advice, to Jeffrey Weeks and Beverley Skeggs for their encouragement to publish and to Alison Shaw at The Policy Press for her patience. This endeavour was made possible by Sheena McGrellis and Sue Sharpe, who generously shared their interviews, and the young people who shared their lives – I hope to have done you justice. Gerry Bernbaum gave me a day a week to do this work and Rebecca Taylor gave me cover – thank you both. I have had the benefit of three readers, one anonymous and two dear friends – Mary Jane Kehily and Brian Heaphy. Finally, I acknowledge Sean, whose support and care makes these things possible, and Isaac, who has taught me so much about change.

> Can one tell – that is to say, narrate – time, time itself, as such, for its own sake? That surely would be an absurd undertaking. (Thomas Mann, *The Magic Mountain*)

ONE

The breadth and depth of youth transitions

In 1996, with a group of colleagues, I began what was to become a 10-year longitudinal study following a generation of young people making the transition to adulthood. The research began in secondary schools in five contrasting areas within the UK, reflecting the very different environments and opportunities that shape young people's destinies. When we first met them, the young people were aged between 11 and 16. The last time we interviewed them, in 2006, they were all in their twenties.

The Inventing Adulthoods study has generated a unique record of the lives and times of a generation of young people who came of age at the turn of the millennium. They are a generation shaped by an explosion in new communications technologies, the expansion of higher education, the 'extension' of youth from the teens through the twenties. Yet they are also a less socially mobile generation than those who have come before them, for whom old forms of inequalities are remade in new kinds of ways. And while they may speak a 'can do' language, in practice many struggle to achieve the forms of autonomy, independence and integrity traditionally associated with adulthood in the West.

The research team responsible for this study has realised this extraordinary data set in a range of ways, including a series of journal articles,[1] a book summarising the key findings of the studies (Henderson et al, 2007), teaching materials (Kehily, 2007) and the creation of a digital archive enabling others to work with the data set.[2] We have also collaborated with other researchers to share our data, providing insights for example about how young people experience bereavement (Ribbens McCarthy, 2006). The Inventing Adulthoods study offers a broad perspective on contemporary youth transitions, following 100 young lives in five distinct localities shaped by their own economies, traditions and dynamics. Yet it also offers extraordinary depth, with up to six research encounters with each young person conducted over the teenage years – providing a document of transitions through puberty, leaving school and home and into adulthood.

In this book I realise the *depth* of the project, focusing on examples that are emblematic of the kinds of situations that young people find and make, and the responses and pathways that are available to them. In presenting the way in which four young people's lives unfold over a period of several years I show how a singular life is forged from a range of possible destinies. It is my view that these kinds of in-depth longitudinal case histories can provide a different kind of insight than we are used to in social science and social policy research. Life chances may be constrained, yet choices and events are not determined – something captured in words such as 'coincidence' and 'serendipity'. It is never possible to map the route that a person's life will take, even though in retrospect we can see logic – even a sense of inevitability. This book is an exercise in story telling, of attending to the detail of a life as lived, problems faced, legacies realised and escaped. It tells stories of people, yet these are also stories about places, about a wider culture and an era.

Although I do not explicitly seek to generalise about the youth of today or the impact of particular policies on their transitions to adulthood, I do propose insights that go beyond the four cases, pointing to the interplay of personal, social and historical processes. The transformation of what it means to be a man or a woman may be the most profound of the many changes that have characterised the post-war period. Sociological accounts of detraditionalisation and individualisation suggest that we no longer have blueprints of what it means to be a typical girl or boy. It is argued that the very meaning of intimacy has undergone a revolution, with commitments negotiated on a rolling programme rather than in relation to notions of duty and obligation. *Unfolding lives* addresses the question of how gender identities are made within late modern culture, exploring both the constraints that shape these possibilities and the consequences of choices made, strategies pursued and compromises struck. The 'case histories' provide a medium for understanding how gender identities work with and through social class, ethnicity, locality and sexuality – vividly bringing into view the significance of intergenerational obligations, more and less conscious emotional attachments and processes of upward and downward social mobility. The unfolding accounts revealed by the case history method provide a fresh perspective on the relationship between personal agency, family history and social structure – in which tradition and innovation are not alternatives but, rather, operate in conversation. I show the way in which experimentation is an inescapable part of young people's experiences and the extent to which they must invent in order to maintain continuity with the past and with those who give their lives meaning.

The book is also about methods, and the way in which researching lives as they unfold reveals temporal processes. Longitudinal research is one of a family of methods suited to the investigation of social change, alongside memory work, life history, ethnography, intergenerational and revisiting studies (McLeod and Thomson, 2009). A characteristic of these approaches is the impossibility of separating the research process and the data record. This means refusing the conventions of sociological genres that gloss over the messy business of real–life research, the collisions between data collection and analysis, the provisionality of interpretation and the presumption and closures involved in writing. One of my objectives is to reveal the process through which the data on which this book is based was generated, analysed and represented. This is realised through the formal structure of the book and, in keeping with the overall tone, is achieved through a process of revelation rather than explication. It is my hope that the result is accessible – with the young people's stories speaking directly to readers and resonating with what they know as well as with what they did not realise that they knew. The way in which it is read and interpreted may change over time and with different readerships.

I also hope that, in a subtle yet serious way, the book provides a challenge to established forms of sociological account: showing the importance of depth, duration and changing perspective to the ways in which we understand the world around us and what become framed as 'social problems'. It may seem that this approach is a long way from the evidence-based culture of social policy research that dominates the contemporary agenda, yet there is a growing sense that policy makers urgently need understandings of processes, decision making and the relationship between aspirations and the lives that are lived (Corden and Millar, 2007). There is more than one route to generalisation, and by engaging in the detail of four contrasting lives I will capture something of the character and feel of contemporary youth that goes beyond and beneath what is possible when working on a larger canvas. This book joins an honourable tradition within the social sciences in which a focus on the *particular* enables insight into the complex interaction between psychological and social factors, over time. It is an approach in which depth rather than breadth provides a route towards generalisation, giving rise to a generative understanding of social change in which agency, timing and the ghosts of possible destinies are all very much in play (Bertaux and Bertaux-Wiame, 1997/2003).

Inventing adulthood in uncertain times

Technology is a sensitive barometer of social change. The 10-year period over which the Inventing Adulthoods study took place witnessed a revolution in personalised information communication technology. When my colleagues and I began fieldwork with young people in 1997, only a few had mobile telephones, and these were a status symbol. A year later, more had them and everyone was talking about them. Girls described new forms of freedom and privacy that the phones made possible. Boys were more likely to complain about the losses that were associated with being contactable, experiencing the surveillance of parents and friends (Henderson et al, 2003). This was also a time of moral panic, with reports of phone-related stories filling the newspapers, including 'happy slapping', cancer scares, exam cheating and muggings. By the end of the study in 2006, no one had much to say about mobile phones – because they had become a necessity, integrated into everyday life and enabling new patterns of sociality based around the individual to emerge. Over the same period the internet has shifted from an adult-centred, work-related technology to the epicentre of youthful sociality, consumption and cultural production.

Karl Mannheim, the sociologist of generation, argued that in periods of stability the relations between generations are characterised by 'piety', with the young aping the style and character of their elders. In periods of rapid social change this relationship is reversed: youth is valorised and imitated by the old, who fear being left behind. The contemporary period is one in which youth (if not the young) is desired by all. Technological change has been the driving force of economic and cultural globalisation that has transformed the national economy, providing a new landscape for the transition to adulthood. By and large, young people face the task of creating lives that are very different from those of their parents. At the centre of this transformation is the effective disappearance of the youth labour market. It is no longer possible to leave school at 16, to find work and to begin the process of building an independent life. The impact of this change is most explicit in the lives of working-class young people, who must navigate either a new pathway into higher education and training or the challenge of economic dependency on family or dwindling state benefits. The expansion of higher education has also impacted on the middle classes, for whom privilege must be secured in new ways. As universities open up to non-traditional students, there is a corresponding inflation in what it takes to succeed, with the spectre of downward social mobility becoming a powerful presence in the middle-class psyche.

The norm is now to stay in education post 16, and the sequence of transition is no longer to leave school, enter work and establish an independent home, partnership and family in quick succession. The markers of transition are increasingly fragmented, and youth transitions are more starkly shaped by social class in the UK than many other European economies (Bynner, 2001; Holdsworth, 2004). Whatever their background, the contemporary generational struggle is to find ways in which to feel autonomous while also negotiating the extended forms of dependency that are a feature of the landscape. What it means to be grown-up is contested. Certain forms of experience are framed within policy terms as growing up too quickly – teenage parenthood, homelessness and involvement in criminal careers. Yet cultural manifestations of extended youth are also problematised – such as the growth of a binge-drinking culture – as young adults who are unable to secure mortgages or to afford to start families spend what disposable income they have on partying (Hollands, 1995; Jones and Martin, 1999). Securing the future of your children is increasingly recognised as a family project, placing new financial and emotional demands on parents and seriously disadvantaging those without familial support (Jones et al, 2006).

Within this changing landscape there are winners and losers. Young women's employment prospects and incomes improved over the 1980s, partly due to their increased participation in higher education (Crompton, 1992, 1997). Yet there was also a polarisation of life chances along class lines during this period, giving rise to the emergence of a group of relatively disadvantaged young men, and a growing gap between the prospects of young female manual workers and professionals (Egerton and Savage, 2000: 46). The picture is also complicated by ethnicity, with minorities producing a greater proportion of applications and admissions to higher education than in the rest of the population (Modood and Acland, 1998), and with young women performing significantly better than young men in Caribbean and black African groups (Platt, 2005).

One hundred lives over 10 years

The 100 young lives that constitute the Inventing Adulthoods study were diverse, reflecting the kinds of social divisions and inequalities that are a feature of contemporary British society. Over the 10 years, the young people followed a variety of routes to adulthood. At the end of the study we concluded that it is no longer possible to talk in terms of standard youth transitions, and that the ways in which young people seek to feel grown-up reflect the resources that are available to them and the kind of recognition that they receive from others. We attempted to synthesise this complex data set in two ways. First, we explored the key areas of social policy interest, including education, work and well-being. Second, we identified and explored the biographical themes that had the most salience for young people themselves: mobility and belonging, home and intimacy. Here I summarise these findings in order to contextualise the four lives explored in detail in the book.

Education

In 1954 just 6% of the British population went to university. By 2010 the UK government aims that 50% of young people will participate in higher education. This dramatic expansion initially privileged the middle class and girls, yet is increasingly impacting on working-class young people, who are often the first generation in their family to go to university. Those who pursue higher education are faced with extended dependency on parents who may not understand or be able to support them. High levels of part-time work and juggling of responsibilities characterised these young people's accounts, and most contend with competing ideas of success – the immediate gratification of wages, fun and romance could make the long educational haul very hard. Some also struggled with the pursuit of a path that would take them on a journey of social mobility that undermined their sense of belonging to family and neighbourhood. Studies of trends in educational achievement suggest that girls outperform boys, and minority ethnic groups outperform the majority white population. Due largely to bullying, lesbian and gay young people, whatever their social class location, tend to leave education early in order to gravitate to more cosmopolitan environments (MacNamee et al, 2003). In the Inventing Adulthoods study it was working-class young women who were most likely to be breaking into higher education, and in the inner city site these young women were often from minority ethnic families and drew on considerable moral support in the pursuit of personal and family self-improvement. For middle-class young people of both genders, further and higher education was taken for granted, although there was widespread fear as to the consequences of educational failure. The pressure to excel could produce high levels of anxiety and was associated with mental health problems for some young people. Those in the middle class who dropped out of education tended to be young men and pursued alternative careers, often in music, the media or skilled manual work. Working-class young men and women out of education tended to move between low-paid work, training and unemployment, sometimes being drawn into competing black market 'careers' or early parenthood.

Work

The effective disappearance of the youth labour market means that full-time employment with prospects is not a realistic option for most school leavers. Nevertheless, many continue to be involved in paid employment alongside their studies and as a way of generating money, experience, friends/contacts and fun. Labour markets are local and the amount and kind of work engaged in by the young people in the study varied according to area and age. Comparatively high levels of middle-class young people had part-time and holiday jobs, yet these were often dropped in order to make way for exams and revision. Work experience was also more likely to be undertaken in such a way as to strengthen a developing CV, linked to possible university specialisms. The relative costs and benefits of pursuing education, training or employment were not clear to many young people, and their decisions were contingent on a shifting set of factors. For working-class young people the desire to contribute financially to family budgets and to have money in the here-and-now could be powerful. In many cases these young people dropped out of education in order to pursue work full time, yet such jobs tended to be low paid and insecure. Several young people returned to an educational pathway after several years in such employment. Yet work was also an important space within which young people experienced themselves as adult, enjoying responsibility and recognition as 'workers', providing a new space separate from home, school and neighbourhood for exploring an emergent sense of self.

Well-being

Risks to young people's well-being are shaped by a range of factors, including the kinds of neighbourhoods within which they live, poverty, the pressures of family life and the different kinds of support offered by families. Although young people are regularly portrayed as a source of antisocial behaviour, in practice they are more at risk of violent crime, assault and robbery than older people (Nicholas et al, 2005). In the Inventing Adulthoods study the Northern Irish city and the Northern estate were characterised by a culture of violence, with higher levels of domestic and street violence, and young people living in these places were more likely to consider revenge and fighting as normal activities. In both places, the spaces of the neighbourhood were territorialised, and young women moved more freely across symbolic divides than young men, whose identities tended to be bound more closely to local and family affiliations (McGrellis, 2005a, 2005b). Urban localities were also associated with criminal (and in Northern Ireland, paramilitary) gang culture, a direct or indirect feature in many young people's lives.

Drinking and drug taking are ubiquitous features of teenage life, and were found in each of the research sites, although shaped in large part by the particular leisure landscapes of the environment. Although drugs might be more readily available in urban environments, accounts of drug taking and drinking to excess were more central to the accounts of suburban and rural young people (Henderson, 2005). While most young people experiment for periods with losing control, some became 'stuck' in drinking and drug-taking patterns. In the Inventing Adulthoods study it tended to be middle-class young men who had rejected a respectable educational route who had integrated drug taking into their everyday lives. A perceived rise in psychological disorders among young people has been linked to late-modern uncertainty arising from the possibilities, choices and decisions associated with the extension of education, financial pressures on students, extended unemployment and insecure parenting (Rutter and Smith, 1995; West and Sweeting, 1996; Furlong and Cartmel 1997/2006). The ways that young people cope with challenging events depend on the resources that they have available to them, which include their dispositions, family support, material resources and social networks through which to seek help. Among the middle-class young people in the study it was the nature of family relationships and the demands of educational achievement that were most associated with emotional problems. Ill-health, bereavement, depression and mental illness were more prevalent in the accounts of young people in the more disadvantaged sites within the Inventing Adulthoods study, and the cultures of violence within these places could be both a cause and an outcome of ill-being.

Mobility and belonging

When we considered the transition to adulthood from young people's own perspectives, some other themes emerged, themes that spoke directly to the subjective experience of gaining autonomy and responsibility. Those living in more rural areas often relied heavily on parents for transport, and having one's own wheels was a central marker of becoming adult – whether that be a bicycle, moped, motorbike or car. In more urban environments, with better public transport, learning to drive was less likely to be a marker of adulthood, yet the ability to negotiate the physical environment safely and to move beyond the neighbourhood to the wider city or town was an important marker of change. As young people faced higher education the dilemma of studying away or staying local became increasingly significant. Some places were easier to leave than others (for example the rural area and the leafy suburb), and where geographical mobility was entangled with social mobility questions of loyalty and allegiance were central to young people's deliberations (Jones, 1999; Jamieson, 2000). Travel abroad – in terms of holidays, gap years or visits to the ancestral 'home' – were also important markers of adulthood, and 'other' places were central to the way in which young people negotiated between notions of localism and cosmopolitanism and the dilemmas as to whether you have to 'get out' in order to 'get on' (Thomson and

Taylor, 2005). While middle-class young people tended to 'collect places' and the new social networks that they made available, working-class young people were more tied to localities and were wary of isolating themselves from the support of family and friends. A sense of belonging was central to young people's identities, and such belonging could be fixed on locality. It might also be more mobile, through investments in a family project, in a religious identity or an affiliation to a particular community of choice.

Home and intimacy

The 'home' was at the centre of the experiences of all the young people in the Inventing Adulthood study, however disrupted this home might be. The task of securing an independent home is perhaps the most challenging goal of the transition to adulthood, as extended dependency forces young people into long-term reliance on the uneven and sometimes unreliable resources of parents (Heath and Cleaver, 2003; Holdsworth and Morgan, 2005). Where the parental home was disrupted by divorce, conflict and economic turbulence young people could experience acute vulnerability and sometimes homelessness. Young people often played a central role in maintaining families, providing domestic labour and financial support. Where families were strong, supportive and flexible they made an enormous difference to young people's abilities to pursue long-term educational projects. The kinds of couple relationships that young people invested in existed in conversation with family resources. Young people were more likely to invest in intense couple relationships where families were unstable. Strong families provided young people with the space to take a more experimental and instrumental approach to intimate relationships, prioritising their own needs over those of the couple. Becoming a young parent was one way in which young people could access forms of responsibility and recognition associated with adult status, yet doing so generally confirmed economic dependence, even if it might also galvanise ambitions for the future. Accepting obligations for the care of others was an important aspect of adult identity for many young people, especially working-class young women, and could come into conflict with the pursuit of more individual goals. Young people recognised the ways in which a couple relationship could jeopardise their individual chances, yet sometimes relied on such relationships to provide them with emotional and psychological security. Nearly all the young people in the study felt that adulthood is only truly achieved when one is settled in a home and a relationship and accepts responsibility for the care and support of others.

Biographical challenges and emergent forms

Each of the young lives that make up the Inventing Adulthoods study is unique, yet they are patterned in systematic ways by location, common values, comparable resources and shared experience. Growing up poor in multicultural inner-city

London gives rise to certain identities and responses, which are very different from those found among teenagers growing up affluent in the suburbs or isolated in the country. Following Mannheim (1952), these distinct youth cultures can be understood as generational 'units' – reflecting shared social locations, values and affinities of responses – and which together constitute a heterogeneous historical generation. As a generation, young people are faced with challenges that arise from the material and social conditions that define their era. For the Inventing Adulthoods cohort these include:

- managing extended dependency on parents and family resources;
- creating new life patterns demanded by the expansion of higher education;
- balancing autonomy and dependence as adult status is acquired in a piecemeal way;
- maintaining a sense of belonging and security against the demand to expose the self to risks and new experiences;
- negotiating the demands of deferred gratification against the acquisition of resources and recognition within the present.

These challenges were present within all the young people's lives within the study. Yet their responses were situated, shaped by the dynamics of family lives, the intergenerational trajectory of family projects and the intersection of social class, ethnicity, gender and sexuality.

As a field, youth studies has struggled to find ways of expressing the relationship between trends or patterns in youth transitions and the character of particular youth cultures (Cohen and Ainley, 2000). A recent development has been to use large data sets in order to create typologies of youth transitions and associated biographical forms – ideal types, or typical lives that capture and caricature the values and practices of groups following similar trajectories. Examples include distinctions between slow and fast transitions (Bynner, 2001), normal and choice biographies (Du Bois Reymond, 1998; Dwyer and Wyn 2003) and biographies characterised by different orientations towards time and the future (Brannen and Nilsen, 2002). An alternative approach has been to document the cultural life of distinct groups of young people or subcultures, capturing what is particular about their collective lives and how this speaks to wider social and historical processes such as deindustrialisation, individualisation and globalisation (Hollands, 1995; Back, 1996; Alexander, 2000; Nayak and Kehily, 2008). Rather than suggesting biographical typologies, this work tends to focus on relationships with peers and situated cultural practices, commenting on how the lives of particular groups can be understood as exemplifying specific social processes. The approach that I adopt in this book does not fit neatly into either of these traditions – focusing on individuals rather than peer groups and on case histories rather than an aggregate of cases. Yet I aim to speak to both traditions through a focus on biographical form, cultural resource and the particular as a route into generalisation.

The young lives that I have chosen for this book each point to a hotspot in contemporary youth transitions: emergent biographical forms shaped by an affinity of responses to the challenges arising from the material and social conditions that define the contemporary era. These hotspots have attracted the attention of youth researchers, and have incited popular representation through narratives of the educational success of black girls (Mirza, 1992, 1997, 2008), the downward social mobility of the new middle class (Dwyer and Wyn, 2003), young women making gender trouble (Aapola et al, 2004; Nayak and Kehily, 2008), and the 'mainstreaming' of gay lives (Roseneil, 1999; Weeks, 2007). The cases enable me to engage with existing literatures and to illustrate how generational challenges play out over time within individual lives, reflecting the experiences of generational units in relation to contrasting social locations. The cases are both typical and unusual. Typical in that each reflects a pattern within the broader data; unusual in that my choice of particular lives has been guided by the quality of the data and my personal response to it.

Outline of the book

Unfolding lives uses four in-depth case histories to explore emergent biographical patterns in youth transitions as well as provide a demonstration of an innovative method-in-practice. The book begins with a discussion of methodology, outlining the value of biographical and longitudinal approaches and explaining how case histories can be forged from the data archive of repeat in-depth interviews. This is followed in Chapter Three by an extended discussion of the theoretical lens through which the case histories are realised – an examination of gender and social change, including the theoretical claims of detraditionalisation and reflections on how this current generation of young people may be expressing the changes that are claimed. The four case histories are then presented in Chapters Four to Eight. First onto the stage is Sherleen, second-generation British of African Caribbean descent, the only child of a single mother, growing up in an urban environment. In social policy terms, Sherleen would be understood as 'achieving against the odds' and her story provides insights into some of the intimate and familial processes involved in the educational success of young black British women. Chapter Five introduces Stan, a middle-class, young white man growing up in the affluent commuter belt but struggling for a sense of purpose. This portrait focuses on his 'experiments' with consumption, religion and work, providing insight into the identity work that is necessary for the new middle class to maintain social privilege. In Chapter Six we meet Devon, a white, working-class city dweller whose late childhood is characterised by family violence and homophobic bullying. Devon negotiates a series of risks and exclusions, eventually learning to become a confident and competent gay man. As with many gay teenagers, this is achieved at the expense of completing his education. Chapter Seven tells the story of Karin, a Northern Irish Protestant girl, raging against the prejudices of her community and investing her time and creativity into youth cultural rebellion. Karin is typical of a new generation of upwardly mobile girls, acting out and entering higher education. Her story illustrates the costs of social and geographical mobility as well as the way in which rebellions can be employed in the service of continuity.

In Chapter Eight the temporal character of the research process is made explicit, with the introduction of further interview accounts from both Devon and Sherleen. These 'interruptions' provide insight into the twists and turns that lives can take, and the importance of keeping on looking. Chapter Nine explores how it might be possible to move from an analysis of individual cases to an understanding of wider social processes. The four case histories are placed in conversation and interrogated from two directions. The first privileges a longitudinal and narrative reading of the data; the second privileges a focus on social and spatial features. In Chapter Ten theoretical, methodological and empirical themes are brought together in an exploration of the ways in which reflexivity and agency operate within the four young lives. In this final chapter I question the opposition of tradition and innovation that is so central to late-modern debates about agency and social change, and the argument is made that longitudinal biographical methods can enable us to understand continuity and change as existing in a necessary and productive dynamic.

I am conscious that this book may be read by different audiences for different reasons. Those interested in the lives of young people may approach it as a source of insight into contemporary youth transitions. They may find both more and less than they expected, with breadth sacrificed for depth, yet enabling insights into the unfolding and serendipitous character of personal change. Others may be interested in the methods and the book as an exemplar of a particular approach to the analysis and presentation of qualitative longitudinal data. A third audience may be drawn in by the theoretical flavour of the work, the focus on identities-in-making, intimacies, relationalities and detraditionalisation. I hope that this audience is convinced by the value of an empirical approach that can capture flux and duration, encouraging the development of less-static theoretical tools. But perhaps most exciting of all is the unanticipated audience, whose interest and perspective I have not imagined, and who may come to this text some time in the future, with needs, questions and insights shaped by another time and place.

Notes

[1] Thomson and Holland, 2002, 2003a; Thomson et al, 2002, 2004; McGrellis 2005a, 2005b; Holland and Thomson, 2009.

[2] The archive is accessible at www.lsbu.ac.uk/inventingadulthoods.

TWO

A method-in-practice: constructing longitudinal case histories

One of the aims of this book is to outline a method-in-practice, to show how it is possible to construct in-depth case histories from a qualitative longitudinal archive. This chapter introduces the field of biographical methods, formulating some of the challenges of working with repeat interviews, and explores the boundaries between primary and secondary analysis that are a feature of longitudinal research. It then outlines the design of the original Inventing Adulthoods study, before describing and evaluating the analytic strategies employed in producing the case histories presented in Chapters Four to Seven.

Biographical methods

There has been a resurgence of interest in biographical methods, reflected in the publication of several volumes that seek to map the field (Chamberlayne et al, 2000; Miller, 2000; Plummer, 2001; Roberts, 2002). In each, the authors or editors refer to a 'biographical turn', commenting on the movement of such methods from the margins towards the centre in social science, paralleling the process through which the examination of the self has become a key feature of the modern world and of social policy and practice.

The terms 'biographical methods' and 'life-history research' encompass a wide range of approaches, defined most simply through a common methodological starting point – the collection and analysis of biographical or autobiographical accounts. This includes a number of research traditions, often with distinct aims, fields and methods of enquiry. Several attempts have been made to formalise these differences – for example Miller (2000) suggests a typology of realist, neo-positivist and narrative positions, yet admits that most researchers take elements from each. Roberts (2002) takes a more descriptive approach, focused on disciplinary boundaries, distinguishing auto/biographical, life-history, oral-history and literary approaches. Bertaux and Thompson (1997: 14) demarcate an Anglo-French tradition which seeks to document the past (and in which they situate themselves) from a German approach (associated with the work of Gabriele Rosenthal (1993, 1998) concerned primarily with subjectivity. Common to each typology is a distinction between realist and constructionist positions – the question of the relationship between the life that has been led and the story that is told.

Proponents of biographical methods distinguish them by virtue of their facility to engage with *temporal processes*. This is well expressed by Paul Thompson in an essay on researching social change:

> Through the intrinsic nature of life history as evidence, whether intentionally or not, the dimension of time is reintroduced to sociological enquiry: the life cycle, social mobility, or 'tradition and change' can no longer be artificially arrested and taken apart like clocks, but must be analyzed as they are, in perpetual growth and decay. (1981: 290)

Yet, with the exception of a lengthy footnote in Miller (2000: 109), there is little reference to specifically *longitudinal* methods within the biographical methods literature, even though the practice of reinterviewing is relatively commonplace and relationships between researchers and the research change over time (Thompson, 1981; Temple, 1996). Plummer (2001) notes that a single life-history work may entail many interviews with the individual over a period of years, and Miller comments that it may be possible to achieve 'saturation' with a single individual, over time. But although biographical methods seek to grasp a temporal process, they tend to do so retrospectively, through a *reconstruction* of events. The primary aim is to understand what has happened rather than to explore what is happening or will happen. Consequently, much of the methodological attention in the life-history literature has been concentrated on the vagaries and constructions of memory (Thompson, 1981) and on disentangling the impact of age, lifecourse, generational and period effects (Giele and Elder, 1998; Miller, 2000: 21–41). This contrasts with the idea of 'walking alongside' a research subject in the unfolding present, which has been used to characterise prospective longitudinal methods (Walker and Leisering, 1998; Neale and Flowerdew, 2003; McLeod and Thomson, 2009).

The emergence of an explicitly named 'qualitative longitudinal method' is a recent development (Thomson et al, 2003; Saldana, 2003). Interest in such an approach has been fuelled by a range of factors. First, such methods offer the potential to escape the limitations of qualitative interview-based studies. By generating a 'movie' as opposed to a 'snapshot' (Neale and Flowerdew, 2003), the longitudinal method appears to get beneath accounts, making visible contradictions between successive accounts and between intentions and practices (Plumridge and Thomson, 2003). Second, longitudinal methods are suited to gaining insight into phenomena that change over time. Where the focus of the research has an important sequential dimension, as with the example of the 'career' (be it educational, sexual, drug, crime, or work related) it is useful to be able to follow individuals or groups over time.

Longitudinal methods are also suited to an exploration of the relationship between agency, structure and serendipity – when questions of *timing* are important to a particular study. In some respects the model here comes from quantitative methods, where a longitudinal approach captures the accumulation and interplay of different factors in the determination of outcomes (Elliot et al, 2007). But qualitative longitudinal studies can do more than putting flesh on the bones of quantitative knowledge: such studies may also provide insight into the human *methodology* through which risks and opportunities are mediated – 'the art of life' (Rutherford, 2000), 'the reflexive project of self' (Giddens, 1991), 'the temporality of action' (Adkins, 2005). It has been argued that the current emphasis on change and contingency in political and theoretical discourse can be seen as part of a paradigm shift to a sociology 'post social structure' (Urry, 2000; Adkins, 2002a). If this is the case, then longitudinal and qualitative research could be seen as an important methodology for shifting attention from the synchronic analyses that privilege the representation of social structure, towards diachronic analyses which privilege processual and temporal themes such as the interplay of risk and resilience in the context of biography (Thomson and Holland, 2003b).

Researching identity in process

A longitudinal approach to life-history methods also brings to the fore the question of the subject and, more exactly, the *subject in process*. Those qualitative longitudinal studies that do exist have struggled with this question (Pollard and Filer, 1996, 1999; McLeod, 2000a; McLeod and Yates, 2007). For example, in a study of young people passing between the ages of 12 and 18, Julie McLeod experiments with a number of concepts, including a temporalising of Bourdieu's concept of the habitus, writing in terms of the 'formation of habitus over time' within which individuals may 'improvise' (McLeod, 2000a). In order to make psychological themes more visible, McLeod draws on Harriet Bjerrum Nielsen's appropriation of Freud's metaphor of the 'magic writing pad', through which resources are gleaned from experience and cultural forms to elaborate the kind of person that one wants to be. These inscriptions are made metaphorically onto a page, to be overlaid with others as they become available. Yet each inscription leaves a mark, or indentation, on a soft, wax block behind the sheet of paper. While the page is wiped and overlaid with new inscriptions, all are accumulated onto the wax block that represents subjectivity, a less-conscious yet more enduring record. At different stages of a young person's life inscriptions are made using particular calligraphies, relevant to her developmental stage. Bjerrum Nielsen's interest is in historically contingent formations of femininity, and she distinguished between gender identity and gender subjectivity, which exist in a dynamic and dialectic relationship over time, giving rise to gender as a process. It is a 'dialectic which results in the "magic" situation that change does not exclude permanence, and permanence does not exclude change. Without inscription there is no change in subjectivity, without the wax block there is no subject for the identity work' (Bjerrum Nielsen, 1996: 10).

Another strategy employed to animate the subject within qualitative longitudinal research is the notion of the reflexive project of self described by Giddens (1991) but bearing strong similarities to Schutz's notion of 'the project of action', within which the actor propels themselves into the future by reflecting on and remaking the past (Schutz, 1982; Reiter, 2000). In this approach the subject is the author of their own biography, self-conscious, constantly engaged in identity work, and seeking narrative coherence, if only on a transitory basis. As I will go on to discuss in Chapter Three, there are many problems with this particular construction, yet it facilitates a temporal exploration of change. Such an approach is attractive because it recognises the specificity of the interview context in which particular stories are created, yet also maintains a sense of the narrative coherence of the subject (Plumridge and Thomson, 2003). Margaret Archer has conceptualised the reflexive subject in a similar way, yet through the lens of critical realism, outlining a temporal sequence of discernment, deliberation and dedication underpinned by a dynamic interplay between agency and structure (2007: 20–1). In the case histories presented in this book I develop an approach to the subject in process that draws loosely on the notion of the reflexive project of self, but which elaborates this with ideas taken from Bjerrum Nielsen, Archer and others in order to capture psychological depth and the situatedness of individual projects within families, generations and wider social processes.

Working through narratives

Many commentators in the field of biographical methods have commented on the facility with which interviewees 'produce' life stories, even when it appears that they have never told the story before (for example, Finnegan, 1997). Most agree that life stories are never simple reflections of reality or experience, but are 'occasioned accounts' (Morgan, 2002) that draw on a wide range of cultural resources, both local and global. Interviewees' narrative styles vary across and within cultures (Plummer, 2001), between generations (Bjerrum Nielsen and Rudberg, 2000) and at different time points within studies (Bailey, 1999).

Commentators also agree that there has been a proliferation of the autobiographical form in popular culture through the 'mass produced confessional tales' of reality television shows and self-help manuals – 'the self on the shelf' (Plummer, 2001: 97). Silverman (1993) has coined the term the 'interview society', pointing to the institutionalisation of the autobiographical form through practices such as the curriculum vitae, the job interview and the doctor's consultation. Plummer writes of the 'autobiographical society' which enables the expression of marginal voices but also results in the commodification of the life story form where 'life stories become controllable, calculable, predictable, efficient' (2001: 98). For Lawler, autobiography or the telling of a life does not so much reflect 'a pre-given identity: rather identities are *produced* through the autobiographical work in which all of us engage every day' (Lawler, 2008: 13). The ways in which we narrate ourselves are shaped by cultural positions and resources. Catherine Reissman (1987) has observed that what appears to be 'narrative failure' may in fact reflect a failure on the part of the interviewer to recognise the particular subject position and narrative style of the interviewee. More recently, Bridget Byrne has cautioned against a reliance on the 'storied narrative genre' in interview-based research, suggesting that 'asking people to produce stories of their lives ... might enable some, but also silence other accounts that are not so easily produced in this genre' (2003: 47).

There is disagreement among those involved in the analysis of life stories as to the limits and consequences of the style of narratives, generally posed in terms of a distinction between a story of a life lived and a life told. This divide has been conceived in terms of a distinction between realism and constructionism (Roberts, 2002), between nomological and narrative explanations (Stephenson, 2000) and between a correspondence and coherence theory of truth (Finnegan, 1997). Narrative style is not a methodological problem to be overcome, but plays a part in what it is possible for an interviewee to say. Bruner describes this in terms of a mimetic, two-way relationship between a life and a story in which ways of telling correspond to ways of being (Bruner, 1987). Plummer provides a more sociological perspective in which narrative forms are understood as cultural resources and are associated with particular storytelling identities. From his perspective, storytelling is an inherently conservative form, alerting us to the potential of stories that are not yet heard, identities that are yet to coalesce and audiences which are not yet formed.

This is a productive tension that cannot be resolved either theoretically or empirically. The epistemological problem of the relationship between the story told and the life lived has not prevented most of those engaged with the collection and analysis of life stories from finding ways of working with and through particular narrative styles. In a methodological note to his final work, Pierre Bourdieu demonstrates an acute awareness of how the techniques of life-storytelling may be utilised as a form of cultural capital, pointing to the ways that 'authenticity' is constructed through mutual recognition with the interviewer. He counterposes this kind of complicity with a form of interview interaction that he describes as 'an induced and accompanied self-analysis' (1999: 615). Bourdieu describes his team as having to throw away many of the interview accounts that they collected, as they failed to capture the 'joy of expression' that is the potential of every interview encounter, 'an extraordinary discourse, which might never have been spoken, but which was already there, merely awaiting conditions for its actualization' (1999: 614). I am more suspicious about the search for authentic voices within interviews, but I do believe that all research encounters have the potential for profound insight, especially those encounters that form part of longitudinal studies where depth, contradiction and trust can be the dividend of research relationships built up over time.

Creating case histories from an archive

The original studies

This book takes as its point of departure a qualitative longitudinal investigation of young people's transitions to adulthood, growing up in contrasting locations in the UK. The origins of the longitudinal component lie in a mixed-method study of young people's moral landscapes, 'Youth Values: Identity, diversity and social change', funded as part of the Economic and Social Research Council's *Children 5–16: Growing up in the 21st century* programme and undertaken between 1996 and 1999. This initial study accessed mixed-ability groups of young people aged 11–16 through eight different schools located in five contrasting locations in England: a southern inner-city site; a leafy suburb in an affluent area near a commuter-belt town; an isolated rural area in the east; and a disadvantaged public housing estate in the north. In Northern Ireland young people were accessed through four schools in one city: a Catholic and a Protestant secondary modern school located in predominantly working-class communities; a formally 'integrated' school with a mixed population in terms of social class and religion; and an informally mixed school with a predominantly working-class student population. The original study employed an initial questionnaire (n=1,800) with mixed-ability classes and from this sample were drawn volunteers who participated in 62 focus groups, and subsequently 57 young people were interviewed (Table 2.1). Additional groups of young people were also accessed through a unit for children excluded from school, marginal youth groups, leaving care projects and lesbian and gay youth groups – the latter group being older than the main sample at the time of their first interview (17–19).

The longitudinal component of the study was also funded by the Economic and Social Research Council as part of its *Youth, citizenship and social change* programme. 'Inventing Adulthoods: Young people's strategies for transition' drew a sample of 121 young people from the initial 'Youth Values' study. The main methods of this stage of the study were in-depth, one-to-one interviews employed at roughly nine-month intervals and including a life-line exercise (Thomson and Holland, 2002), the compilation of a memory book (a kind of diary, see Thomson and Holland, 2005), and participation in cross-site focus groups towards the end of the study exploring issues of 'leaving' (school, home, locality, travel, etc).

A further two rounds of interviews were made possible by further funding from the Economic and Social Research Council as part of the Families & Social Capital ESRC Research Group based at London South Bank University. This third phase of the overall project (involving the same researchers and participants) was called 'Youth Transitions and Social Change'. Interviews took place in the autumn of 2002 and again, after an 18-month interval, in 2004/05. Over the period of the studies the same group of young people was followed for up to eight years, with an overall interview sample of 62 at the final round of fieldwork. Up to six interviews were undertaken with each young person. Questionnaire data were collected for all in 1996/97, and for many at a later point in 2000.

Table 2.1 The original studies: time frames and methods

Dates	Study	Methods
1996–99	Youth Values: Identity, diversity and social change Sample aged 11–17	Questionnaire (n =1,800) Focus groups (n = 62) 1:1 interviews (n = 57)
1999–2001	Inventing Adulthoods: Young people's strategies for transition Sample aged 14–23	Three in-depth 1:1 interviews at 9-month intervals (n = approx 100) Memory books (n = 49) Lifelines (n = 104)
2002–06	Youth Transitions and Social Change Sample aged 17–28	Two in-depth interviews, 18 months apart (n = 67)

Secondary analysis, drawing boundaries

In this book I draw from this huge data set in order to build case histories of individuals. It is possible to understand my orientation to this data set in terms of secondary analysis. In order to 'count' as secondary analysis it is not necessary that you have had no involvement in the original study. Natasha Mauthner and colleagues (1998) have written about revisiting their own data sets after a period of several years, to find themselves estranged or distanced from the original data collection processes and the theoretical frameworks employed. There is an important difference in my situation. The study is longitudinal and ongoing, and while my interests and those of the research team have shifted over time, I am intimately familiar with the data set *at the same time* as revisiting it for different yet related purposes. The 'gap' implied by secondary analysis (whether created by time or space) is not clearly evident (Henderson et al, 2006).

Yet there are gaps in my relationship with the data. I undertook a significant part of the fieldwork in the first 'Youth Values' study. The second 'Inventing Adulthoods' phase coincided with pregnancy and maternity leave, meaning that I concentrated on design, analysis and writing rather than on data generation. So while I have met all the young people in the study, interviewed most of them at least once, or facilitated them in a focus group, I have not been directly responsible for generating all the data in the study as a whole nor all of those selected for analysis and interpretation here. My position in relation to the wider study provides me with easy access to the vital 'contextual data' that Mauthner and colleagues consider to be as important as the transcripts themselves: for example, field notes, coding frames, background documentation on research design. Moreover, I am in a position to talk to the original interviewers, to interrogate their memories of interviews and to seek their views on my interpretations of interview accounts.

The approach that I have taken to the analysis of the cases seeks to maintain boundaries between my role as analyst/interpreter and the role of the original interviewer. Where that interviewer is someone else, I have gathered all relevant field notes and commentaries, analysed them as a form of data in themselves, and taken steps to maintain boundaries between my own interpretations and those contemporaneous interpretations made by interviewers. This has entailed always analysing and interpreting a series of interview accounts *before* I read the interviewers' notes and analysis. Having read the initial interviewer's accounts I have made notes of how our two interpretations compare and differ. In some cases I have discussed these contrasting perspectives with the original interviewer. Where I was the original interviewer (see Chapter Six, Devon) the boundary between analyst/interpreter and interviewer still exists but in a form that draws attention to the significance of writing as an interpretative and ethical act. Readers of the manuscript for this book observed a distinct quality in the writing of Devon's case which can be attributed to my greater confidence in reporting and interpreting data that I had been involved in generating.

Accessing the social through the individual

In the field of biographical research it is common to distinguish between a life story and a life history. The life story is the data – an individual interview or written autobiographical account. The life history is the analytic story that is finally told, drawing on a range of data sources. Drawing on the work of Riceour, Steph Lawler (2002: 245) argues that an archive only becomes a narrative through emplotment, the vehicle through which three forms of synthesis are achieved: between many events and one story; between discordance and concordance; and between different senses of time. In this book I use the term 'case history' to reflect the transformation of the raw materials of the archive through emplotment (see also Bertaux and Delacroix, 2000; Kuhn, 2002). My decision to use a small number of cases was both guided by a desire to do justice to the complexity and scale of these individual data sets, and because a focus on individual identities 'in process' complemented the themes that are the theoretical focus of the book. Yet, in isolating a number of individuals for in-depth study I am still aware of the wider data set and its relationship to these individuals.

Daniel Bertaux has repeatedly made a case for life-history methods to focus on social relations rather than on individuals or groups (Bertaux, 1981). Writing with Catherine Delacroix, he poses a striking methodological challenge, which I will quote in full:

> A single life story, although it may make fascinating hearing and reading, although it may bring to the mind of the researcher many hypotheses about how this or that social world actually functions, needs to be supplemented by other life stories, or by other kinds of materials in order to stand as sociologically relevant 'data'. Five life stories of individuals not connected to each other constitutes five separate pieces, perhaps five gems, but with no cumulative power unless they are from the same social world' (Bertaux and Delacroix, 2000: 74).

This statement reflects Bertaux's view of the appropriate uses of life-history research and his grounding in a realist epistemology which, in conjunction with grounded theory, suggests that through an intensive and cumulative process of eliciting and understanding what people know about life it is possible to understand a particular social relation. The aim of sampling, then, is to facilitate movement towards 'saturation'. It is such an approach that Liz Stanley has characterised as the 'microscope approach', in which more and more detail will enable one to get closer to the truth. She contrasts this with the 'kaleidoscope approach', in which 'each time you look you see something rather different, composed mainly of the same elements but in a new configuration' (Stanley, 1992: 158). It is interesting to compare Bertaux's comments to those of Jerome Bruner, firmly situated at the constructionist end of the epistemological continuum. Reporting on four narratives taken from members of a single family, Bruner is clear that, despite coming from a 'common landscape', the accounts can confirm neither each other nor the analysis. Rather, he suggests that, following Geertz (1973), they can 'thicken' it (Bruner, 1987: 24).

My decision to use individual life histories as a way of exploring questions about gender identity and processes of social change was inspired in part by Bob Connell's 1995 book *Masculinities*, in which he seeks to adapt Sartre's progressive–regressive methods, which aim to reconcile the universal and the singular within social science method. This is an approach to life history that has been influential among sociologists. For example, Ken Plummer cites Sartre as establishing the case for the documentation of lives:

> A man [sic] is never an individual: it would be more fitting to call him a universal singular. Summed up and for this reason universalised by his epoch, he in turn resumes it by reproducing himself in its singularity. Universal by the singular universality of human history, singular by the universalising singularity of his projects, he requires simultaneously examination at both ends. (Sartre, 1968, cited in Plummer, 2001: 165)

Connell responds to this challenge by examining 'both ends' of the gender order: the social and the biographical. He begins with the identification of 'crisis tendencies' in the gender order and goes on to identify four clusters of Australian men likely to be experiencing these crisis tendencies around being a man. He selectively samples 36 individuals within these clusters and conducts life-history interviews. These interviews are analysed individually, then as a cluster and finally comparatively. Through this iterative process he seeks to bring together the singular (life history) and the universal (gender order). Although working with fewer cases in greater depth, I was interested in this same connection between the biographical and the social/political context.

In selecting these four cases for in-depth analysis I have gone through a similar process. While I threw nothing away, I was able to select from an existing body of data examples of series of interviews in which the quality of the exchange was remarkable in terms of the insights it offers into 'the point within this world from which they see themselves' (Bourdieu, 1999: 615). In the cases that I have selected for this book, the quality of the interview encounters gave rise to a particular quality in the data that makes it suitable for my particular purposes. Clearly, narrative style both reflects the resources on which individuals draw and operates as a resource in its own right (Thomson et al, 2002; Plumridge and Thomson, 2003). Moreover, it may be that this kind of 'intangible' resource may be increasingly central to the production of new forms of privilege and exclusion (Adkins, 2003; Skeggs, 2004). I hope that, in selecting individuals who have such resources, I am able to maintain a focus on how reflexive resources are generated, deployed and received. Focusing on individuals who are all relatively fluent, yet whose social locations differ in many ways, also has the potential to generate insights into whether and how being 'reflexive' goes beyond the personal style of middle-class culture (Adkins, 2002b).

From reading to writing: stages of analysis

In the introduction to this book I have contextualised the four cases in relation to the Inventing Adulthoods data set. The data that constitute the archive for each individual case are outlined in an appendix. The process of moving from a longitudinal archive to a case history involves a massive condensation of data, but also a structured analysis. My particular approach sought to find a way of combining cross-sectional and longitudinal analyses. In the first stage of the analysis of individual cases I took a very grounded approach to the analysis of the data, identifying themes inductively. I did not deliberately seek to draw connections between interview accounts, but inevitably found my analysis of the second and third interviews reflecting back, drawing my attention to earlier statements that had not previously seemed to be important. This process can be described as initially incremental, progressively cumulative and ultimately recursive. The outcome of this first stage of analysis was a series of in-depth analyses of interviews for a single individual and an emergent sense of the dynamic relationship between them. These analyses are very close to the interview text, with insights associated with particular passages of text. My experience of this stage of analysis was a sense of 'saturation' in the data from an individual, the aim of which was simply to hold and begin to digest the data archive for that person (Miller, 2000: 121).

The second stage of the analysis entailed moving from the component parts of the data for a single individual towards the re-creation of a whole in the form of an analytic narrative. My choice of approach was also a choice of a mode of representation. Initially I was very uncertain about how to do this and reviewed the literature on life-history research for guidance. For example, Plummer (2001) comments on the different ways in which life stories have been presented, ranging from the approach of Studs Terkel in which unedited text is presented without commentary, to the presentation of life stories followed by analysis, to various forms in which the voice of the central subject is taken over by the author. At this stage of analysis I would also have to commit myself to a particular mode of writing. I made many false starts, experimenting with different approaches which privileged different aspects of my analysis and the data itself. These struggles to find a writing style were also the struggles of forming an interpretation, which is always highly selective and provisional. I needed both to find a structure through which I could 'show' the rich longitudinal interview material and to work out the 'story' that I wanted to privilege though it.

Eventually my struggles to find a structure for writing and a model for interpretation were assisted by my work on the wider data set, where I had developed a simple yet holistic model for capturing the relationship between an individual's accounts of self and different arenas of their life (see Thomson et al, 2004). The origins of the model lie in a coincidence of reading about Foucault's ideas on 'techniques of the self' and searching for a means to represent biographical data. Foucault's later work explores the notion of daily 'aesthetics of existence' which provide structures, material and economies for the development of a relation of the self with the self (Rabinow, 1984; Martin et al, 1988; Foucault, 1994). His account derives from an interest in the world of the citizens of ancient Greece, and thus he distinguishes the relevant realms of truth, erotics, dietics and economics, each of which brings a particular 'aesthetics of existence' that resources the individual's relation with the self. What attracted me to these ideas was the way in which the connected individual (rather than the institution or discursive figuration) lies at the centre of the analysis. It is this way of capturing the range of discursive resources available to the individual while enquiring as to how that person constructs an identity *from these* that I found so useful. A holistic model centred on the connected individual was compatible with the biographical character of the data, enabling me to capture the range of resources that the young people drew on in making their gender identities. By animating this model in time, it would be possible to then see what the young people actually 'did' with the resources.

Theoretical resources

Foucault's work on the care of the self has been criticised for failing to account for the social embeddedness of 'practices of existence', simply juxtaposing micropractices of the self and social horizons rather than relating them (McNay, 1992: 155). For example, McNay argues that Foucault's insistence on the practical character of an ethics of the self and the local and contingent character of reflexivity discourages the search for an analytic relationship between the self and social structure. Within my model I was looking to find ways of locating 'techniques of self' in relation to specific arenas of life – representing both material 'spaces' and symbolically important 'places' (Massey, 1994: 168). Eventually I adopted the term 'field of existence', capturing something of both Foucault's notion of 'aesthetics of existence' and Bourdieu's notion of social field (see Chapter Nine for a full discussion).

For Bourdieu, fields can be understood as arenas of social life that operate 'according to their own internal logics and dynamics' with 'particular stakes at issue (e.g. cultural goods (lifestyle), intellectual distinction (education), power (politics) etc.' (Williams, 1995: 587). Fields are mapped from particular social locations and individuals may define and access them differently. For example, Hall (1995) describes five cultural fields in which British-Sikh teenagers play out their identities, including the temple, the home, the shopping mall, the school and 'English' night life. For my purposes a 'field of existence' refers to a specific arena of an individual's *biography*, likely to be coterminous with specific spaces, places and institutions, and making available particular technologies of the self. The exact categories employed for each case arose from the initial analysis of the data set but tended to reflect the domains of the domestic, paid work, leisure and education. For each of these biographical domains I forged a longitudinal account. This entailed drawing together all the data relevant to each field across the different interviews and sketching a narrative of change and continuity over time, an approach that is similar to Saldana's idea of the 'through lines' that can structure a longitudinal analysis. Combining and relating these biographical parts back into a narrative whole constituted the written histories.

Using this model I then returned to the analyses of individual interviews and transposed insights and fragments of data under each of the relevant 'fields'. Within each field I began to forge an analytic narrative that took in the insights and data from successive interviews, paying attention to how particular technologies of the self operated and where such technologies might be transposed between fields. The model enabled me to translate a series of holistic snapshots into a collection of temporal narratives: stories of family, of education, of work and of play. The final stage of moving from the data to the case history was to find a way of sequencing and relating these part narratives into an overall whole which constitutes the analytic story for that particular young person. Although I have used the same model in order to structure and analyse each of the data archives, I have approached the 'telling' of the stories through different sequences, responding unconsciously to the aesthetic and formal imperatives that shape how stories can be told.

The aim of the case history is to provide a compelling account of the connected individual, of how and why events unfolded as they did, the transformation of the individual over time, and the dance between personal agency and relationships of interdependence (Thomson, 2007). As Daniel Bertaux and Catherine Delacroix explain, the purpose of this kind of life history is not so much to predict how a life will develop, but to explain why a life was lived as it was, accounting for the number of 'unlived lives' that did not transpire (Bertaux and Delacroix, 2000). Theory is one of the main tools that the analyst employs in this task and will dictate the character of the 'through lines' that become the focus for the analysis. The longitudinal character of the data provides 'some check against over or misreading remarks' (McLeod, 2000b: 50), as events do not necessarily turn out as anticipated or desired. But there remains a strong temptation towards narrative and theoretical coherence which has to be balanced with the disjointed character of three separate interview encounters.

Validity and the interview data

The process described above is both theoretically informed and highly pragmatic. My overriding concern with each case history was to find a structure and an analytic thread with which to synthesise and present a complex set of data. On the basis of such pragmatics it is more than possible to fail. A case history may be incoherent, contradictory, repetitive, badly expressed. So too may be the interview account. However, as analysts of qualitative data, we come to expect that 'data' is like this; it does not take away from the data's validity. In fact, we tend to be suspicious of interview data that is fluent, that could pass for written text, presuming that we are being 'fed' a well-rehearsed story or have encountered a 'quasi-professional' storyteller (see Plummer, 2001 on the commodification of stories). I make this point to draw attention to the different criteria that are employed when making judgements in qualitative research about the validity and reliability of the data and the interpretation of that data.

The realist approach to life-history research has been associated with a grounded theory approach to qualitative analysis and the notion of 'saturation', by which is meant that no new findings are forthcoming from continuing data collection. Miller (2000) has suggested that it may be possible to reach 'saturation' with one individual interviewed on several occasions. My experience of analysing this kind of longitudinal data set encourages me to think that, rather than moving towards saturation, the analyst in fact develops an increasingly 'thick' account, which resists analytic closure, documenting as it does a dynamic process of change and identity construction. As the account thickens, it simultaneously acquires greater complexity, yet there is also a growing sense of familiarity as narrative themes recur and a form of biographical triangulation sheds light on phenomena and relationships from different vantage points.

The vantage point offered by this kind of longitudinal interview data offers a privileged perspective on a life that can be problematic. Bourdieu (1999) insists that the analyst should seek to capture the social logic of the interviewee's position rather than to portray their views as 'absurd' or as examples of psychoanalytic displacement. It is also important to recognise that the 'perspective' that the analyst forges is informed, more or less consciously, by their own particular class and cultural location (Skeggs, 2004). As Walkerdine and colleagues observe, it is impossible to keep interpretations free from projections (Walkerdine et al, 2002: 190). In placing interview accounts together and reading them retrospectively, the analyst's role can easily shift from that of interpreter to legislator (Finnegan, 1997: 100), producing accounts based on explanation rather than on an attempt at understanding.

Although Bourdieu may understand the research subject as little more than the effects of their social position, his approach nevertheless recognises the integrity of that position. Approaches to the analysis of life histories that assume a 'defended subject' (Hollway and Jefferson, 2000) or even a 'storied self' (Bruner, 1987; Polkinghorne, 1995) can also privilege the account of the analyst over that of the interviewee in such a way that the account itself or the life behind it are less relevant. For example, Polkinghorne (1995) rejects the notion that providing a narrative account of the data is a case of imposing a structure. Taking the position that experience is already storied, and that putting experience in language imposes order, he argues that 'the move to narrative configuration is a still higher order from the fullness of lived experience' (1995: 19). The character of longitudinal data sets makes such a shift very seductive.

In the process of creating a single analytic narrative from component parts I have inevitably engaged in what Polkinghorne (1995: 16) describes as 'narrative smoothing', in which data that do not contradict the plot and are not necessary for its telling are dropped. I have imposed a structure and I have drawn attention to relationships and configurations of events that the interview subjects did not present as the focus of their accounts. My interpretation represents a narrative analysis rather than an analysis of narratives (as distinguished by Polkinghorne, 1995). It draws on a range of data sources in a bounded system of study. The outcome is a story configured around a plot told retrospectively, 'not just a description but a history', exploring intentional and unintentional outcomes (Polkinghorne, 1995: 19). I have sought to tell a story that is embedded in, yet distinct from, the individual interview accounts that have informed it. In constructing this story I have captured a process of change over time as well as a sense of the subjects as positioned within distinct social locations. These localities give them access to local resources, scripts and recipes for structuring experience (Bruner, 1987), drawn from a 'store of accepted resources for personal story telling' (Finnegan, 1997: 91). In turn, this story is structured by the 'possible lives available to them', the particular gender, race, age and sexual identities that they inhabit (Appiah, cited in Stephenson, 2000: 118) and the way it meshes with those around them (Finnegan, 1997; Plummer, 2001).

My analytic account is interested in both the content and the formal characteristics of the interview narratives on which it draws, recognising the role of stories in mediating between experience, identity and expression. I have sought to maintain as much as possible of the 'complex tangle of causality and self-determination' (Bertaux and Thompson, 1997: 18), possibly at the expense of a coherent or entertaining story. I have struggled to stay true to an aim of understanding rather than explanation, 'describing in-depth' (Bertaux, 1981: 41) rather than engaging in diagnosis. I have tried to avoid the temptation to provide the story with a beginning, middle and end, being aware of the other ways in which it could have been told (Bruner, 1987) and increasingly conscious that these stories will be revised in further rounds of interviewing. I have also written these analytic narratives within my own local conventions of storytelling – an academic style in anticipation of a particular audience (Clifford and Marcus, 1986). In the next chapter I sketch the theoretical framework that shaped the way in which I constructed the case histories.

THREE

Gender and social change

This book is concerned with the ways that lives unfold over time and identities change as young people grow into adulthood. Questions of gender are at the centre of the account: what it means to move from a being a boy into a man, from a girl into a woman. This chapter sketches the conceptual landscape for the book, framing the overall project and introducing a theoretical vocabulary. It is organised in two parts: the first considers the argument that gender identities have been subject to a process of detraditionalisation, outlining late-modern and feminist accounts as well as arguments emerging from studies of masculinities, sexualities and social change. The second locates young people within these debates about gender and sexual transformation.

Sociological interpretations of changing gender relations

The 'fact' of changing gender relations has become a key motif for a range of contemporary sociological theories of social change. Theories of individualisation (Beck, 1992; Beck and Beck-Gernsheim, 1995) and detraditionalisation (Heelas et al, 1996) identify a transformation in the relations between the genders (in particular a transformation of the lives and expectations of women) as both evidence for and explanation of the processes of change that they seek to explain. Ulrich Beck describes the Risk Society as somewhere 'people are being removed from the constraints of gender ... traditional forms and ascribed roles' (1992: 105). Writing with Elizabeth Beck-Gernsheim, he uses marriage and divorce as a case study for an account of the expansion of individualisation. Divorce, they suggest, can be explained by the mismatch of two individualised work biographies, the integration of which 'is a feat' (Beck and Beck-Gernsheim 1995: 6).

The continuing centrality of gender in contemporary life is not dismissed by the theorists of detraditionalisation. In Beck's view, 'we are situated at the very beginning of a liberation from the feudally ascribed roles for the sexes' (1992: 104) in which the mechanisms of reflexive modernisation undermine the very structures that industrial society was founded upon and has produced, such as the public/private divide and the sexual division of labour. Although he describes men and women as being freed from 'gender fates', in practice, consciousness of change outstrips material changes. In particular, the arenas of work and the division of labour in the home may be the sites of continuing inequality. What is new is an 'equalisation of prerequisites' in education and law, and raised expectations among women.

The resulting contradiction between expectations of equality and experiences of inequality means that 'the positions of men and women become more unequal, more conscious and less legitimated' (Beck, 1992: 104). For Beck, the process of detraditionalisation is not simple. In his terms, individualisation dislodges women from traditional roles, yet the same process serves to confirm and strengthen traditional masculinity. This gives rise to new tensions over responsibilities for housework and childcare. Although women may take up individualised work biographies, they have the 'double-burden' of continued responsibility for childcare and the home. Thus 'the lives of women are pulled back and forth by this contradiction between liberation from and reconnection to the old ascribed roles' (1992: 112). The overall result is that conflict over gender inequalities increasingly comes to the political centre. Paradoxically, 'the more equal the sexes seem, the more we become aware of the persistent and pernicious inequalities between them' (Beck and Beck-Gernsheim, 1995: 14).

In the account of social change provided by Anthony Giddens (1992, 1994), women have been the vanguard of the transformation of intimacy, while men are the laggards. Giddens does not see this as a completed revolution, acknowledging that 'deep psychological as well as economic differences between the sexes stand in the way' (1992: 188). He is careful not to go so far as to suggest that gender divisions no longer exist; rather, he observes that such divisions no longer have authority, so that traditional gender roles now 'demand discursive justification' (1994: 105).

> No longer can someone say in effect 'I am a man and this is how men are', 'I refuse to discuss things further' ... Behaviour and attitudes have to be justified ... where reasons have to be provided, differential power starts to dissolve, or alternatively power begins to become translated into authority. (Giddens, 1994: 106)

Although Giddens acknowledges the continuing existence of gendered inequalities, he looks to a future where gender becomes an increasingly irrelevant factor in negotiations between equals. His argument about legitimacy could be seen as consistent with the position of Bob Connell, who identifies 'crisis tendencies' in the gender order, as demanding responses in the forms of masculinity achieving legitimacy and hegemony (Connell, 1995). Connell makes a stronger case for the resilience and defence of male privilege than does Giddens. Yet he also remarks on the historical impact of feminism and lesbian and gay movements alongside material and cultural changes in the gender order, observing that:

> the change of which there is so much awareness is not the crumbling of the material and institutional structures of patriarchy. What has crumbled, in the industrial countries, is the legitimation of patriarchy ... In all public forums, and increasingly in private forums, it is now the denial of equality for women and the maintenance of homophobia that demands justifications. (Connell, 1995: 226)

The notion that these social changes are associated with a changing relationship between the private and public spheres is also central to theories of late modernity. Women have moved in increasing numbers into the public sphere of work, 'transposing a feminine habitus' (McNay, 1999), and those such as Giddens (1992) and Weeks (1995) argue that this movement has been paralleled by a *democratisation* of the private, part and parcel of a transformation of intimacy. Commentators such as Richard Sennett (1986) and Christopher Lasch (1980), among others, have lamented this muddying of the private/public divide, identifying an associated loss of public virtue and rise in narcissism. Nikolas Rose has gone further, to question the relationship between psychotherapeutic discourses and political power, noting that 'the distinction between the public and the private is not a stable analytic tool, but is itself a mobile resource in these systems of power knowledge' (Rose, 1999: 221).

But although there may continue to be a case for understanding late-modern gender identities as underwritten by a public/private divide (Adkins, 2003), in practice such distinctions are difficult to maintain. There are always overlaps and interactions. There are public spaces and practices within the private and private spaces and practices within the public (Sheller and Urry, 2003). In an exploration of these overlaps Fahey (1995) argues that the interesting question is *how* and *why* public/private divides are created, rather than the essential meaning of the realms they delineate. In his view, the public and private are far from discrete, but are boundary-drawing processes that are endemic to social life.

It is in this context that terms such as 'intimacy' have value. From this perspective, intimacy need not be a euphemism for the 'private' but, rather, could be understood as another relevant term in play in these kinds of interactions. As Weeks (1995) observes, private acts are not necessarily intimate, and intimate acts are not necessarily private. Attention then may shift to the *quality* of the interaction rather than the particular location in which it takes place. This view is consistent with the typology offered by Barbara Misztal (2000) that conceptualises the traditional public/private divide as transcended through three distinct styles of interaction: civility, sociability and intimacy, each defined by the particular form of types of roles, motivations and regulations that shape different arenas of the social. Lois McNay makes a similar observation about how intimate relations are becoming 'increasingly unbounded and having variable effects across different fields' (2000: 71). She encourages the adoption of Bourdieu's conceptual framework of the field and habitus as a way of capturing the ways that gender relations may be undergoing restructuring in realms other than the domestic.

Feminist accounts of continuity and change

Anthony Giddens' case for the transformation of intimacy has been criticised on both empirical and theoretical grounds. Lynn Jamieson (1998) suggests that he fails to engage with literature on the resilience of gender inequality. She sees little empirical evidence of 'plastic sexuality' or experimentation, citing that research among young people 'conclusively documents' the absence of the fusion of sex and emotional intimacy and mutual pleasure, and observing that among older heterosexuals equality and intimacy are 'outweighed by sex and gender trouble' (Jamieson, 1999: 484). Feminist commentators, in particular, have criticised the privileging of the individual psyche and the couple relationship at the expense of the more collective and material dimensions of gendered inequality, such as the responsibility that women tend to hold for childcare and the home (Jamieson, 1998; Ribbens McCarthy and Edwards, 2001, 2002). As Jamieson (1998) points out, 'change is undoubtedly occurring but how to characterise the nature and significance of the change remains deeply contested' (1998: 2). For Lois McNay (2000) this overstatement is explained by the way in which late-modern theory works from a primarily symbolic account of identity, disregarding the more entrenched embodied and psychic aspects (see also Heaphy, 2007).

The privileging of the gendered dimensions of social change in mainstream social theory stands in some tension with contemporary agendas in academic feminism. Western feminist academia spent much of the 1970s and 1980s working through the theoretical and political implications of inequalities in relation to the workplace, the home and sexual relationships (Maynard, 1989). This theoretical agenda focused on the task of documenting inequality and deconstructing the neutrality of modern institutions such as the family, work, the public/private divide. In this sense, academic feminism was involved in exposing what Beck has called the 'feudal gender relations' that are integral to modern industrial society. Theorists such as Carole Pateman (1988) sought to show that modernity itself is constituted through the exclusion of women and that apparently neutral categories such as 'worker' are dependent on the unpaid labour of women and children in the private sphere. Liberal feminist approaches that sought to gain equity between men and women within and through existing institutions were critiqued from both Marxist and radical feminist positions as failing to recognise the necessity of inequality within patriarchal capitalist society (Maynard, 1995; Whelehan, 1995).

The 1990s were characterised by two linked trends in academic feminism. First, a recognition of diversity among women, precipitated by a critique of feminism as speaking from and for white and middle-class positions (Spellman, 1990; hooks, 1981). Second, a 'textual turn' in academic feminism, involving an engagement with post-structuralism and giving rise to an intellectual agenda dominated by questions of language, epistemology and the ontological status of gender itself (Maynard, 1995; Segal, 1999). Both these trends demanded a critical engagement with what it means to be a woman. One of the consequences of this trajectory was a progressive disengagement of academic feminism from popular discussions of changing gender relations. Writing at the end of the millennium, British-based feminist Lynne Segal (1999) reflected on a mainstream popular and political discourse that characterises change in terms of a net gain for women and a net loss for men. In her view this discourse masks the realities of a withdrawal of state support and an increasing polarisation of life chances by class. She bemoans the lack of influence that academic feminism has had on this debate, suggesting that it has been preoccupied with internal differences. Yet gender, she argues, continues to be a relevant political category, pointing to the

> disruptions and strains caused by changing gender relations, everywhere apparent yet everywhere unresolved. Whether we notice them in the underachievement and misdeeds of boys, potential sexual hazards facing girls, the failures and uncertainties of men, the bitterness or overwork of married women, the impoverishment of lone mothers and their children, the deliberate provocations of sexual dissidents, daily fears of violence or simply in the continuing debates within and about feminism itself, gender is part of our very existence, our social being. (1999: 225)

Lois McNay (2000) has questioned the 'negative paradigm' within feminism that accounts primarily for the resilience of gender inequality rather than explaining change. She associates this negative paradigm with a focus on the symbolic realm, on discourses, subject positions. In her view, a shift to a more materialist and embodied account of gender as a 'historical matrix rather than static structure' (p 13) brings with it a more generative account of agency that facilitates dialogue with mainstream social theories on gender transformation.

As yet, the conversation between feminist academics and theorists of detraditionalisation is relatively undeveloped, although there are signs that we are moving into the generative paradigm that McNay envisages (see, for example, Rahman and Witz, 2003; Lovell, 2003; Adkins, 2003; Archer, 2007). One of the first feminist scholars to engage directly with such theories was Lisa Adkins, who asked what feminism might lose by ignoring late-modern theories: 'A revitalised empirical purchase? A new political salience?' (Adkins, 1998: 36). Adkins agreed that 'processes associated with individualisation may be key to the current organisation of gender', and in this sense supports Beck's view that 'many sociological categories (especially those associated with industrial society) are now inadequate' (Adkins, 1998: 47). However, her argument also suggests that 'individualisation itself has a gendered productivity' – that far from being transgressive of the social categories of gender, individualisation may 're-embed' women in the social: 'Individualisation is therefore not emptying out gender but may be creating new lines of social domination, for instance those of community, of networks and of new knowledges and forms of communications' (p 47).

Building on her established work on female labour and the family, Adkins argued that:

> in terms of gender, individualisation and the attendant processes of traditionalisation in the labour market, could, therefore, be said to represent a process of re-traditionalisation both in terms of the labour market and the family: the exclusion of women from reflexive

occupation and an intensification of the appropriation of family labour. (Adkins, 1998: 44)

Adkins distinguishes between a 'radical thesis' which stresses a break between a traditional past and a detraditional present and future (a position associated with the work of Beck and Giddens) and 'a coexistence thesis' in which the 'traditionalism' of the past is questioned, as is the absence of tradition from the present and future. Here, ideas of complexity, retraditionalisation and contradiction are stressed, and she considers this to be fertile territory for feminist description of the ongoing production of gender. In subsequent work Adkins has developed and extended these arguments, suggesting that 'a critical reflexive stance towards gender is increasingly characteristic of gender in late modernity – a habit of gender in late modernity' (2003: 32).

The contradictions of individualisation as it affects women are also explored by Norwegian feminists Harriet Bjerrum Nielsen and Monica Rudberg (1994), who suggest that the picture of social change presented by late-modern theorists is too simplistic. In their view, modernity can be traced through the creation of *phases* of the gender order. First, a phase of gender polarisation; second, a phase characterised by a battle between the sexes; and third, the emergence of a specifically female individualisation. In their view, male individualisation is synonymous with modernity and women were spectators of the process. Female individualisation happens at a later stage where the costs of progress are more visible, and where 'there is nobody at home when she too leaves the house except the children' (p 48).

Bjerrum Nielsen and Rudberg develop a nuanced understanding of changing gender relations as well as capturing the factors that may interact to constrain change. Drawing on an empirical study of three generations of women, they distinguish between *gender identity* (the gender I have – I am a woman and therefore act in this particular way), *gender subjectivity* (the gender I am – I am me, and therefore I act in this particular way, laid down in childhood and unconsciously influenced by the gendered subjectivity of my mother) and cultural and social possibilities offered by society at any time (1994: 92). They argue that at the point of adolescence there is always a lack of 'contemporaneity' or 'fit' between these dimensions. The character of this lack of contemporaneity is different for different generations. For example, girls growing up in the 1960s and 1970s experienced contradictions between a modernised gender identity and an 'old-fashioned gendered subjectivity (development of autonomy through relationships with men)' (p 109). For their mothers, who were girls in the 1940s and 1950s, the contradiction was between a modern gender identity and restricted cultural possibilities. For girls in the 1980s and 1990s the contradiction was between gendered subjectivity and cultural and social possibilities. So the modern girl may not 'acknowledge her sex as a limitation – she wants everything and believes she can do anything. But is that possible?' (p 111).

Sarah Irwin and Wendy Bottero (2000) also take issue with the focus on the individual within theories of individualisation, arguing that the recognition that modern industrial society afforded individual economic freedom for men only should caution us from accepting a model that stresses the growing dominance of market forces. Rather than viewing recent changes in the family and employment as the consequence of the triumph of market forces, they suggest that we pay greater attention both now and in the past to the particular social relations through which specific forms of family and employment were achieved. Suggesting a theoretical model of the 'moral economy' derived from the work of E.P. Thompson, they draw attention to relationships of interdependence between men, women and children, and the moral claims that they make in different historical circumstances. They characterise the current family and employment model as the 'co-resourced household', which, with the demise of a family wage, is dependent on both adults working, and depended on by children and young adults for security and support. In their words, 'the decline of familiar social patterns should not be equated with the decline of social structuring itself ... but a move to new forms of social structuring' (2000: 263). In their view the focus for understanding such social changes should not be in gender per se, but in shifting claims in terms of gender and generational groups. This should not be theorised as the 'dissolution of social bonds, or the emergence of individualization, but as the move from one set of social arrangements and moral claims to another'. Such an approach is open to a historical exploration of the interaction of class, ethnicity and other dimensions of social location as factors shaping the moral economies within which such claims have meaning. More recently, Irwin has described this perspective as focusing on 'social configuration':

> a metaphor of society as a social space in which groups are positioned differently in a web of social relations and interdependencies. Values are an integral component, influencing the ways in which social differences and interdependencies are configured and reconfigured. (Irwin, 2003: 567)

Thinking through resistance

The character of gender detraditionalisation is uneven and undetermined. Changes in expectations are not consonant with changes in practices, drawing attention to the emotional investments that individuals have in tradition. In this book I am interested in exploring the microprocesses that are involved in the process of gender detraditionalisation, the ways in which gender projects develop over time and how these are constrained by and disrupt wider formations of class, gender, sexuality and ethnicity. The methodology of repeat interview both privileges and decentres the individual. Through the accumulation of accounts it becomes possible to understand the self as situated, enmeshed and saturated in circumstance and obligation. Ironically, it is precisely through the focus on the operations of agency that it becomes possible to discern the factors contributing to individuals' ability to improvise and innovate in the construction of gendered identities, and the extent to which these innovations have resonance with or are recognised by others.

Nikolas Rose describes detraditionalisation as a seductive sociological 'just so story of how the human being got its individuality' (Rose, 1996: 295). But for Rose, 'subjectivity has its own history, and it is a history that is more heterogenous, more practical and more technical than these accounts suggest' (p 295). He argues that:

> the notion of the 'detraditionalized self' is of little use because it fails to engage with the ways that different localized practices – of domesticity and sexuality, of consumption and marketing, of production and management, of punishment and reformation, of health and illness, of security and insurance, of conflict and warfare, of management and rule – presuppose, represent and act upon human beings as if they were persons of a certain sort. (1996: 312)

Rather than simply narrativising the ways of being human, Rose suggests that we also need to spatialise them, rendering them 'intelligible in terms of the localization of repertoires of habit, routines and images of self understanding and self-cultivation within specific domains of thought, action and value' (1996: 304).

I have already referred to problems inherent in an overly spatialised account of subjectivity explored by Lois McNay's critique of constructionist understandings of identity which focus on the symbolic dimension of what she calls 'subjectification'. In her view, such an approach 'does not explain adequately how individuals may be attached to their subjugation, or the investments, conscious or otherwise, that individuals may hold in deeply irrational and oppressive gender identities' (2000: 77). While the late-modern approach to the project of self may overplay the temporal features of narrative, from her perspective, the post-structural account of identity is 'temporally underdeveloped and cannot explain why certain forms of gendered behaviour endure long after the historical circumstances in which they emerge have faded' (2000: 79).

Various commentators have sought to account for this cultural lag, including the distinction drawn by Bjerrum Nielsen and Rudberg between gender identity, gender subjectivity and the available social and cultural possibilities. McNay herself talks in terms of the 'non-synchronicity' of change in gender relations (2000: 112), suggesting that through the narrative mode individuals seek to integrate the non-synchronous and often conflictual elements of their lives in different ways. It is thus vitally important both to understand the particular local and historical expressions of gender identity, as well as to enquire into the specific ways in which individuals compose gender identities and the reception that these identities receive in particular times and places (see also Plummer, 1995). For McNay, a narrative approach to the formation of identity not only provides a much-needed depth to post-structuralist accounts, but also animates agency by attending to the temporal methodology through which self-formation becomes meaningful.

While the problem of the intractability of (or lack of change in) gender identities has provided an important theoretical project for feminist scholarship, attention is also beginning to be paid to the ways in which change *does* take place. Moves towards a more 'generative' understanding of agency have to contend with enduring theoretical debates about the relationship between agency and structure and the limits of choice. Building on Judith Butler's ideas of performativity, Terry Lovell suggests that it is important to understand transgressive or resistant practices in a wider context, taking into account 'the social relations of political (inter)action, and the specific historical conditions of particular interactions' (2003: 2). The important question for Lovell is not simply whether individuals are able to act in a transgressive way, but whether those transgressions have authority. Lovell argues that individuals cannot endow their own actions with authority, but that the authorisation of their actions must be a result of a wider historical configuration.

Using the example of the civil rights activist Rosa Parks, Lovell argues that (unlike other possible candidates) Parks was chosen by the civil rights leadership as the right kind of person (respectable working class) at the right time, and thus her heroic actions on the bus provided a symbolic catalyst for a wider political and social change. So while Parks had agency, the authority of her act of resistance did not reside in her person but in the wider social movement that endorsed her actions and invested them with historical significance. Moreover, Parks' particular project of self (including her class and gender identity) was crucial in determining her suitability for this role. Lovell suggests that Parks' subsequent marginalisation within the civil rights movement might be explained by her role as a symbol rather than an agent of change for a movement based on the recognition of manhood, which is not easily reconciled with female authority.

This more nuanced understanding of the social conditions and indeterminacy of resistance alerts us to the relations within which agency is constituted and enacted, and how gender, class, sexuality and ethnicity may be implicated in the ways that agency is (or is not) authorised. If we return to the arguments put forward by both Lovell and McNay, it becomes important to understand the 'distantiation of action'; in McNay's words, 'agency cannot be reduced to the intentionality of actors but becomes exteriorized and sedimented within social time' (McNay, 2000: 114). We might also add that spatial boundaries and movement between fields and across public and private boundaries are significant factors in this process of authorisation. It is the authorisation of private innovations by wider collectivities within the sphere of the public that is problematic for women. As Lovell observes, agency is 'a function of ensemble performances – often with very large casts of others' (2003: 2).

Masculinities, sexualities and social change

Academic feminism and gender studies provide us with different conceptual palettes for the exploration of masculinities and femininities. The 'problem of men' has always formed part of the feminist sociological project, yet explored primarily as an exercise in understanding the character and resilience of male power. A sustained feminist (and feminist influenced) engagement with the study of men and masculinity began in the late 1980s, exemplified by Segal's (1990) *Slow motion*, Hearn and Morgan's *Men, masculinity and social theory* (1990) and Connell's *Gender and power* (1987) and *Masculinities* (1995). These studies moved beyond attempting to fit men into theories of the oppression of women, towards an attempt to understand the operations of masculinity in its own terms. Such studies were instrumental in documenting the existence and importance of diversity within the cultures of men, and giving rise to a theoretical framework that sought to make sense of the relationships between these masculinities within wider theories of gendered power relations. Connell's theory of hegemonic masculinity argues that, while all forms of masculinity are in some way complicit in the production and reproduction of male dominance vis-à-vis women, masculinities also exist within a hierarchy. Positions of dominance, subordination and marginalisation between men are maintained through relations of complicity, desire and competition.

There is a powerful popular and academic narrative in which women are the motors of much of the social change that has shaken the gender order, moving into the workplace, gaining education, demanding better relationships and more from sex. Accounts of men's responses to these changes reflect a mixed picture. Commentators such as Anthony Giddens (1992) consider men to be a recalcitrant group, experiencing a loss in agency and power, resenting their dependence on women and in some cases resorting to anger and violence. Connell provides a more finely drawn picture, distinguishing between responses of men shaped by their place within the relational gender hierarchy and the biographical constraints and resources on which they draw.

The ways that men and women make sense of and respond to change are inevitably shaped by generation. Studies of young men suggest a widespread awareness of the impact of feminism and relatively widespread comfort with the rhetoric of equality (O'Donnell and Sharpe, 2000; Frosh et al, 2002). Yet, as several accounts argue, in practice the exercise of equality may be highly threatening (Holland et al, 1993; Wilkinson and Mulgan, 1995). While young men may seek to accommodate the changing lives of women on an individual basis, it appears that the process they are engaged in is characterised as much by reaction, resistance and accommodation as it is by 'reinvention' – pointing to an important distinction between the kinds of reflexivity that are conscious and critical and forms of reflexion that are impulsive (Heaphy, 2007). It is only recently that the conflation of masculinities and men that has characterised much of the literature in this area is beginning to open up, with new work exploring the extent to which some men, in some circumstances, may be 'performing' (or read as performing) feminine styles and being rewarded for this (for example, Nixon, 1996; McDowell, 1997). This shift towards seeing masculinity and femininity as cultural styles has been associated with a corresponding shift in attention from the identity of the performer to the ways in which particular performances come to be authorised/recognised or not (Halberstam, 1998; Adkins, 2002a; Skeggs, 2004; Nayak and Kehily, 2007).

A number of commentators have pointed to the experience of lesbians and gay men as central to processes of detraditionalisation, suggesting that exclusion from the rewards, sanctions and regulations of normative heterosexual culture demands individual and collective inventiveness. Giddens (1992), for example, portrays lesbian and gay cultures as pioneering relationship practices that are characteristic of a wider 'transformation of intimacy'. This is a view that has found support in the work of Weeks, Heaphy and Donnovan, who point to a convergence of trends in heterosexual and lesbian and gay family life (2001) and in the work of Bech (1999), who points to the disappearance of the modern 'homosexual' as a consequence of the homogenisation of hetero/homosexual culture. Others talk of a 'normalisation' and 'routinisation' of lesbian and gay sexuality in developed western countries, in which individuals can be described as being 'beyond the closet' (Seidman et al, 1999; Reynolds, 1999).

All of these accounts share in common the view that lesbian and gay cultures have made an important contribution to detraditionalisation, one of the consequences of which is that the hetero/homo binary which characterises modern sexuality is in the process of deconstruction (Roseneil, 2000; Nayak and Kehily, 2007). There are many criticisms of this view, including challenges to the empirical base for claims of detraditionalisation of sexual cultures (Jamieson, 1998), the view that the fluidity claimed by queer theorists may be the exclusive province of the urban middle classes (Hennessey, 1995; Jackson, 1999), and an emerging argument that this optimistic vision of progress may in fact be complicated by counter processes of retraditionalisation (Adkins, 2002a). It appears that the biographical pattern of lesbian and gay lives is in flux, and that this flux is in conversation with flux in the shape, authority and coherence of gendered lifecourse narratives.

Situating young people within an account of detraditionalisation

During the 1980s there was a dramatic improvement in UK young women's employment prospects, their incomes, and thus the incomes of the young men living with them (Crompton, 1997). These improvements were partly related to the expansion in women's participation in higher education (Crompton, 1992). Egerton and Savage (2000) comment that if we add to this the trend towards the postponement of child rearing among many women until their thirties during the same period, 'then we are clearly able to see that the fortunes of these young adults in the early 1980s soared in economic terms'. During the same period there was also a polarisation along class lines, most distinct among men, giving rise to the emergence of a group of relatively disadvantaged young men; yet also significant was the inability of the fortunes of young female manual workers to keep pace with young female professionals (Egerton and Savage, 2000: 46).

Despite a number of reservations, the model of changing gender relations offered by the theorists of detraditionalisation has been productive within youth research, with young people being taken up as an illustrative case of individualisation (Chisholm et al, 1990; Wilkinson and Mulgan, 1995). In many ways young people and the young 'couple' fit easily into the model of the individualised and detraditionalised social actor, having relatively few commitments or responsibilities at this point in their lives. The distinction between 'normal' and 'choice' biographies, coined by Beck, has been elaborated by a range of youth researchers to make sense of increasingly fragmented pathways in the transition to adulthood (Du Bois-Reymond, 1998; Dwyer and Wyn, 2003). These distinctive biographical paths are distinguished by gender. Du Bois-Reymond talks in terms of a 'gender specific normal biography' where young people 'aim for a clearly defined profession and employment at an early stage and enter fixed relationships in order to start a family – or at least they intend to' (1998: 66) and contrasts this with a 'non-gender specific choice biography'.

Du Bois-Reymond argues that, through the process of detraditionalisation, gender is losing its determining influence, yet in practice the pulls of tradition still operate and are most acutely felt by young women, who are more willing to accommodate their careers with family demands than are young men. She comments on the 'doubleness' of the female biography which 'even in its modern shape carries with it the burden of traditional female destination and definition' (1998: 75). Drawing on Giddens' notion of 'life projects', she explores how young people develop partial projects, 'drafts for a desirable future' (1998: 63). Young people may move between normal and choice biographies as they revise these projects and adapt to the demands of their changing circumstances. In her recognition of the difficulties that young women may have in living out a choice biography, we again encounter the contradictory character of female individualisation.

Du Bois-Reymond is also careful to observe the interface between these processes of individualisation and social class. In her study of post-adolescents she focuses on what she considers to be a cultural elite, and within this elite the 'trendsetters'. It is these young people who are most likely to take up choice biographies and blur the boundaries between work and leisure. While this blurring of spheres was originally characteristic of an elite male post-adolescence, she suggest that such tendencies are increasingly popular. In contrast, disadvantaged young people may, in her terms, 'be unable to take advantage of the benefits of modernization' (1998: 67), and consequently the arenas of work and leisure tend to be more separate, as in the gender-specific normal biography. Wilkinson and Mulgan (1995) also distinguish between two trends among 18 to 34-year-olds. On the one hand they identify a move towards androgyny and away from tradition among the majority, yet they also identify a group they call the 'underwolves', excluded from mainstream values and structures. Other data from young people challenge this picture of expanding androgyny. For example, in interpreting the data from the British Young People's Social Attitudes Survey, Ann Oakley concludes:

> The experiences and underlying beliefs and values glimpsed through the elliptic lens of the YPSA survey questions do not suggest an androgynous youth culture. What they suggest, instead, is a pattern of endemic difference, and a continued fundamental tension between the ideology of gender equality, on the one hand, and the realities of learning to live in a gendered world on the other. (1996: 39)

The changing balance between agency and structure in sociological accounts as well as in society becomes central to accounts of changing gender relations. In her critique of Anthony Giddens' *Transformation of intimacy*, Lynn Jamieson criticises him for taking assertions of agency at face value, suggesting that he fails to distinguish between practices and experiences that could be empirically verified, and accounts which could be normative or aspirational. Furlong and Cartmel (1997/2006) make a similar criticism, suggesting that Giddens overemphasises the significance of individual reflexivity, disconnecting subjects from social and political contexts. While they accept Beck's conclusion that collective social identities are weakening and social divisions are more increasingly obscure, young people's objective life chances and biographical paths continue to be shaped by structural factors beyond their control, including gender (Furlong and Cartmel 1997/2006). What is new is our lack of consciousness of this process. Young people may speak an increasingly individualised 'can do' rhetoric, but 'blind to the existence of powerful chains of interdependency, young people frequently attempt to resolve collective problems through individual action and hold themselves responsible for their inevitable failure' (1997: 114).

Feminist commentaries on girlhood have also begun to engage critically with ideas of individualisation and detraditionalisation. For example, Angela McRobbie (2001, 2004) argues that young women can be seen as the symbolic spearhead of a new meritocracy. The young female worker who is flexible, focused on success, self-sustaining and self-disciplined has become a key subject for the New Labour project. McRobbie contrasts the subject position of this 'good girl' with the representations of the 'bad girl' who is increasingly at centre stage of social policy – the teenage mother. The subject position of the 'good girl' not only excludes the experiences of many young women who fail to live up to its exacting standards, but it also excludes an awareness of and responsibility for the costs of such success within a highly individualised discourse of self-improvement and social mobility. In their study of the lives of girls over a 17-year period, Walkerdine, Lucey and Melody (2001) have observed how social class structures the trajectories of young women and the meaning of success in the UK. They portray a regulated and constraining middle-class femininity in which the fear of failure operates as a disciplinary practice, producing a highly standardised model of academic excellence at the expense of embodiment and personal happiness. In contrast, they observe that working-class girls' trajectories are more varied and individualised, informed by differing notions of success and competence.

Diminishing opportunities for social mobility alongside these polarising biographies also give rise to new lines of inequality, such as the 'right' to parenthood (Ferri and Smith, 2003). As the subject of neoliberalism increasingly takes the form of the young female worker, the 'familiar exploitation' (Leonard and Delphy, 1992) necessary to support families and children has to be negotiated between partners and families or has to be accommodated within individualised biographies (Beck, 1992). Even where it is possible for young men and women to pursue parallel individualised life projects, tensions become explicit in relation to the institutional forms of heterosexuality – in particular, negotiations over the balance between the division of labour in public and domestic arenas (Van Every, 1995; Thomson and Holland, 2002). Extended dependency on parents makes this an intergenerational affair (Jones et al, 2006). Evidence of the resequencing of the transition to adulthood in this area is increasingly evident, with the majority delaying childbirth into their thirties and with a minority using parenthood as their first step towards adulthood in their late teens.

The extent to which such changes can be seen as a form of 'progress' are increasingly at the centre of academic feminist discussions in the UK (Walkerdine et al, 2001; McRobbie, 2004). The apparent rejection of a feminist project by a generation of younger women, and the embracing of forms of femininity resisted and critiqued by earlier feminists, has been a source of some confusion and debate (Frith, 2001; Nayak and Kehily, 2007). McRobbie (2001) describes an emerging sentiment of 'anti-sisterhood' as a generational reaction to mothers. And in the United States generational tensions between second- and third-wave feminists have become explicit, with third-wavers portraying relationship in terms of mother/daughter conflict (Baumberger and Richards, 2000). Second-wave feminists (mothers) are charged with telling a negative story, focusing on loss, while third-wavers portray a more positive and resistant image of girls. Aapola and colleagues (2001, 2004) characterise these different approaches in terms of a second-wave concern with 'Ophelia' (following Mary Piper's influential work in the US) and third-wave interest in 'Girl Power', observing problematic aspects of both positions. In the words of Walkerdine and colleagues:

> discourses of 'girl power', which stress the possibility of having and being what you want, provide an ideal that is almost impossible to live up to, and through which young women read their own failure as personal pathology. (2001: 178)

Where the US and Australian debates appear to bring questions of generation in feminism to the foreground, debates in the UK are increasingly drawing attention to the impact of social class in polarising the lives of women. When compounded with effects of generation (Walby, 1997), this gives rise to very different female biographies and an uneven access to opportunities brought about by feminism. Diversity exists in women's lives both within and between cultures. In a comparative study of young people's lives and expectations of the future, contrasting European and Scandinavian countries, Brannen and colleagues explored the range of ways that young people experience disjunctions between gendered realities and the discourses of individual choice (Brannen et al, 2002: 89). They observe that discourses of equality operate differently in different countries, relating to national welfare regimes and policy languages. In Scandinavian countries they observe a 'silent' discourse of equality, premised on a normalisation of expectation which nevertheless makes the contradictions between normative expectations and actual practices difficult to name. In the UK they suggest that equality is translated into the 'language of individual choice, and contradictions between expectations and realities are also attributed to individual tastes' (p 106).

In summary, a story of changing gender identity lies at the centre of the dominant sociological accounts of late modernity. This stands in some tension with feminist paradigms that have tended to privilege an understanding of the production and reproduction of inequality. Yet within feminist analyses and analyses of masculinity there is a shift towards seeing gender as a cultural formation that may be cultivated and exchanged in the pursuit of privilege. This shift opens up not only possibilities for understanding diversities in the ways in which gender is made, but also differences in how gender is rewarded. This has significance for what 'counts' as change, innovation, progressive practice, and what may be read as reactionary and fixed (Walkerdine, 1995).

Conclusion

The 20th century witnessed a transformation in the position of women and thus in gender relations (Ferri et al, 2003). Improved life expectancy, the ability to control their fertility and the increasing possibility of financial independence have enabled women to transform their lives and, in doing so, change society. Mainstream sociological theorists have located these changes as part of wider processes of individualisation and detraditionalisation. While gender is central to these theses, the accounts of change provided by different theorists place different degrees of emphasis on agency, structure, resilience and change. Feminist commentaries on changing gender relations have tended to emphasise resilience, and until relatively recently have not engaged with discussions of detraditionalisation. Youth researchers have adopted the conceptual tools of the detraditionalisation theorists to some effect, but empirical evidence suggests that changes in gender relations may not be as advanced, nor as simple as some of the theorists of detraditionalisation suggest. Recent work exploring the operations and limitations of reflexivity suggest that it is not sufficient to ask how innovations in the gender order are forged: we must also understand why only some innovations are noticed, authorised and rewarded. These are questions that I will take up throughout this book, seeking to understand the impulses that shape the creation of particular gender identities and the internal and external audiences involved in their authorisation. In the following chapters I will showcase a series of case histories of young lives through which I explore the dynamic character of gender identities over a period of several years, and between generations within a family.

FOUR

Going up! Discipline and opportunism

In this chapter I will explore the successive accounts of Sherleen, a young woman of African Caribbean heritage living in inner-city London. Sherleen was interviewed four times between the ages of 13 and 16 by Sue Sharpe, who conducted each of the interviews in a room at Sherleen's school. I approach this material as a secondary analyst and have spent time absorbed with audio tapes and interview transcripts, looking for ways in which to tell the series of linked narratives that are within this body of data. A fifth interview was undertaken with Sherleen in 2002, after the first draft of this chapter was written, and in keeping with the temporal structure of this book, it is considered in Chapter Eight. The detail of the data set is outlined in the Appendix (see p 181).

The changes that take place in Sherleen's life over this period may appear modest. She continued at school, working hard, being entered early for one of her GCSEs and doing well in her mock exams. She continued to live with her mother in a flat, spending most of her time with her extended family and occasionally seeing her father and half-brother. Her social activities developed and contracted as school work claimed more of her time and attention. Two boyfriends came and went, and her mother split up from her long-term partner. Yet this was also a period of intense identity work for Sherleen through which she explored the kind of person she wanted to be and negotiated her relationships with others.

The reader will not find a singular chronological story in this chapter, but rather a series of partial narratives, each of which captures a 'field' of Sherleen's 'existence' (education, family and leisure). These fields, which represent the spaces through which Sherleen's project of self is constructed, give rise to the narrative threads of a wider biography. As the partial narratives unfold the reader may feel caught within, in a temporal loop – moving repeatedly through the same four-year cycle – but this incremental approach allows for an accumulation of complexity, meaning and insight.

Education: from diligence to determination

We begin Sherleen's story with school, the place where she spends a large part of most of her days, the demands of which also structure much of her 'free time'. All four of Sherleen's interviews were marked by an educational temporality. In her first she was making sense of the transition from primary to secondary school, in her second she was reflecting on her SATs results and choice of GCSE subjects, in her third she was absorbed with her early entry for GCSE maths and in her fourth she meditated on the results of her mock-GCSE results and her plans for further education. From the outset, Sherleen communicated a sense of 'educational urgency' where 'doing well can become a radical strategy; an act of social transformation' (Mirza, 1997: 274). Succeeding is not simply about individual success but involves the interests of a wider collectivity. Her account resonates with Heidi Mirza's account of a 'West Indian, migrant working class ethos' that 'filters down' and is subsequently 'adapted' (1992: 181), which she contrasts to the 'subculture of resistance' described by Fuller (1982). Sherleen's enactment of 'doing well' develops over time, and transcends the boundaries of the school.

The official school

When interviewed at the age of 15 Sherleen was still absorbed in reflections on the transition from primary to secondary school, a process that she had found empowering.

> **I came out** of primary school thinking that I wasn't that smart, it's only when I got to secondary school I realised that I was quite smart 'cause like there were people who in my primary school were smarter than me and it kind of, I kind of like watched them and how they act, how they was acting and I thought, well I'm never gonna be that smart so I may as well sit down and be quiet. But then I started to do some work and like, in Year 6 I did SATs, in Year 6, and that went quite alright and I was picked to do the top set. [...] I thought okay, so I am smart then. [1999, aged 14]

Yet being in the top set brings pressures. In this interview Sherleen talks at length about the results of her SATs, and although she understands herself as doing well – 'I got just above average, average is like a 5 and I got straight 6s in all my lessons' – she is aware that she could have done better, explaining that 'you take certain streams [...] the highest I could have got was a 6. I took the 4 to 6 test and two other people in my class took the 5 to 7 test'. While Sherleen embraces the technologies of self made available within this educational setting she also remarks on the energy and discipline that it takes to achieve the necessary demeanour to be a successful pupil (see also Reay, 2002). In the context of the interview she is prepared to express her ambivalence about these ways of seeing oneself and being seen by others. Her comments suggest that while the techniques of streaming and testing offer possible subject positions, these are not taken up in absolute terms.

Notions of a career also begin to take shape in Sherleen's second interview, and with them the idea of an educational project as a 'long haul', with her goals located elusively in the future. Consistent with this metaphor is the danger that she is unable to 'keep on track' long enough to realise her ambitions. Here she questions her ability to hang in for the duration:

> **Law school's too** long. (*laugh*) Probably because of that, I'm a patient person but to some extent I couldn't wait all those years for that law

degree. I could not wait that long, I'd go crazy, I think I'd go mad waiting all that time. But I think if it's gonna take that long, then it's gonna have to produce a lot for all that time without any money or anything. [...] it'll have to have a really good outcome, for me to stay at it for so long. [1999, aged 14]

She presents her motivation as fuelled by a critical understanding of her life chances:

If I keep on working, I think I'll have good chances, other than that, if I don't, don't think I'll have any chances. Working hard, education really. [...] if I do well in school, then I can get quite far, but if I don't, I'm gonna have to try a bit harder than someone who lives in a posher area really, but I don't mind [...] I am a determined person, everyone says that, I am determined. [1999, aged 14]

At her third interview, a year later, Sherleen experiments with ideas of a career in leisure and tourism, expressing doubts over her plans to be a lawyer:

It [training to be a lawyer] is long time, and somehow I think I can't do this. But I think I could probably do it, but then I think about money and stuff, where's it gonna come from. 'Cause I know I'm gonna have to study, it's just the money side of it really. [2000, aged 15]

During this interview she explains that she has been entered a year early for her maths GCSE, which means 'I'll probably have A level maths by the time I'm 17'. Yet being identified as 'early entry' places her under considerable pressure and she expresses her anxiety about keeping up with the requisite workload:

I really can't stand being behind, that's one thing. I don't like not knowing things that other people know, I really can't stand that. It scares me, it doesn't scare me but it just makes me think, why don't I know this 'cause I like if I wanna know something and someone else knows it, and I think I should know it, that I should have learnt it. [2000, aged 15]

When interviewed the following year she expresses disappointment in her performance. She did not do as well as she thought, explaining that 'I was doubting myself too much, I didn't think I would do too well'. On the advice of her teacher she is retaking the exam, attempting to turn her 'D' into a 'B'. Her account emphasises the personal attention that she is receiving from her teacher:

She says, you're the only girl that I know in a class that actually is taking (...) 'cause I'm the only girl, well, I was last year, but this year there's another girl doing it (...) but she says you're the only one that I can actually say has got a head on her shoulders. So make sure you pass. Always pressuring me. [2001, aged 16]

Here she is rewarded by individual attention and an educational identity that is given traction by discourses of equity. In this same interview Sherleen's comments suggest how another teacher has provided her with narrative resources to imagine herself achieving against the odds:

> **I know I** really do wanna be successful and I don't think I'll let anything hold me back, 'cause even one of my teachers, 'cause she's black and she said, she used to be, what was it, accountant and she had a lot of racism, come into a lot of racism, and she said that it didn't let her hold her back basically, can't let anything hold me back right now, or in the future. [2001, aged 16]

In this fourth interview Sherleen reflects on the changes in her own experience of school since the research began, commenting that she used to like school in Year 7 and 8. Now she is 'just trying to keep on track'. In retrospect, she wishes that she could have 'taken it easier' in Year 7 and 8, noting that 'I really pushed myself'. She reports no longer enjoying school in the same way, but is well aware that she has to do well in order to realise her ambitions. Although her determination is renewed, it is tempered by recognition of the costs of living for the future. Sherleen describes herself as being 'a bit frustrated. I want to be doing law already.' Her plans continue to be hard work: 'If I work hard I'll make progress. Doors are open and if I work hard I'll get to them. But if I don't work hard I won't'.

Over the course of the four years Sherleen moves from being a diligent pupil, complying with the demands of the educational structure and comparing herself to others, to being an individual success, developing an educational identity that is self-consciously informed by being a 'determined' black woman, achieving against the odds. It is an identity that finds support within the official school. She is chosen by one of her teachers for a special work experience placement at a top barrister's chambers. She recognises the particular opportunities available to her through the school (such as a university scholarship scheme) and the value placed by the school on black history and culture. Asked if she sees herself as fortunate, she responds, 'No, determined and obstinate.' She explains that many of her friends are not sure of themselves, but when she starts thinking of where she 'wants to be going, I get that determination and self-confidence back'. Asked if she experiences discrimination she responds, 'I know it's there but I know if I'm educated and have the knowledge that I don't see why that should bother me.' 'I'm nowhere near rich, but I wouldn't say I'm destitute. I know if I want it I've gotta work for it.' Recently she had been unnerved by witnessing friends dropping out of school, and she comments, 'I know I need to come to school to be a barrister. Now I'm near the end I've really seen what I want to do' [2001, aged 16].

The informal school

Sherleen's ability to observe and learn from her environment was also reflected in her account of the informal school culture. Aged 13, she provided a detailed account of the gender dynamics of the pupil culture:

> **Boys play more** games, and when they're playing games it's always, he's on my team, he's on my team, so they get to like be friends more at the end of the day. But girls [...] they think it's like hypocritical to have an argument with one girl and then, like be her friend the next day. They won't do it, but boys, they don't care, they just (...) they'll do it anyway. [...] with girls they hang around in like uhm, more tighter groups, and even though they might like hang around with one person and a few people, their groups are like tighter and more close together. But with boys they speak to everyone, they do this, 'cause this – like when they play their games like football and patball and all that, they uhm (...), like spread their groups around a bit more. So it's different with boys. [...] boys they will never tell on another boy [...] 'cause they think that if they say anything they're gonna get like excluded, but girls they're a bit more self-conscious. [1998, aged 13]

These kinds of insights clearly affected the way in which Sherleen positioned herself in relation to friendship groups and informal peer hierarchies. While it may be necessary to work hard to be a successful pupil, when it comes to popularity this has little value.

> **I think that** in school with the children it's like more popular people, they have like more say in what they're doing, and it's always the prettier girls, and like the smartest girls they don't really have a say. So unless you're smart and you're pretty then that's the only way you do actually get a say into things. [1998, aged 13]

Sherleen is aware that different rules govern the popularity of boys. While these rules also lead boys into their own dead ends (eg, excelling at football at the expense of academic achievement: Connolly, 1998), the very fact that there are different ways of playing the game suggests possibilities for Sherleen, who is frustrated by the constraining models of femininity offered by the informal school culture. Her solution to this situation is to learn from boys, and an opportunity to do this is offered by a (different) research study that was conducted in the school, where the usual classroom seating formation based on student choice was disrupted and replaced by girl/boy couples:

When I did sit next to this boy, I did actually like learn a lot. 'Cause I learnt a lot about what boys think as well, and how they like carry themselves, what they do, what they think, like why they play football, why they like things so much, and stuff like that. I did learn a lot 'cause I thought, oh sitting next to a boy – so boring, but when you do actually talk to them, it's different, you think they're gonna be so boring – chatting about rubbish, football all the time, but they don't, not all the time. [1998, aged 13]

Not only does Sherleen learn from the individual boy sitting next to her, but she also observes the significance of the official educational culture making an intervention into the informal gender culture of the classroom through the research.

I think there's more of girls that are really trying than boys, that's why they've done all that research to put us next to each other and stuff like that. [1998, aged 13]

By her second interview Sherleen is drawing a line between her school and non-school identities. In school she identifies primarily with the formal school, and places little value on her friendships, which she presents as immature:

I'll talk to one friend one way and talk to another friend another way, like my friends outside of school 'cause they're more mature so like I have to change the way I speak and the language I use and everything, that changes. [1999, aged 14]

Her 'real' friendships exist outside, and these are primarily relationships with boys:

I prefer being around boys it kinda puts all the stereotypes, it kinda puts them all down so, I prefer to hang around with boys though, to me they're more fun, girls are more worried about what they'll look like in the morning like if they mess up their hair and stuff, but like boys, they'll just go out and do things recklessly so. [1999, aged 14]

In drawing boundaries around school Sherleen can experiment without jeopardising her identity as a good student. By her third interview, what had previously been presented in terms of friendship is articulated through a language of 'boyfriends'. Sherleen reports that she had recently split up with a boyfriend of nine months. The boy, Darren, had not attended her school. She explains:

I made myself a policy, I wouldn't see anyone in school, it's like when you don't go with 'em anymore or anything, I mean you're not with them anymore, it's like you see them and you might have a bit of feeling or anything so I don't like to mix it. [2000, aged 15]

Sherleen is consistent in taking the opportunity to learn what she could from her boyfriend:

> **He was black** and he was a bit, he was like quite (...) he was (...) like (...) I can't think of any word now, he was (...) really (...) um (...) he knew about black history, a lot of it, he knew a lot about it and I think I know some of the things that I know from him, but he was just (...) he was a nice person but like at the end I didn't really see any interest in him anymore so I thought (...) I didn't really wanna go out with him anymore. *(laugh)*. [2000, aged 15]

The relationship was not sexual and she was determined that it shouldn't be. Sex and educational achievement did not mix. In this interview, Sherleen explained that the boundary that she had built between school and non-school identities had been renegotiated and that her friendships were now primarily with school friends:

> **Yeah, they are,** my friends are important to me, but now are more important than anything, 'cause we do a lot of, we do studying together, practically think together. [2000, aged 15]

Yet she continues her identification with boys, even though she observes that these relationships were complicated by the spectre of sex:

> **I'm still close** to a lot of boys, I still talk to, I'm still more friends with boys than anything. [...] I find boys more tolerable, even though most of the boys I know have got sex on the brain right now [...] I do find them more tolerable, every boy in the school has got sex on their brain, it's annoying. [2000, aged 15]

By the time of this interview she had another boyfriend, whom she describes as 'nice, he's safe, just a nice person to talk to'. They had been going out together for two months and the relationship was largely conducted on the telephone, made possible by free evening calls with her mobile phone contract. Asked whether the relationship was sexual she responds, 'No. At the moment I can't think about much else but my exams' [2000, aged 15].

I have included this material on boys and boyfriends within an educational narrative because I believe that Sherleen talks about these relationships with friends and boyfriends pedagogically: she learns from them and employs them as resources in her educational project. By her fourth interview her relationships are much reduced in order to make space for study. She only sees her friends in school, remarking that 'we've all been buckling down with school work'. She had finished with her boyfriend, on her mother's advice, to enable her to focus on study. When asked about sex she replies, 'I've got other things to concentrate on now. Other things can take their time.'

Family: 'doing better – a family trait'

Sherleen's efforts to be a diligent and determined student are complemented by the support and direction offered by her family. Although she lives alone with her mother, she is, by her own, account 'a family person' who likes to be around her extended family network. Most of Sherleen's social life is spent with her cousins, aunts, uncles and grandparents on her mother's side of the family. Family can be understood as constituting another field of existence within Sherleen's biography – making available particular narratives, and being associated with a 'daily aesthetic' that she engages with in the construction of her identity. It is important, however, to distinguish between different dimensions of family life in her account: the family as represented by the extended family network, and the family at the more intimate levels of the 'home' comprising herself and her mother. There is also an absent family which holds a place in Sherleen's emotional landscape, linked to her father, his former relationship with her mother and his new partnership and children. These different dimensions of family life are interdependent and the boundaries that Sherleen constructs between them (and the changes in these over time) are one of the means through which she articulates the kind of woman that she understands herself to be.

Self-improvement – an intergenerational strategy

It was clear from the outset that Sherleen's educational ambitions were embedded within a family culture of self-improvement arising from the experience of migration. She explains that her life will be different from that of her parents, who, due to circumstance and racism, were unable to realise their potential.

> **Uhm, I think** with my parents, I think I will be different because like my mum was born in Jamaica, and she came over here, and she was – like she was bright, but she found it – like 'cause she's a chef and she uhm, works – like she's head chef for a shop. [...] so, I don't think I'll actually turn to cooking, I think like I will do that after I've tried singing, and after I've done my science bits and stuff like that, I think I will do that afterwards, but I don't think I'll actually go for cooking or stuff like that, 'cause I don't really – I like it, but I don't think I'd look to it as a career or anything like that. [1999, aged 14]

In her third interview she was more explicit:

> **I try and** work hard because like I wanna be something that, 'cause like when people in my family, they just, they don't get to be that prestigious, have lots of money, not rich or anything, so I just wanna kind of turn it around. [2000, aged 15]

And later in the same interview:

> **I really do** wanna get somewhere, I really do 'cause like some people in my family they just end up in jobs they don't like. [2000, aged 15]

In this interview she describes a family culture in which three generations are engaged in a collective educational project, with hopes being placed in the youngest:

> **Everyone thinks that** I'm smart and until you meet my cousins, like they're really boffins and egg heads [...] Yeah, (*laugh*), all my family, like my mum pushes me and their mums push them as well so, that's what it's like in my family, you get pushed to do the maximum. [2000, aged 15]

There is a close relationship between recognising the injustices and sacrifices that have shaped the past and valuing the authority of older generations. Sherleen expresses this through a valorising of 'discipline'. She sees herself as different from her peers because she has been parented in this way, and attributes her diligent demeanour in school to these values.

> **[...] like I** was taught about discipline from a young age and I've actually been disciplined quite a lot. [...] I think it may be because of my grandparents as well, 'cause if they discipline me, I always have to do it, I won't argue back because I would never do that 'cause like they're older and you should respect them, and things like that, but uhm, I was taught from a young age that, if someone's older than you, you have to respect them, no matter what. [2000, aged 15]

Sherleen presents herself as situated in benevolent competition with her cousins, who provide each other with support and motivation. She explains that her cousin Steven 'helps me, he knows I'm in early entry, and if he's got any mock papers, exam books, anything, he'll just come and help me'. The articulation of a collective educational strategy is underpinned by a narrative of family return to Jamaica that forms an important yet changeable part of Sherleen's own future plans. At 15 she imagines herself going to Jamaica at the end of her legal training:

I think like I've always wanted to live there, I've wanted to go and live with my nan and granddad for so long, 'cause they should go back there, it's not, they just really need to go back, they miss it, you can see it, they really miss it. But it's the family that's here, they will miss them even more. [2000, aged 15]

Over subsequent interviews it emerged that Sherleen's maternal grandfather was in fact the prime mover in the story of return and that her grandmother stubbornly resisted his exhortations to move back to Jamaica, where he had purchased land, being determined to 'stay with us'. By her final interview, Sherleen's own plans to practise law in Jamaica have been postponed. She is still committed to 'returning' at some point, observing that she would 'want to go sooner than everyone else did. Granddad left it way too long.' She explains that if her mother decided to retire to Jamaica she would take the opportunity to move as well, and she predicts that most of her family will eventually be there, on the grounds that 'they'll have had enough of England by then'.

The technologies of parenting

At 14 Sherleen observes a strict boundary between the generations, finding it difficult to believe that her mother could understand her feelings. Asked if she confides in her mother, she replies: 'I can't tell her how I'm feeling, she's like just tell me but I'm like no, cause you're my mum. (*laugh*).' Sherleen accepts the practices of parenting with little resistance, relying on these interventions to motivate her application to her studies:

She's very strict about my education, very strict, she makes sure, makes sure that I work, she loves it, she loves, 'what did you do at school today', loves asking me about school, I don't know why, I think she's probably checking on me but I'm okay with that, 'cause it makes me, it's makes sure I work, it make sure I'm doing something, 'cause if I don't, if she doesn't check sometimes, I just like not do any work, try to get away with it. [1999, aged 14]

However, by her fourth interview, Sherleen communicates a much closer identification with her mother. She repeatedly claims common personality traits, locating these in a wider family heritage. Her mother is a key resource in maintaining her educational trajectory, helping her 'to think about how to get there'. She talks about their similarities, 'both Taurean, both stubborn', observing that 'All the women in my family are really stubborn'. Her mother is her 'number one role model next to my nan', who is 'four foot eleven with some attitude. Mum says I'm very like my nan.' She describes her mother as the 'toughest' of her aunties, observing 'I'm a lot like her in a way. People notice it as I get older, people say I look like my mum more. She hasn't had it easy.'

The process of becoming 'like' her mother is presented as the result of her mother's parenting practices. In her first interview this was explained in the following terms:

> **I know when** she's gonna tell me off, when she's gonna tell me to do something. So I try and get in there first, 'cause I don't like being told off at all. So I try and get in there first before she has to tell me off, so like with discipline now. [1998, aged 13]

By her fourth interview the process of internalisation has progressed, and with it comes a new identification with family:

> **I have the** kind of drive where mum doesn't have to tell me. Even though my mum wants me to do better, and do kinds of things that she didn't get the opportunity to do, I want to do those things anyway. It's a trait that runs through my family. [2001, aged 16]

Yet being like her mother and other female relations stands in some tension with her ambitions to have a life very different to theirs.

Intimacy, dependency and gender subjectivity

In their discussion of the dynamic relationship between gender identity and gender subjectivity, Bjerrum Nielsen and Rudberg (1994) make the important observation that while a young woman may draw 'inscriptions' as to the kind of woman she might want to be from the culture around her, these are likely to exist in some tension with a less conscious dimension of gender subjectivity that is in great part shaped by her emotional relationship and forms of identification with her parents. In the sections above it is possible to see how Sherleen draws on the resources made available to her by the fields of education and family life to elaborate a relatively conscious identity as a woman. If we now look more closely at her relationship with her mother and her absent father, it is possible to capture some of the contradictions between this emergent gender identity and the investments and emotions that shape her gender subjectivity. While it is difficult to delineate the more or less private aspects of an individual's gender identity, I suggest that this area of identity work can be understood as particularly 'intimate' in that it displays evidence of the kind of 'moral density' (Weeks, 1995) associated with intense and unfinished identity work (Crawford et al, 1992). In order to consider this relationship I will focus on the themes of marriage and dependency.

Sherleen was invited to complete a 'lifeline' in her second and fourth interviews, part of which demanded that she predict her relationship status in three years' time, at the age of 25 and at the age of 35. In her first lifeline, aged 14, Sherleen predicted that in three years' time she would hope to have no boyfriend, remarking that 'they slow you down and they take up too much time. I think those three years of my life I'd like to be selfish a bit.' At the age of 25 she would have a 'serious' boyfriend, but they would not be living together. At the age of 35 she would be 'married with two children *(laugh)*. I aspire to have two children when I started my career in law.' Asked whether marriage was important to her, she replied:

> **Not really, it's** not really important but, I dunno, part of me wants to get married and part of me says, no don't do it. But yeah, I think, it's not that important but it's something I'd like. I wanna have a wedding, I just wanna go through the whole marriage process, I like the sound of it. [1999, aged 14]

At her fourth interview, nearly two years later, she was asked to reflect on her original plans. Her aspirations for three years' time remained intact, and she comments 'hopefully no boyfriend. Slows you down and takes up too much time.' At the age of 25 she reiterates her original sentiments: 'Serious boyfriends but not living together *(laugh)* – I really do need my space.' However, she now sees life at 35 quite differently:

> **I wanna have** the wedding, the trimmings, but not sure about the husband. I like the idea of having a big wedding ceremony [...] It depends on how work situation is. If I'm working hard and don't really have time for it I'll put it off for a couple more years – but not too far down the line. I wouldn't mind just living [...] I don't see marriage as something I need to do ever. Unless I find someone I really want to marry I don't think I will. [2001, aged 16]

Asked about her views on children she remarks:

> **I don't know** if I want kids – I'm not sure. I ought to be like my auntie – keep promising the family I'll have kids and never do it. [2001, aged 16]

At the end of the interview Sherleen explains that doing the first lifeline made her 'think a lot', coming to the realisation that 'I know I'm not too serious about having kids. I've become a lot more independent. If I do have kids it will be because I really want to.' Although she attributes this change to the space offered to her by the research process, the following discussion also suggests that her evolving orientation towards marriage and commitment is closely related to her relationship with her mother. The interviewer asks Sherleen whether the sort of woman she wants to be, 'independent and happy', is different to women in her family. She responds:

Most of the women in my family have got married and had kids and stopped working, or carried on working. My mum hasn't really done that, so I think I'll follow my mum for a little while. Even though she has thought about getting married, she wasn't really into the commitment side of it, I think I'll probably be like her. [2001, aged 16]

Sherleen explains that although her mother married her dad, she 'didn't really want to', concluding that 'I'm not into all the marriage side of things and she knows she doesn't really want to get married. I think I know I'm a lot like that. I don't think I will get married young or have kids young. I want to do everything I want to do first. Live my life before bringing anyone else into this world.'

Here we see slippage between Sherleen's views on marriage and those she attributes to her mother. Given that the marriage status and plans of her mother have major personal significance for Sherleen's security, it can be argued that there is a dynamic relationship between her conscious gender identity (the kind of woman she imagines herself be) and more unconscious dimensions of her gender subjectivity (the feelings and investments that she must contend with). To explore this further it is worthwhile tracing Sherleen's account of her relationship with her mother over the four interviews, and her orientation towards her mother's relationship with men.

From the outset it was apparent that Sherleen's mother was a major figure in her life. Although Sherleen did not want to follow her mother's working life she nevertheless admires her:

She's like really strong minded, and she does like really help me a lot, and like I said, we're more friends, and we do, I do talk to mum about everything, boyfriends, everything, so like with mum I'd like to be like my mum, like if I ever become a mother, I'd like to be as close to my daughter as I am with mum. [1998, aged 13]

It also became apparent in this interview that Sherleen's mother plays an important role in constructing and monitoring her educational identity:

Mum says, don't talk unless you finish your work, because I don't want to see you coming home with loads of detentions, none of this, none of that, for talking. She says if you've finished your work, then you can talk, and don't be disrupting other people ever, because you don't want to stop them from getting a job when they're older. [1998, aged 13]

In her second interview Sherleen said little about her father, other than that her parents split up when she was 6 years old, and that she tries hard to keep in touch with him, his new family and his extended family. In the next interview she was more critical of her father and sought to draw a clear distinction between her relationship with her two parents. She did this by invoking 'friendship' as a quality that can be afforded between her and her mother, but which merely exposes her father's lack of commitment.

> **The relationship between** my dad and me isn't as good as my mum 'cause like he doesn't try to be a dad as much, he tries to be my friend too much so it's like, I would rather have a father first than a friend, cause like my mum's been there, she's been my mum like all of my life so like I'd rather like him to try and be a father to me rather than a friend straight away, I think those kind of things just, they kind of come as time goes by but that's what happened to me and mum, now we're like more friendly, we can talk about things that matter, she talks to me about what happens in her life and I talk to her about what happens in mine, but with my dad it's kind of different. [1999, aged 14]

Her refusal to identify with her father is summed up in her comment, 'I look like my dad (*laugh*) unfortunately (*laugh*).' When asked about how she felt about her father's absence she initially downplayed its significance, but then made a strong statement as to the consequences of this estrangement for her expectations for relationship:

> **It doesn't seem** that much to not have my dad there, like I'm kind of used to it. And even though mum does have a boyfriend, it's like it's not the same. But I'm used to not having like my dad around, I'm used to it now. So, if anything has kind of made me like less dependent on men and in general, becoming any less dependent on people really actually. [1999, aged 14]

Later in the interview she talked about finding it difficult to trust people, and again attributed this to the split between her parents, both her father's absence, and also her mother's ability to manage without him:

> INT: So why do you think you've got a lack of trust?

> **I dunno, sometimes** I actually think 'cause of my dad, I don't know, I think it's just the way that I've kind of been brought up, my mum, she's kind of independent and even though she does trust in people like, it kind of reflects onto me. So it makes me think that I need to be independent and that I don't really, shouldn't trust anyone. [1999, aged 14]

There is a dynamic relationship between Sherleen's admitted dependence on her mother (material, emotional and moral), her desire to model her mother's independent spirit, and her assertion of independence *from* her mother. Again we find tensions between her identification with her mother and her assertion of her difference from her:

> **I don't really** depend on my mum, I don't really, like I depend on her to get money, and like my own food – I make it. She can buy it but I make it. And like we do go shopping together, my mum doesn't do the shopping by herself, although I help her carry the bags and everything but she does like a lot of stuff. And sometimes we go clothes shopping together 'cause she likes the kind of same clothes as me so we just go shopping together, like food and get food for the house, and clothes shopping. And we look at things and we like the same kind of things. So we just like, when we see something we don't like, ugh, so we just laugh and joke a lot when we go out. [1999, aged 14]

Although Sherleen expresses a respect for age-based hierarchies, her comments about her mother tend to emphasise the egalitarian nature of their relationship, they are 'friends', they confide in each other, they like the same clothes. Yet Sherleen is also very vulnerable in relation to her mother. She relies heavily on her support for her educational project, and she is the source of her security. This vulnerability is rarely expressed directly, but is implied in her discussions of her mother's relationship with her boyfriend:

> **My mum wants** a family but she doesn't really. I don't really know what she's waiting for 'cause she's got a boyfriend (*laugh*). I think she's waiting for like the business to come along probably.
>
> INT: Is this like a long-term boyfriend that she's got?
>
> Yeah, since I was about 6.
>
> INT: That's quite long term, isn't it?
>
> Very long term and they haven't had any children. I think he's got two children, but I don't really know them that well.
>
> INT: So would you like her to have a child with him?
>
> I don't know 'cause sometimes I don't like him, that's sometimes though, sometimes I don't like him, but he tries to be nice to me but sometimes I just think, why are you trying so hard (...) I have tried to like him, I really have but sometimes I just don't. [1999, aged 14]

Sherleen went on to explain that her mother's boyfriend teaches Karate, an activity which she herself took up. This 'gives us something to talk about'.

When first reading this interview I noted my own feelings that something was likely to 'give' in her relationship with her mother, having gained the sense that it was associated with intense and contradictory forces. It is important to recognise that these feelings may be associated with my particular perspective, from which I identified a contradiction between Sherleen's identification with her mother and the logic of her educational trajectory, which was based on not being like her mother. I was also sensitive to the contradiction between Sherleen's desire for material and emotional security and her sense of her mother as an independent and uncommitted spirit. It was in Sherleen's discussions of the presence and absence of men in their lives that I sensed that she was giving voice to these uncertainties.

In her third interview there had been a dramatic change in these circumstances. While I had wondered if Sherleen might come into conflict with or withdraw from her mother, I had not anticipated that her mother would withdraw from her. In this interview Sherleen presented her mother as being depressed, and unavailable:

> **She sits in** her room and sleeps all the time, 'cause she's always tired. When she comes back from work she sleeps a lot […] It just gets tense like she'll, sometimes she'll come home and she's tired and I wanna talk and tell her about my day, and she's like, no no (...) I'm like okay, I wanna go to sleep […] So not tense, just sometimes it's like she wants to do her thing and go to sleep and I just wanna talk, or I'll do something else, like I just wanna go out or something, and she'll say I can't take you out now 'cause this that and the other. But then after a while I just leave her to sleep 'cause I know she needs it. [2000, aged 15]

Sherleen explained that her mother suffers from health problems which caused her to put on weight and to become depressed. Her mother's withdrawal triggers a crisis in Sherleen's life. Her educational project was effectively a collaboration between the two, and in her mother's absence Sherleen was searching for alternative sources of support:

> **She does, she** does push me still, but now she expects it of me, without saying much, I know that if I do anything wrong, I've got my mum standing over me, or she'll tell me off or something, so I'm okay now, but I'm alright, kind of I just know that she's there. […] My maths teacher, she helps me a lot, she doesn't tell me, I expect she's busy, I know what I've gotta do, she's like my mum, she's like my second mum, and I've got my aunt, she's another one. [2000, aged 15]

In this same interview Sherleen talks about the increasing importance of her friends in her life. She also voices doubts over her ability to become a lawyer (posing an alternative plan of going into leisure and tourism) and begins to make a significant investment in a boyfriend relationship. It was only when asked about her involvement in Karate that she explained that her mother had split up with her boyfriend.

> **But they broke** up.
>
> INT: Did they?
>
> Yeah, not too long ago, it was about a month, about the same time I left Karate they broke up.
>
> INT: 'Cause wasn't he a Karate teacher?
>
> He was the person that taught Karate. 'Cause they were having (...) they were just not getting on, my mum wasn't really, losing interest basically.
>
> INT: What, she was losing interest in him?
>
> Yeah. But just they broke up.
>
> INT: So she's not depressed about him?
>
> No, but it wasn't 'cause of that why I left Karate. I already had decided to leave before that and I told him that I was leaving and he said okay, go and do other things (...) he understood about my exams and everything, it was getting a bit boring. I didn't think I needed it (...) I didn't need to go as much at that time. [2000, aged 15]

There are a number of slippages in this passage that I find interesting – effecting a parallel account of her mother ending the relationship with the boyfriend and her ending her relationship with him through leaving the Karate class. I also read into this data a 'mirroring' in Sherleen's denial of both the suggestions that her mother might be depressed because of the split with her boyfriend and that Sherleen might have left Karate because of the split-up. I would suggest that at this point Sherleen's earlier identifications are in flux, she begins to look beyond the boundaries of the collaborative educational project to more local resources, and a more local future. My interpretation of this situation was to assume that Sherleen would no longer be able to rely on her mother, wondering how she might achieve her ambitions (if they still were her ambitions) without her mother's support. My attention moved to her boyfriend and the thought that an ambitious partner might help her along her way, while also recognising the dangers posed to her educational project by love and sex.

In her fourth interview Sherleen describes her mother as being 'back' from her depression and herself as back 'on track' educationally. She explains that her mother is now friends with her ex-boyfriend and happy to be alone, adding that she 'might just be saying it'. She characterises her mother as being focused on work and wanting to start her own business. On return to her role as Sherleen's 'coach', her mother intervened to end Sherleen's relationship with her boyfriend. Again, we can see a 'mirroring' in Sherleen's account between her own identity and that which she attributes to her mother. Sherleen's mother ends her relationship with her long-term boyfriend, and with it the prospect of a baby. Sherleen makes sacrifices giving up Karate (severing links with her mother's former partner), accepting her mother's advice to finish with her boyfriend and withdrawing from her locally based peer group. In this interview Sherleen reflects on her decision to give up Karate, observing that 'I had to give it up', even though 'It gave me a lot of confidence and discipline when I was younger, I couldn't picture me the way I am now without it.'

The lifeline exercise provides an explicit marker of change in Sherleen's gender identity between her second and fourth interviews, moving from the position of a 14-year-old who wanted to marry and settle down, to a 16-year-old determined to prioritise career over family life and motherhood. During this period her relationship with her mother underwent a 'crisis', jeopardising her educational project. By making 'sacrifices', the two manage to maintain the project, yet through this process some of Sherleen's ideas about the kind of woman she wants to be have shifted.

Martial arts: a catalyst of identity

In this final section I explore Sherleen's involvement in martial arts, which I suggest can also be understood as a field of existence, giving rise to resources for realising the self. I have already suggested that her involvement in Karate had biographical significance, being taken up and put down in conversation with her mother's relationship. If we look at Sherleen's biography in terms of fields of existence, it is possible to see martial arts operating as a catalyst between the fields of education and family, facilitating movement and the transgression of boundaries.

Sherleen first talked about her involvement in Karate at her second interview, explaining that she had been going to classes for eight years. Her answer to the question of whether she started going to Karate because of her mother's boyfriend is somewhat ambiguous:

> **Well, I was** there before actually, she knew him when she was in college and um (...) they kind of like met up again, but he was telling her about the class and how he's owning his own business, but at the

time they weren't together when I started and then they kind of got together. [1999, aged 14]

Her description of the physical and mental disciplines of Karate fit well with Foucault's approach to the 'techniques' of relating the self to the self:

> **Karate teaches you** discipline and it teaches you like when you're in there, when you're in the class, even from like the age of five some of them, like you're taught to act responsibly so I think 'cause I've been doing it for so many years now, nearly eight years nearly, 'cause I've been doing it that long, it seems like, it seems like it has, I think if I didn't go to Karate, I probably wouldn't be nothing like the way I am now, I think it's like responsible for a lot but I think it's helped me but sometimes it's a burden, sometimes it is. [1999, aged 14]

It is interesting that the term 'discipline' also appears in Sherleen's discussions of her family upbringing, and of the development of her own self-discipline in relation to school work. The extent to which she is able to draw on the techniques of self offered by Karate and to translate them into other realms of her life is most clear in relation to her role as a teacher. As she has been studying for such a long time – in her words, 'I know nearly everything now' – she is able to teach Karate to others. The movement from pupil to teacher was empowering, not only in the context of the Karate class, but also in the context of school.

> **You're like trying** to teach other people what you know and it's like if you don't teach it to them properly, they're not gonna learn it. It's kind of your responsibility. So, now I know how the teachers feel in my school. That's why I like, when the class is like loud and everything, I try not to be too loud 'cause I know how it feels. I know like when people aren't paying attention what it feels like, to have to try and get their attention. But like when I'm teaching, even if I'm kind of quite strict, I still try and make it fun, 'cause I'm teaching like younger children, I try and make it fun for them 'cause I know what keeps me interested in lessons so I can like put it onto them. […] it's not that hard when you put your mind to it, you've gotta just treat them how you would expect to be treated really and teach them what you would like to learn so it's not that bad. [2000, aged 15]

The experience of teaching Karate affects how Sherleen relates within the realm of education. Her movement from being a 'diligent' to a 'determined' student, drawing more directly on the resources offered by teachers, may be partly indebted to the insights provided by this experience. Occupation of the subject position of teacher in Karate enables Sherleen to gain insight into the position in the context of school, but her attempts to secure comparable movement in relation to her mother are not so effective. Although she has offered to teach her mother Karate many times, she recognises that to be in a position of tutelage to her daughter would be embarrassing for her.

> **She goes okay,** I'll do one lesson, so I ask her when. She'll say one time soon and one time soon drags on and on and she will never go. She knows that she wouldn't do it even though, like Peter teaches it and I'm doing it and I teach it, she will never go. I think the most she would do is let me teach her a little bit at home. That's the most, because I think like being in a lesson for her is embarrassing. I don't know why, it's just embarrassing having to learn and not knowing, but that's like for all, for everyone. [2001, aged 16]

Although it was acceptable for Sherleen to be taught by her mother's boyfriend, it was not acceptable for her mother to be taught by either of them. So while the techniques of self associated with Karate could transcend some of the boundaries between the fields of Sherleen's existence, other boundaries were defended, and not only by Sherleen. Her decision to give up Karate, reported in her fourth interview, can be understood as a significant sacrifice, even though she presented it as a positive decision made for her own reasons – namely the need to devote more time to study.

> **I used to** like it a lot, but now I just realised that there's other things, 'cause my exams, I was gonna leave anyway, I was gonna take time out, but 'cause of my exams, they were coming up closer, I had loads of mocks, and it clashed with things in Karate that I was supposed to be doing, so I wasn't allowed to do a lot of things, so I said I was gonna leave, and I'll probably go back to that after my exams. [2001, aged 16]

She resisted her mother's attempts to make her stay:

> **My mum didn't** want me to leave, but I said that's something that I wanted to do. She didn't want me to leave at all. I said I wanted to leave. She thought I had just given up, but it wasn't like that. I weren't giving up, I just had too much on my plate at the time and I didn't think I would really stay at it. I just left really, I told her about it and I talked to him and he said, if you need to then go. [2001, aged 16]

In this interview Sherleen reflects back on the practice of Karate, prompted by a photograph in her memory book of her receiving her fourth gold medal. While she expressed pride in her achievements, she also described the burdens associated with the discipline:

When you're training you have to diet, you have to do a lot. It's a lot of training, it's hard training, and my muscles were aching, most of the time. I was sleeping a lot, trying to regain my strength. Sometimes I was sleeping, sometimes I was really hyper, 'cause you're eating no fat. You're not allowed no fat and no sugar or added salt, so basically you're only allowed to eat potatoes, basically carbohydrate foods. [2001, aged 16]

It is clearly important to her to assert that the decision to leave Karate was hers alone, an exercise of agency:

No really, it's just sometimes I won't do what's predicted of me. I won't do what's predicted of me and I'll change and do another thing. Like Karate, everyone was expecting me to stay there for ages, and I said, basically I just said no. It wasn't a split decision, but I did think about it. I said no I'm not gonna stay. [2001, aged 16]

Sherleen looks back at this as a significant moment for her. She acknowledges that she wasn't sure of the decision, it was 'such a regular part of my life. Stopping was weird. I still miss it.' In the end she explains that her mother was the main reason that she went to Karate in the first place and that she made her stay when she wanted to leave. She says nothing more about why she finally left, other than to comment of her mother: 'She only makes me do things that are good for me. She makes me stay on track.'

Conclusions

In this chapter I have presented a series of interviews with a young woman undertaken between the ages of 12 and 16 years. I have structured my interpretation of her accounts through the identification of three biographical 'fields of existence': education, family life and martial arts. In each section I have traced narrative changes and continuities, identifying techniques of the self that are drawn upon in the construction of identity. I have also distinguished between more and less conscious dimensions of identity formation, pointing to tensions and movements. In this way I have hoped to realise the potential of a longitudinal data set for seeing identity making in process, charting the exercise and constraint of agency and the self as embedded in relationships.

Sherleen's case history provides insights into the ways that social change is expressed at the level of family relationships. Being different from your parents is not an easy thing – especially in the context of a single-parent family and an extended period of dependency demanded by higher education. Sherleen is self-conscious about this process. This is not an individual project, but involves others – the extended family and (more intensely) her relationship with her mother. Here we see the coincidence of class and gender transformations, articulated through the experience of migration and discrimination. In this context much of the identity work is dedicated to the maintenance of continuity.

This case history also suggests that change in relation to gender is likely to be much more messy, contradictory and varied than is implied by the models used in theories of detraditionalisation. The extent of the complexity becomes apparent over time, where it is possible to see movement from one provisional identity solution to another. Most striking here is the extent to which the gender projects of different generations are linked. Although we are focusing on the story of Sherleen, it is impossible to separate out the story of her mother, with her grandmother also an important figure on the horizon. Her story also reinforces the critique made by black feminists that female individualisation is not new for black women, for whom full-time work and economic independence are the historical norm (Reynolds, 1997). In terms of understanding intergenerational change in this example, we do not see a young woman rebelling against a domestic version of femininity; rather, we see someone who expects to work and whose subjectivity is constructed in and through notions of work, discipline and application. 'Doing well' for Sherleen demands that she adopt a strategy and stick with it, navigating her way through a sea of potential dangers and distractions. The following case history provides a stark contrast, an example of a life oriented towards distractions and responsive to the demands and desires of others.

In terms of the biographical challenges outlined in the introduction of this book, it is possible to see how an extended family can support and manage the extended dependency demanded by tertiary education. As the first generation to anticipate university, Sherleen and her cousin are consciously forging new biographical patterns that give rise to intergenerational obligations. The period between ages 13 and 16 captured in this chapter suggests some of the complexity involved in balancing immediate and deferred forms of gratification and the need for both security and risk taking. Becoming an adult is revealed as an emergent accomplishment that is both fragile and flexible – something that will be revisited in Chapter Eight.

FIVE

Going down? Caught between stasis and mobility

We first made contact with Stan in 1997 when he was aged 16 and attending one of the schools in which the Youth Values study was conducted, a high-achieving state school located in an affluent, leafy suburb in the commuter belt. Stan completed a questionnaire and took part in a focus group discussion but was not selected to be interviewed. We made contact with him again in 1999, when he was invited and agreed to participate in the second stage of the study. He was interviewed three times, at ages 18 (1999), 19 (2000) and 20 (2001). In addition, he completed a memory book between the first and second interviews. This case history draws primarily on data from these three interviews and his memory book. Each of the interviews was conducted by Sue Sharpe and all took place in the sitting room of his family's home.

The study captured a period of intense personal change and identity work for Stan. When we first met him he was in the school sixth form, studying for A levels, expecting that, like most of his peers, he would go on to university and a profession. By the end of the study he was working as an apprentice joiner in a local firm. This transformation in his working plans occurred alongside a transformation in his personal life, wherein he found God and romantic love on the same weekend – finding his way from being 'a spotty youth in a fast car' to a 'family man' and a leader in his local church. Although I did not expect Stan to be an articulate commentator on his own life, his successive interviews are marked by intense personal reflection and introspection, and he valued the opportunity to keep a diary for the research.

The data that form the basis of this case history are slighter than others in this book, yet nevertheless capture an intense and revealing period in a young man's life. In this chapter I trace a series of experiments in masculinity, exploring in turn the fields of existence represented by work, consumption and family life. In each I identify how particular techniques of the self contribute over time to the narrative threads of a project of self. These threads are longitudinal, and contribute to a layered analysis in which it is possible to discern contradictions and instabilities, as well as repetitions and recurrent motifs.

Work and the motivation crisis

At first sight, Stan appears to have a classic white, new middle-class pedigree. His father works as a 'troubleshooter' for an international investment company and his mother works part time as a fundraiser for a local charity. The family's roots in the middle class are relatively shallow. His maternal grandfather was a cabinet maker and before his present incarnation as a corporate businessman his father was actively involved with the church and travelled, doing missionary work. Social class represents unfinished and mostly unspoken business for Stan. As we will see, he has access to a range of alternative family histories which resource investments in different identities and practices.

At his first interview Stan was in the midst of a 'motivation crisis'. He explains that he had dropped out of sixth form:

> **I made the** wrong decisions in my A levels, eh, didn't really get on with the teachers and decided it'd be better if I left 'cause I wasn't doing my work, so I wasn't really fooling anyone, so decided to jack it all in. [1999, aged 18]

He had started working full time at the supermarket where he had previously been working part time for a couple of years. While many of his peers had similar part-time jobs, they saw these exclusively in terms of short-term expediency. To work at the supermarket full time and on a long-term basis was to consider the possibility of a different kind of future in which he counted as a 'school leaver'.

> **The managers and** stuff are from the uni and they're good at their job and then most of the workers are just school leavers so, but um, it's alright, I'm working hard, they can see me working hard and there's a possible chance of promotion there to departmental manager so [...] if I was still there, be the first one up for the job so, be handy, look good on the CV as well. [1999, aged 18]

Stan is extremely aware that in contemplating such a pathway he is disrupting the highly constrained timeframe of the university route. He talks about the year working at the supermarket as a 'year out' in which he has time 'to think about which direction' he wants to go in. These directions ranged from 'full-time work and sort of just working with GCSEs to trying to go to do my A levels and then getting on to university'. In the end he decided to enrol for a different set of A levels at sixth-form college, with the view that he could 'get three A levels, yeah, so I can go to uni after that, if I feel like it'.

At this point in his life, Stan aspires to reproduce the status and life-style attained by his father, what Connell describes as the corporate masculinity of the new middle class for whom education, qualifications and professional credentials are *the* route to authority and social status (1995: 164–91). For Connell, this is a 'tamed' masculinity which fits the needs of the corporate economy. Yet crisis tendencies in the gender order mean that such masculinities are likely to be subject to conflicts between authority and expertise – the kinds of knowledge, skills and credentials really 'count' in making you a man.

Such conflicts are evident in Stan's ambivalence about university. When he is asked to describe the sort of person that he wants to be, he replies 'I wanna be an interesting person', and he sees that this may be incompatible with the conscientiousness and deferred gratification necessary to get to university and a profession. The year out of school has encouraged him to see himself as different from his peers.

> **People my age** group and most of the majority of them, they're people who just do all their GCSEs and work and go on to A levels. 'Cause that's what you're supposed to do if you get good GCSE results, do your A levels and then go on to uni. And then like, I think people will turn around after they've done uni and think, I've got to work now and I haven't done anything. I think you can kind of get caught up in it all, kind of like just get caught up with the flow. And just, what you think is what you want isn't really what you want. Um, see what I mean. And so by thinking ahead and thinking, well I wanna do this, when am I gonna do it, you can kind of have a (...) bit more varied and rich life, you know. [1999, aged 18]

Stan draws on the example of his father, whose pathway to the new middle class was complicated:

> **My dad didn't** do his degree until his late twenties and he's done a lot of different stuff. 'Cause they're involved quite heavily with the church and they did in their younger life. I wasn't even on the scene. They did a lot to do with kind of Christianity and stuff and kind of lot of travelling round the world with that kind of. My dad worked for a Christian kind of charity and so he's been to places like South Africa and working with that so kind of a different way. He wanted to do that in the first part of his life so he did it. Then he settled down. So it's quite good, but I think, yeah I think if I go to uni first, I think my life would be a bit easier than theirs. [1999, aged 18]

At this point, Stan faces two linked problems, one is how to sequence his life (what order to do things in) and the other relates to motivation – how to sustain himself on the pathway that he has chosen. Even though he has made a self-conscious decision to try the A level/university path again, he is not convinced that he will be able to motivate himself to complete it. The example of his parents both inspires and worries him, as they went through periods of financial hardship that he would like to avoid. So, although he is excited by the possibility of disrupting the traditional pathway, he is not contemplating the possibility of downward mobility. In this way Stan could be understood as seeking to remake privilege (Adkins, 2002a), combining work, pleasure and travel, and cultivating the 'mobile' and 'cosmopolitan' subjectivity demanded by a reflexive economy (Lash, 1994; Hannerz, 1996; Urry, 2000).

> **I met a** guy this year and I was chatting to him. And every five years he drops everything and buys a round-the-world ticket and he just does that. And it's like ideal, yeah, you know, someone's got the right idea. It's kind of, a lot of people talk about but not a lot of people do it, put it through. So I would like to be one of those people that put it through. [1999, aged 18]

When Stan engaged with the lifeline exercise, contradictions in his plans became apparent. He felt certain that at the age of 35 he would be married and settled, living 'somewhere like here'. Yet he was in some turmoil as to the route to this destination. He tentatively commits himself to a plan of being at university in three years' time:

> **By 21, I** think if I'm not at university, then I'll definitely be travelling or something, I think I'll definitely be in another country I think, snowboarding, scuba diving or just seeing sights, bumming around. [1999, aged 18]

And starting a year in accountancy by 25:

> **I've got quite** a few kind of ideas and I change my mind every day to what I wanna do. Eh, but like I wouldn't, if I was to go to university, I'd definitely do an accounting kind of business course and try and get my accountant's exam or part way to that and become an accountant. [1999, aged 18]

From accountant to artisan

At Stan's second interview, nine months later, it emerged that college had not gone very well. He explains that he 'never really got to grips with A levels', dropping two subjects, including Accountancy, which he describes as flying over his head. He is still studying for his A level in Business Studies, which he describes himself as being 'naturally good at', explaining that 'I'm more of a practical person'. Most significantly, he announces:

> **No, I mean** it's just a simple fact that I can't see myself, well, I'm not going to university [...] I think they [parents] could see it was quite inevitable really. 'Cause I hadn't filled out a UCAS form this year. I was going to, kind of did all the research. At the last minute I just decided I didn't wanna go, and I still maintain that view. I don't wanna go to

university. After doing A levels, I just haven't got the motivation really, to sit down and do three years of writing. [2000, aged 19]

Stan reports that he had recently seen a careers adviser who suggested that he consider cabinet making, furniture design or an apprenticeship as a joiner. He had enjoyed woodwork at GCSE.

> **That's the only** subject I've ever done – I've ever enjoyed. And my granddad's a carpenter and I tend to go up there sometimes and help him and do a bit of turning on his lathe and stuff. I love it, and so I've perhaps been thinking about going into something like that so. [2000, aged 19]

The prospect of doing a job that he actually enjoyed was very important to Stan, as was the prospect of some certainty as to his immediate future. He explained that he had felt that he was drifting without a clear sense of direction:

> **I think I'll** be happier when I'm settled and doing something I enjoy, kind of can see the kind of road if you like [...] I think you've kind of gotta look down the road a bit and see what you wanna achieve and then kind of work for it. [2000, aged 19]

In moving from an imagined future as an accountant to becoming a carpenter, Stan is reorienting himself to a new model of masculinity, representing a different relationship between expertise and authority. In his eyes, the dividend of accountancy would be financial security. He invests the work itself with no intrinsic value, unlike carpentry, the value of which may not be reflected in financial terms.

> **'Cause I always** talked about money as well, and kind of like always thought I was capable of earning quite a bit of money. And although I didn't necessarily think I needed loads, I don't wanna earn little. Kind of not much. I think my views have changed to kind of more happiness [...] Yeah, that's something I was always mulling over in my head, kind of do I go for like big bucks and be bored, or do I go for kind of not so much cash, and enjoy what I'm doing. I think do the latter. [2000, aged 19]

This shift from accountant to artisan can be understood as the culmination of Stan's growing critique of a corporate masculinity as well as his own feelings of inadequacy in struggling to fulfil the demands of the knowledge economy. One of the pages of his memory book (completed between the first and second interviews) was devoted to this theme. Selecting 'education', 'boring' and 'failure' from a range of stickers provided by the research project, he elaborated his feelings concerning academic study in handwriting:

<<BORING>>   **<<EDUCATION>>**

I think education is poo. I dropped out of my first year of A levels (History, Business, CDT) because I hated them, only to go to college the following year and do Business, Law and Accounts. This was a worse choice and I should have joined the dole queue! After dropping Accounts I am taking my Law and Business exams in summer 2000. I hope I am not a

<<FAILURE>>

At his third interview, 10 months later, it became clear that Stan had put this decision into practice and was busy reworking his understandings of work accordingly. In order to explain how life had changed, he went back to advice given to him by his grandfather when he was contemplating spending the summer putting up marquees in order to raise the money to go off travelling:

> **He said, 'It's** all alright you're earning money but you're not learning anything.' He says, 'It's not gonna be a useful thing at all.' You know, 'it's not gonna get you through life'. He said, 'Go and learn something,' you know, 'while you're working.' So I thought, oh mm fair enough, that's kind of a kick up the backside. [2001, aged 20]

By the end of that week Stan had a job at a local joiner's where he has been working full time ever since. In contrast to his A levels, where he saw himself as incompetent, he is able to draw on existing knowledge gained by helping his grandfather over the years. He was not learning from scratch, but he was learning in a new way, and in doing so establishing a new relationship of self with self.

> **At work 'cause** you're learning all the time. You are quite dependent on people at work showing you stuff, but um, but obviously like for me every day's getting more like do my own thing. But not dependent in a kind of childish way, dependent in a kind of like knowledgeable way. Like, 'I don't know how to do this, could you show me?'. Yeah that's fine but not at college, I'm not depending on anyone or anything. [2001, aged 20]

His attitude towards work was transformed. For the moment, his motivation crisis had been resolved.

> **I thoroughly enjoy** what I do. It's not, you know, obviously everyone has bad days. But I get out of bed and go to work. And, you know,

> I used to be someone who would uh (...) when I worked full-time for the supermarket I think there wasn't a week that went by I didn't phone in sick. You know, um (...) lack of motivation. But now it's kind of (...) I don't take any days off. I love what I do and it's fantastic and it's kind of a release as well. [2001, aged 20]

Previously, Stan held back from making personal investments in either education or the supermarket work. Yet skilled manual work offers a relationship between expertise and authority that is more accessible and comfortable for Stan than that associated with corporate masculinity. Craft can be understood as a technique of self that enables immediate gratification in the fruits of one's labour through the realisation of embodied knowledge. In the carpentry trade, expertise lies in physical skill, pricing a job, selling your labour and 'making your money work for you'.

> **We'll price the** job and we'll quote and you [...] some people are happy for you to work on a day rate. If they know you and they know how you work then they'll pay you a day rate until they know the job's done. Some people want a priced job. So you could put a sky high price in and it could take you half a day, or it could take you a week, depending what problems you hit and stuff. But it generally, generally it's kind of 50, 60 quid a day, which isn't, it's not bad. [2001, aged 20]

Although Stan has no regrets about his earlier decisions in relation to education and work, it is only when he begins carpentry that he is able to make an investment in his working identity and to integrate these techniques of self into his wider project of self. When invited to revisit his lifelines, Stan is amused by the changes, commenting: 'I was gonna be a rich accountant with 17 children.'

Consumption: from fun to faith

In his journey from accountant-in-waiting to practising joiner, Stan works hard at renegotiating the meaning of success and achievement. He moves from seeing himself as a failure to a potential success. This process of renegotiation was well under way at the point of his first interview, and was mediated by the investments that he was making in the field of his existence that can be broadly understood as consumption. In this section I draw attention to the techniques of self made available within this field, suggesting how they are deployed as part of the biographical and identity work that is captured by the notion of the project of self.

'The most important thing is enjoyment'

At 18 Stan doubted his ability to last the course of the A level/university pathway, yet consumption and leisure were fields within which he experienced himself as competent (Thomson et al, 2004). At this point Stan's life centred on his fast red car. He had bought the car before he had been able to afford to put it onto the road, spending a year working on it in the garage, acquiring a practical understanding of the workings of the car engine:

> **It was sitting** on the drive at the back of the old house, not being driven or anything, just being looked after.
>
> INT: Stroked and polished.
>
> Yeah, that's it (*laugh*), no money to spend so I could just clean it, yeah. It was good fun. Learnt a lot about cars in that time as well so. [1999, aged 18]

The labour that he expends on the car is counted as fun or play, and he identifies the freedom that driving gives him as central to his transition to adulthood, enabling independence from family and participation in wider social collectivities (Thomson et al, 2002).

> **[...] 'cause most** of my life I was looking forward to driving. It's one of my biggest ambitions, always wanted to get behind the wheel. And as soon as I did, I kind of, that changed me a bit. 'Cause suddenly I went from the person who kind of relies on his parents, didn't really have much of a social life 'cause he could never get out, to someone who could suddenly, whack, you know, I could get everywhere, the sky's the limit. And that kind of changes you 'cause you can get out more and see more people. Eh, I think that breeds change so, yeah, that was good. [1999, aged 18]

While dropping out of school and working at the supermarket distinguished Stan from his erstwhile peers, the immediate gratification provided by full-time wages enabled him to achieve a level of physical and financial independence that eluded those on the qualifications track. He proudly explains that

> **Um, no, I'm** totally self-financed now. Yeah, kind of, bought some wheels for my car and I did it through direct debit. And so my pocket money stopped and they were paying my direct debits for the car's finance – which I shouldn't have done. And after that they kind of, my pocket money didn't start up again. So they don't pay my petrol, don't give me anything now so, it's quite good. [1999, aged 18]

Going back to college had been a shock to his system. He observes that 'after earning lots of money, it's difficult, taking a cut in pay, kind of get used to it after a while'. His life-style included regular drinking sessions with friends that 'burns a hole in your pocket'. He also played in a band with friends, which involved significant expenses.

If caring for and driving a car provided Stan with short-term pleasure and purpose, planning and dreaming of snowboarding holidays with his friends provided him with motivation for the future. Snowboarding and travel even provided an alternative future to the university route. He is at his most eloquent when describing the pleasures of the sport:

> **[...] the snowboarding** I think, you don't think about that when you're out on the board. 'Cause I mean eh, the people I snowboard with, they get such an adrenalin rush from doing it like. At the bottom of the hill you kind of can't wait to get back up to the top and do it all over again. I dunno, it's amazing, it's like a drug, yeah. [1999, aged 18]

In contrast to the highly individualised project of qualifications and university, snowboarding, dangerous sports and travelling offer an alternative within which values of immediacy, risk, embodiment and male solidarity are prioritised over diligence and deferral. Thus, hedonism can be seen to operate as a technique of self through which it is possible to defend against the responsibility and rationality demanded by corporate success and the burden of parental expectation.

> **Parents see it** like, oh, we've gotta make sure you get qualifications so that you can earn a living and stuff. But friends come to see it as, well, are you enjoying yourself? No? Quit then, go and do something you'll enjoy. And I've got a few good friends that always talk about going travelling and we're always trying to plan like next year and stuff, what to go and do [...] we all kind of encourage each other which is a good thing, yeah, yeah, that's good. [1999, aged 18]

When asked to recount any moments of significance in the recent past, Stan counterposes 'dropping out' of school and going to college with a near-death experience while diving:

> **Last summer I** did a bit of scuba diving and I had a kind of a bit of a close scrape under water. And that changed my outlook quite considerably – for the better. Kind of, see things now, kind of bit live for the moment – now. Um, and there's a few things I wanna do in the near future that I'll do, like travelling and snowboarding, eh. [1999, aged 18]

Conflicts between these life paths and associated values and temporalities are made explicit by Stan's lifeline exercise. The possibility of travel disrupts each life stage. While he is committed to being an accountant at the age of 25, he anticipates little pleasure:

> **Yeah, I think** it'll be a slog, yeah. But I mean, by then I'll probably need to earn some cash to wipe out loads of debts. So (*laugh*) probably be more compulsory than anything. [1999, aged 18]

Although he is open to alternatives (explaining 'I see somebody doing this and I think that could be a laugh, just totally swap life-styles'), Stan is anxious as to whether he will be able to secure the goals of a stable and affluent family life further down the line. So while he is opposing the demands of the technocratic route to corporate masculinity by investing in more immediate and collective embodied practices, he nevertheless remains committed to the goal of family life that it would support. At this point Stan does not choose between ideals of mobility and 'settling', hoping that he can combine the two by deferring heterosexual commitments, having fun while he has 'no ties'.

> **I think people** get a bit short-sighted when they stay in sort of like this country, you know, kind of get into the way of life and dunno if it is the right way of life.
>
> INT: No, no, 'cause you can get sort of stuck in.
>
> Yeah, work, pension, you know.
>
> INT: And it seems more and more difficult to actually break out of that.
>
> Yeah, once you've got more and more ties holding you back, you can't, when you're young it doesn't matter. [1999, aged 18]

'I've really been given a gift there so I intend to use it'

At his second interview Stan explains that there has been a thorough-going transformation in his life since he was last interviewed, involving both falling in love and a religious conversion. He introduces the events in the following way:

> **The time I'd** spoke to you, I'd been snowboarding, and a guy there he's my age, good friends with (...) he'd become a Christian. And he was kind of into (...) he was a gang member and he got asked to go to this Bible week (...) where he took weapons. And I was with him and stuff (*laugh*), and he said he didn't want any Christians telling

him how to live his life and stuff. But he became a Christian and the change that kind of took place in his life was quite amazing actually. And they invited me along, so I kind of said yes. Dunno why really, and no I just thought, 'cause all my friends were going (...) I thought you know it'll be alright (...) be a good laugh. [2000, aged 19]

At the Bible week Stan struggled with his scepticism and he describes 'testing' the presence of God:

I was kind of thinking (...) well it's all very well if they believe this but I don't really believe there's a God. Kind of didn't tell anyone (...) just kind of asked God a question. I said (...) you know, if you're out there and stuff, how do I get eternal life? And kind of being that that was the main point they were talking about. And that night (...) it was quite strange, I had a dream. I'm not normally into all this sort of thing so it's quite a surprise for me. And I had a dream that I was reading the Bible and I woke up in the morning and this kind of passage was in my head. I just thought rubbish, but later on in the day it was nagging at me, nagging. So I kind of borrowed someone's Bible, crept off into a corner somewhere and read it. And my question was the opening line of this verse. And it went on answering the question and stuff, and it was just like (...) the feeling I had then was just wooo! Kind of, that was heavy (...) but I mean it's great. [2000, aged 19]

He goes on to explain the implications of this change for his relationship with his friends and his commitment to his former life-style of drinking and socialising with the lads:

My friends can't understand it 'cause I kind of stopped smoking pot, stopped drinking as heavily as I was, sold my car. I go to church and I'm a leader down there in kind of youth group and stuff now. [...] And thinking possibly of doing this summer perhaps some street work in the city and stuff. So it's kind of changed my whole outlook. [2000, aged 20]

The significance of Stan's religions conversion is heightened by the coincidence of meeting Nadia;

It's just kind of like a massive change really. And the day I became a Christian, I sat next to her, in a hall of about five thousand people, and she lives three miles away from me. [2000, aged 20]

Stan sums up the experience as shaped by powerful forces beyond his agency: 'the whole thing like that week was just kind of cosmic really'. This combination of falling for love and for God was a self-consciously important moment in his project of self and the interview provided him with an audience for recounting the experience. The notion of a fateful biographical moment is outlined by Giddens (1991), who suggests that moments of crisis are associated with both risk assessment and the reworking of self-narratives. A revision of identifications that have become increasingly troubling or incompatible is much in evidence in this interview and in the 'testimony' that Stan includes in his memory book – written for the audience of his church, and subsequently published in a religious newspaper. Before his conversion, consumption (in the form of snowboarding, travel and his car) had provided Stan with a positive sense of identity, efficacy and community. The account that he gives in his published testimony places a rejection of these practices and of the materialism that underlies them at the heart of his transformation. Yet, in his interview he is more ambivalent, suggesting that his 'fateful moment' was part of a more complicated process (Plumridge and Thomson, 2003; Holland and Thomson, 2009). Although he has sold his car and given up his lucrative Sunday shift at the supermarket so that he can attend church, he is now dreaming of buying a motorbike and doing more dangerous sports. Giving up the identity of the 'bad boy' does not mean giving up risk. He then goes on to employ the motif of risk taking when describing his activities in the church, where he has been recognised as having leadership qualities:

> **I'm kind of,** well, in my element and enjoy doing it. And I come out (...) that was great, she [Nadia] just sits there, rolls her eyes.
>
> INT: So do you get another sort of buzz out of that?
>
> I do actually, yeah, a strange kick I get. It's really kind of (...) as I stood up and did this talk on this Sunday morning, kind of the church is packed, and they come to see, (...) it's not normally that packed. People have heard that our family is doing it, so they're coming along [...] I've really been given a gift there so I intend to use it. [2000, aged 19]

There are echoes here of the ways in which martial arts operated as a catalyst within Sherleen's biography, facilitating the transposition of techniques of self between fields and enabling new combinations of identification. It may be that the church constitutes a new field of existence into which Stan can expand aspects of practices that may have been forged through the fields of work and consumption, reworking boundaries between public and private domains of the self and between individualised and collective identities.

A rich and fruitful life

By the time of his third interview, 10 months later, Stan is firmly embedded in his identity as part of a heterosexual couple, speaking in terms of 'we' and 'us'. Many of his friends had left the local area in order to go travelling. Two friends with whom he had played in a band and who, like him, had been 'stuck in dead end jobs', had gone off to Australia. Snowboarding had been cancelled that year, due to a lack of funds. Asked whether he was sad to be left behind, Stan responds:

> **No, it's a** kind of money thing that's held us back. And also the fact that I'm a kind of talking (...) I was talking about going travelling a lot and that's still an option. But at the end of the day it came down to like (...) well I could go away but Nadia's at home and like I know that I'd badly miss her (*laugh*). So the only reason I've (...) the only (...) the only real reason I got sucked down in a job was cause, uh (...) the Mrs. So yeah, waiting around you know. [2001, aged 20]

Stan also reveals that he has been working hard to get himself out of the debt incurred during his days working at the supermarket. Although he had referred to how expensive his life-style was in earlier interviews, he had not mentioned the spending spree that is now narrated as a moment of madness:

> **I got myself** in a bit of a financial muddle really. I spent a bit too much money, yeah (...) A few too many nights out and lots of expensive new toys and that. But I put it all on my credit card and kind of suffered. But that's nearly taken care of (...) I learnt my lesson so (*laugh*). [2001, aged 20]

In order to gradually pay off these debts, Stan had been working extra hours and staying in with Nadia in the evenings:

> **Yeah in fact** I've gone a bit middle aged really. I've um, 'cause I (...) I dunno (...) I did myself a mischief like when I was working full time. Before I used to go out every night and just get wrecked and get up and go to work. And it's (...) kind of like, it's boring. And I don't like, you know, I'm happy to sit in front, like sit in front of the TV or get a video out or just sit in with Nadia and just have a quiet night. It doesn't bother me at all, I prefer it really. [2001, aged 20]

At this interview it appeared that Stan's approach to money and consumption had changed. He talks about being more cautious, committed to saving and 'getting the money you've been working for working for you'. His new-found respect for the value of money was paralleled with some frustration at his relatively meagre wages. Yet he also recognised that in his old persona, saving was not on the agenda. Money continues to be a central part of Stan's identity, yet now money is directly related to securing a future for himself and Nadia. Here he seeks to accommodate his concern with financial security with his commitment to the value of the non-material aspects of the world.

Um very well done, quite (...) you know, very rich, lots of debt but very rich, yeah. But then you know, it could only take a few things, and I could say (...) it could all turn on its head you know. Say I become a monk or something, (...) I dunno. Yeah that's it, 'Saint Stan' and all that. No, I'm very fortunate. Friends, relationship, job and all equates to, I don't have very much money, but it all equates to being rich and fruitful and stuff. [2001, aged 20]

The conflation of falling in love with his religious conversion has disentangled over time. Stan no longer toys with ideas of becoming a minister and he and Nadia are beginning to distance themselves from the intense introspection that characterises the culture of his religious peers:

When you last spoke to me I was a person that used to do a lot of worrying and a lot of thinking about all that, and um, like think about stuff like that immensely. And me and the friends would just have all these deep, really deep discussions and it didn't do me any favours at all. I used to get worried and you know, I used to drink too much partly and all this. You'd have highs and lows and it's (...) and now I'm just kind of well, no one I know can answer any questions. Until someone can then I'm just not gonna think about it, you know. And Nadia's of the same opinion. It's like you know, we're in this cell. And the cell, they call it cells, it's a kind of home church if you like, but it's youth. But you know there's loads of us and they're all great but they're just obsessed with asking all these difficult questions.

INT: Without getting the answers?

Yeah just ask them all the time (*laugh*). And me and Nadia are just, well (...) you know, gonna crack on have a laugh while we're here. You only live once and all that, so make the most of it. [2001, aged 20]

Here we can see the ethic of hedonism reasserted, employed to temper the demands of faith and to establish the boundaries of the couple. Stan is wistful when talking about his old loves of snowboarding and travel, joking that he will have to build a chalet in the Swiss Alps for family snowboarding trips. When he reflects on the lifeline exercise that he had completed in his first interview he remarks:

I think I was planning to do snowboarding for a lot of my life. I would still, I'd love it. But it's, I dunno, the realism has kind of kicked me in the face [...] Um, I suppose it made you stop and think. But back then I didn't think about my life plan. Well I did, but I had no idea. I didn't even know what I wanted to do. I know I know what two things that come out of that are kind of – family and um, you know, wife and stuff. And that, that hasn't changed, I'd still like to be quite a young dad you know. But um, yeah now I've got a bit more kind of something. A bit more stable work-wise. I hate to (...) I think about it now, I'd hate travelling, coming home and washing dishes and then travelling my whole life. I'd (...) I'd like to settle down a bit yeah. But not settle settle if you see what I mean (*laugh*). [2001, aged 20]

Family life: 'it is in the genes'

The way in which Stan draws on his family as a resource in the construction of his identity shifts over the course of the interviews. Overall it is possible to understand the objective of establishing a family and becoming a father as consistent features of his narratives over the course of the research. They even feature in his initial questionnaire, completed in 1997, where he lists his hopes for the future as 'get a job, get a wife, get a family'. Although he experiments with different forms of masculine identity, the ultimate objective of 'settling down' is never questioned. In fact, it could be argued that establishing his own family is the guiding light of his project of self and that the very distance of this goal is part of what makes the route offered by corporate masculinity so long, lonely and unattractive. His passage from son, to lover, towards father and husband then lies at the centre of his account of his transition to adulthood.

In his first interview Stan's approach to family is from the position of being a son. He talks frequently of a family taste for travel, arguing that travel 'kind of runs in the family', and, speaking of an uncle who was staying at his house until a visa came through, he says '[he] travelled all his life, it is in the genes'. He also talks positively about the importance of travel in his father's work, signalling a continuity between the missionary work of his past and the jet-setting of his present. Yet Stan expresses an awareness of the costs of this current life-style, observing that his father's regular absences from the household on business trips mean that his son becomes responsible for some of the duties that have been abandoned, such as DIY and providing lifts. Throughout Stan's narratives, we find a more embedded, embodied and domesticated form of masculinity being associated not with his father but his maternal grandfather:

> **My mum's dad** has been a cabinet maker all his life, and I've always been interested in that, playing with wood. And so whenever something like that comes round the house, a shelf needs fitting, it's always me that does it so (...) I kinda help that way, things like that. [...] My dad being away a lot, kind of lot of handy jobs that (...) say something goes wrong and dad's away and mum can't do it, it kind of all falls to me. [1999, aged 18]

The ways in which Stan identifies with and seeks to distance himself from his parents are complex. In the interviews he reflects frequently on his father's untraditional career path, from church work, through a period of unemployment and financial hardship, to re-education and a corporate career. Over the course of the three interviews he values and rejects different elements of this trajectory, including travel, postponing 'career' and religion (describing it as 'their thing' in his first interview). Yet Stan is deeply ambivalent as to whether it is either possible or desirable for him to live a life like that of his father.

My feeling is that Stan identifies more easily with his mother, drawing on her for advice and commenting approvingly on her values towards work. When conducting the lifeline exercise, it also became apparent that he used her biography as his model for family life:

> **My mum was** married at 18 and she had me at 20 so she was quite young. And that's kind of (...) a lot of all my friends and I think, I think that's probably the way (...) I do want kids and I'd like kids and when I have them, I'd like to be quite young. [1999, aged 18]

The desire to make a family at an early age does not fit with the model of deferred parenthood increasingly characteristic of the new middle classes, where qualifications and financial security come at the cost of extended dependence and deferred gratification (Kiernan, 1997). Stan struggles to draw on his own experience of family life in order to imagine a financially secure future. These anxieties are already apparent in his first interview, when he is single but hopeful:

> **I would like** to earn, 'cause both my parents were unemployed for a while, quite like to earn enough so that if I have kids and can easily support a family and a house and you know all the creature comforts. But nothing extravagant. [1999, aged 18]

By his third interview, he is in a committed relationship, yet with a four-year age gap. Again he draws on his parents' example as a model, and in doing so articulates anxieties about fulfilling the role of the breadwinner more clearly:

> **The fact that** they've got exactly the same age gap between Nadia and me and the fact that they were married quite early (...) um it's a bit weird. But I think my dad took out quite a lot of time to become a church minister and stuff. And for a while there was not a lot of food on the table and stuff. And I remember as (...) and also he went through a time of unemployment. I remember as a kid I always had this worry about money. And it's always always been embedded in my head 'cause when I talked about accountants, it was just money. And um always as a kid I remember, like you know scared at (...) obviously

they had it under control, but I was (...) I'm a worrying person anyway
and I worried. And um, but I think I think that's one thing I'm gonna
strive to do is to make sure I don't have to – not so much be spoilt
or anything, cause they won't be – but not just not have to have that
as a worry [2001, aged 20]

'A match made in heaven'

Commentators such as Giddens, Beck and Beck-Gernsheim have pointed to the
increasing importance of the couple as a social unit. For Beck (1992) and Beck and
Beck-Gernsheim (1995) the growing uncertainty of life makes us progressively
more reliant on couple relationships and the elusive satisfactions of romantic love.
Within these partnerships, it is argued that processes of individualisation erode
the legitimacy of gendered division of labour, forcing individuals to confront the
existence of inequalities. For Giddens (1992), the couple is increasingly the vehicle
for the expression of the pure relationship, contingent and negotiated commitment,
free from the securities of tradition and naturalised gender roles. None of these
commentators dwells on the coexistence of tradition and individualised forms of
relationship, nor on the practices and processes that couples may engage with in
order to live with contradictions and inequalities. It is left to feminist commentators
such as Lynn Jamieson (1998, 1999) to draw our attention to the 'costs' of couple
relationships for women of all ages, in the form of deep and shallow emotion work,
violence and resignation, while also recognising the possibility of a movement
towards the democratisation of the intimate.

The relationship between Stan and Nadia reflects the tensions between tradition
and the contingency of the couple in interesting ways. Romantic love plays an
important part in establishing the relationship – notions of fate, love at first sight
and even divine intervention frame Stan's narrative of their meeting:

People say do you believe in love at first sight, but we both kind
of like, I laid eyes on her I knew that that was something I wanted
(*laugh*), I wasn't gonna kind of let anything get in the way of that
[2000, aged 19]

The location of this relationship within the context of the church can be
understood as providing a structure for the negotiation of gendered roles within
the relationship. At his second interview Stan talked about the difficulties that he
and Nadia experienced in maintaining a chaste relationship. Stan explains that
in theory he would like to wait until marriage for sex, more realistically, they
would wait until Nadia is 16. By committing himself to what might be seen as
an old-fashioned or traditional form of masculinity, in which sexual access is
deferred until legitimised by marriage (or in this case age), space is created in the
relationship for a recognition of both their sexual agencies.

> **Yeah, some people** say that and I honestly respect them if they can do that. I dunno whether that's realistic with us (*laugh*), 'cause we're quite physical anyway. No, I mean she's also, she's 15, she's 16 in November and that's a factor (...) I have to fend her off with a stick (*laugh*). It's funny 'cause like she was the one that came up to me and asked me, and I've never had that before [2000, aged 19]

Stan is aware of his movement from a male friendship culture to a heterosexual couple relationship. When asked whether his friends resented Nadia, Stan replies:

> **Probably, but they** haven't said anything, because I had a friend of mine and he was with a girl for a year and a half, and basically they didn't leave the bedroom. And me and a friend were kind of ahhhh, you know flicking heck, dumping your mates for a girl and stuff. And I was yeah, that's terrible kind of thing, and now (*laugh*), I see her a lot and they're kind of, 'Not coming out?' But no, I think they understand, I reckon they do. [2000, aged 19]

While the transition is not entirely easy (for example, he regrets the limitations that the relationship makes on his freedom to travel), he enthusiastically embraces the opportunity to imagine a shared future. Nadia's young age and lack of career plans mean that Stan is able to assume mutuality, yet within a traditionally gendered division of labour.

> **No, she's a** lot like me, I think that's why we get on so well. I mean concerned about it and we just kind of both wanna do something we both enjoy, but at the same time, have a laugh. And her only ambition is have kids and go travelling. The other way round. She's great, yeah. She has got no kind of career kind of prospects or anything. She said to me the only thing she'd really stick at, she would like to work with kind of like teenagers with learning difficulties. You know, she'd like that sort of challenge. [2000, aged 19]

By the third interview, Stan and Nadia's relationship had become sexual:

> **Since her 16th** birthday I haven't, keep our hands off each other or whatever it is (*laugh*). [2001, aged 20]

Their relationship had also become independent of the church and the circumstances of their meeting. Stan describes a process of increasing intimacy – the result of intense mutual exploration:

We've become amazingly strong, got really really close. But not like chokingly close. Not, we did, we have done before and we got kind of – I dunno, I suppose when we were – 'cause when we met we didn't know each other at all. Never knew each other before, so it was kind of, the whole getting to know each other process. But now we know each other really well and it's, you know, it's just I dunno a match made in heaven and all that. You know, everyone's always joking about it. [2001, aged 20]

He continues to position himself as caught between identification with homosocial masculinity and a traditional form of heterosexual commitment that enables him to acknowledge and welcome his growing dependence on Nadia.

My views on marriage? Um, I used to be really scared of it actually. But um, I'm scared of it I suppose when I'm in front of my friends. But um, I like the idea of, it's important for me 'cause I need someone there standing over me to sort me out. I couldn't live in a house on my own and actually cope, I don't think. 'Cause nothing would ever get done and then you know (*laugh*), sounds a bit sad really, but um it's true. Not in terms of marriage I, I think it's an important thing. I think if you find someone you like and you love and – I think committing yourself to them is, can do a lot for the relationship. [2001, aged 20]

Stan explicitly invokes metaphors of stasis and mobility to describe their relationship. His words suggest that their couple relationship constitutes a distinct field of existence with associated techniques of self:

She was very solid at the time when I was kind of buoyant and kind of fluctuating as a personality you know. She brought stability to me and something to latch onto I suppose.

INT: She kind of earthed you in a way?

Yeah did, kind of brought me back together. 'Come on, Stan, sort it out', yeah. She didn't even have to do that really, I kind of did it all myself. Well not all, but 'cause of her you know. [2001, aged 20]

It is not the contingent, balanced and labour-intensive commitment of the pure relationship that is described by Stan, but a form of interdependency, characterised by a division of labour. The asymmetry that might characterise a relationship with a significant age difference is inverted through romantic discourse. By falling in love he becomes the object in a discourse of romance (Hollway, 1984; Holland et al, 1998/2004), and in doing so accesses a very traditional route to becoming a man.

> **You know the** cliché, got knocked off my feet and that was about it
> really. Had to take a deep, big deep breath. But um no, no I suppose it
> gave me a reason to sort myself out really, grow up a bit. Couldn't act
> like that with a girlfriend who's a lady you know. So uh, but she's very
> patient with me. So you know, she's great. So yeah. [...] I suppose I just
> stopped and took stock and like uh, you know. Perhaps that happens
> to everyone at that age. But I dunno, it just seemed that the event of
> having a girlfriend is what happened to me yeah. [2001, aged 20]

In acknowledging his dependency within the couple relationship (and ignoring
Nadia's vulnerability), Stan is also claiming the privileges of adulthood. This
becomes clearer when we see the shifts that have taken place in his relationship
with his family of origin in the account he provides at his third interview. In
moving into the subject position of lover/husband, he also moves out of the subject
position of son: he has begun to plan another home for himself and Nadia.

> **This isn't my** place and I'm not (...) it's not my life if you know
> what I mean. It's my mum and dad's, um, it's, I suppose it's a family
> whole life but it's kind of (...) I wanna start my own somewhere else,
> you know. Be involved in this one, you know when I choose (*laugh*),
> Sunday afternoons when I'm hungry yeah. [2001, aged 20]

In moving from a middle-class university trajectory to a more traditional skilled,
working-class niche, Stan manages to deal creatively with tensions between his
own aspirations, the resources provided to him by his family and milieu, and the
social and cultural possibilities available to him. If we return to Bjerrum Nielsen
and Rudberg's (1994) model we could argue that his gender identity – the kind
of man that he wants to be – is very much in flux and he has to struggle to attain
it. The model of corporate masculinity that he starts with proves unattainable
and unsatisfactory. An alternative model of artisan masculinity is accessed, and
licensed by existing familial resources. Issues of generation feature powerfully in
his struggle to bring his gender subjectivity and identity into line. He must deal
with his 'failure' to hold on to the social mobility achieved by his parents as well
as the apparent parallels between his own trajectory and theirs. While there may
be some comfort in intergenerational continuities, the transformation of social
and cultural conditions that frame these different biographies would appear to
demand some form of change. The ease with which Stan will be able to inhabit
the traditional form of masculine identity that he has created will, in part, be
dependent on the demands, or lack of them, made by Nadia. Clearly, these are
early days. It is an improvisation which will give rise to consequences, which may
or may not accumulate as anticipated.

Conclusions

In this chapter I have traced changes and continuities in the interview accounts of one young man over a four-year period. My account has been structured by the fields of existence that feature most clearly in his biography: work, consumption and family life. In each I have considered the techniques of self which he draws on in his identity work. This is not to say that Stan presents a coherent project of self. Rather, I hope to have traced some of the narrative threads, contradictions and resonances that arise from a layered analysis of successive interview accounts.

The story that I have told about Stan is explicitly concerned with masculinities and social class. Preoccupations about the kind of man he could or should be dominate his accounts. Within his deliberations it is possible to detect considerable uncertainty and anxiety about work, career and money, reflecting the dynamic processes through which particular masculinities are privileged over others. At the same time, he expresses certainty in relation to love, intimacy and parenthood, yet seeks to realise these hopes with a woman much younger than himself. In this way Stan's case history provides a sense of both the fragility and resilience of late-modern masculinities, played out in tensions between mobility and stasis.

Although I initially located Stan in relation to the corporate masculinity of the new middle class (fitting into the 'dominant and complicit' category of Connell's 1995 schema), over the course of the three interviews a more complicated and dynamic picture emerged. Corporate masculinity was certainly the norm against which Stan was judging himself and the destination to which the majority of his school friends were heading. It also reflected his father's current social location and occupation. Yet there was no simple process of social reproduction taking place. Stan is highly ambivalent about the gender identity represented by his father. As the child of socially mobile parents, he faces the contradictions that arise from his parents' choices as biographical and intimate problems (for example, privileging of material over emotional or spiritual riches). That Stan privileges geographical mobility (in the form of travel) rather than social mobility is an interesting example of how such dynamics are played out at the level of identity practices.

Even though Stan can, at moments, be understood to be cultivating a mobile and reflexive gender identity, he is also dominated by desires for security, belonging and dependency, demonstrating what Walkerdine et al (2002) refer to as a split subject position. If we consider Stan's family case history from an intergenerational perspective, there is little evidence of a simple movement from traditional to detraditionalised forms of masculinity. Rather, it is possible to see traditional forms such as 'the artisan' and the 'breadwinner' as being *remade* within the present, alongside identifications with 'risk', 'mobility' and 'faith'. The ways in which these negotiations are enacted occur in conversation with parental subjectivities and are supported (or not) by social and cultural opportunity. So, although Stan may be able to perform this amalgam of old and new masculinities, the extent to which these performances are authorised and rewarded largely depends on external factors that have to be tested. Thus, narratives of success and failure have an urgency in Stan's accounts, with the pursuit of competence in one field of existence being offset by a sense of failure in others. These fields of existence make available distinct techniques of self through which different competencies can be produced, recognised and rewarded. Like Sherleen, he attempts to transpose techniques of self, resources and skills between fields, for example by blurring boundaries between play and work and between religion and intimacy. Yet he also redraws boundaries as part of his ongoing and provisional identity work, separating himself from his parents' generation and separating himself and Nadia as a couple from his wider peer group.

Stan positively rejects the challenge to forge and manage the extended dependency on parents that is demanded by higher education. Yet he embraces other forms of dependency: on the couple; on the authority of skilled craftsmen; and on the excitement and rewards of snowboarding and fast cars. Stan is not a compliant neoliberal subject, yet nor is he a dissident. The 'motivational crisis' that Connell suggests is characteristic of new middle-class masculinities is a motif of Stan's biography, and a search for meaning and purpose shapes his accounts of work, consumption and religion. However, his particular strategy is highly dependent on a distinct and complementary female role, showing how central heterosexual identification is for the closure of gender identities. A movement from primarily homosocial to heterosexual identifications lies at the centre of Stan's case history. Girls and women do not feature explicitly as friends, competitors or role models. And femininity is off bounds as an identity resource that could be drawn on, consciously. This makes Stan vulnerable and dependent. He needs to be needed, in order to be the kind of man that he wants to be.

SIX

Coming out: from the closet to stepping stones

In this chapter I develop the case history of Devon, drawing on interviews that took place over a four-year period between the ages of 18 and 21 and a memory book. I first met Devon in 1997, when he participated in a focus group as part of the Youth Values study, held at a lesbian and gay youth group. His first interview took place in January 1999 as part of the Youth Values study. Subsequently he was interviewed in March 2000 and November 2001. After this chapter was written Devon was interviewed again, in February 2003, and an account of this interview is featured in Chapter Eight. This is the only case history in the book where I, the author, was also the interviewer, and this is discernible in the tone and depth of analysis presented. Each of the interviews took place in my office at the university.

In describing and interpreting Devon's successive accounts I focus on the process through which he becomes increasingly familiar with gay culture, the way he manages the boundaries between gay and straight life and the articulation of sexual, gender, class and ethnic dimensions within his identity. I am interested in understanding Devon as being part of the same generation as Sherleen and Stan, yet, as white, gay and working class, managing very particular forms of identity work. Devon left school without taking his GCSEs, some time before I first met him in 1998. When first interviewed, he was living in a shared house (a gay foster placement), working as an office junior and beginning to explore commercial gay culture. Over the course of the research his circumstances were relatively unsettled, and he moved between four different jobs and an extended period of unemployment, paralleled by movements between independent living and his parents' home. Continuity during this period was provided by his involvement in a lesbian and gay youth group and the support of his family.

The case history is structured by the three fields of existence that I consider to be most important in Devon's evolving biography: family, work and play. These three arenas characterise each of his interviews in different ways, family being the dominant theme of the first, work and the boundaries between work and other parts of his life dominating the second, and play dominating the discussion in the third. In addressing each arena in turn I will move through the successive interview encounters, conveying a sense of temporal movement.

Home: 'a future other than my family'

Devon's first interview focused on his family of origin and on the turbulent events that resulted in him and his younger sister going into the care of social services when he was 15. The story that Devon told in this interview was fragmented, even though it bore many of the marks of an 'enforced narrative' (Steedman, 2000) created through discussion with family members and social workers. At the heart of Devon's story were his still highly ambivalent feelings about disclosing to a teacher that his father was violent:

> **I was sort** of the one that blabbed. That's all I can think of it as. It was because of me that they'd come in and erm (...) things like that. I just felt so guilty and so (...) ashamed of what I'd done and I just hated myself at the time as well. Because now, looking back, I know that it was for the best and I'm glad I did it. But erm, you know, at the time, even though I could see it was like, nobody else could, nobody else was blaming me. But I wanted them to, you know. [1999, aged 18]

In practical terms this disclosure resulted in a formal intervention into the family by social workers, enabling his father to access counselling. Devon reflects on the trauma of the period, dominated by his fear that his family would reject him. In this first interview he had already constructed a retrospective account of the positive consequences of events, both for the family as a whole – 'we all changed for the better' – and for himself. In forging an independent voice, distinct from the 'we' of his family, Devon draws on the vocabulary of his social worker, explaining, 'apparently I was close to a nervous breakdown over it'.

His discussions of family disruption are inextricably linked to the 'coming out story' that emerges in this first interview. Separating from the family and coming to terms with his sexuality coincide to form a single experience:

> **She [social worker]** said: 'What are you gonna do for yourself?' And I said: 'Oh, I've seen this advert for er, erm, a youth project, I thought maybe that just you know, somewhere to go that's away from my family, just for me (*clears throat*), and be around people my own age' (*clears throat*), and she's like: 'Oh that's nice. What's it called? Where is it?' And I said: 'Well, it's over west and it's only for gay people, so I'm gay.' And er, she started crying […] Yeah. Just like, oh I'm so happy! [1999, aged 18]

At the time of his first interview Devon was established in a household 'that is totally gay. I can totally be myself.' Previously he had endured an unsuccessful foster placement and difficulties with his family, but was now 'getting on brilliantly' with his family, who were 'getting on brilliantly with everyone else'. For Devon, 'home' was now a safe and a gay space. He explains, 'I found somewhere stable I could go home to [...] I've got my own space I can call home.'

One of the motifs of this first interview is a distinction that Devon negotiates between normality and perversion, the former associated with the domestic practices of his mother, the latter associated with the prejudices of his father. Throughout the interview he asserts an identification with his mother and distinguishes himself from his father. This requires a great deal of work – as he puts it, it is 'still hard to have her on my side in my mind'. The work can be detected in the following extract, where he expresses surprise that his gay household engage in mundane and 'normal' practices such as shopping:

> **I remember going** shopping with my mum and that just seemed
> so normal actually, but when I first moved into erm, a gay household,
> going shopping with them, it was – I know it sounds so stupid, I got
> embarrassed by them, walking round and they were saying sort of the
> same things that my mum'd say like. Talking about the special deals
> that was on like, loaves and bread and like that and [...] Even like the
> points that you get on the cards and that, so (...) oh we've got like er,
> 250 points now or whatever (...) like that (...) and it was just so strange
> and because living in like a gay household, well, over a year, sort of,
> that's just normal. I just go and do my own shopping and now it's
> just, it's hoping sort of talk – influence my dad into thinking that you
> know, we're not all like sex-crazed perverts. [1999, aged 18]

In order to access an inhabitable gay identity it is important for Devon that he gains recognition from his family. There is a complex relationship between the problematising of his father's violent behaviour and Devon's attempts to negotiate normality, a home and a positive gay identity. The stress he places in this interview on his role in 'reforming' his father is inevitably bound up with feelings of guilt about exposing family secrets. Here and elsewhere in this interview Devon speaks of embarrassment caused by his father's racism, his violence, and the consequences of what he characterises as laziness:

> **I had Chinese** friends and Asian friends and black friends and white
> friends and just [...] and dad would come home and he'd sort of call
> people a bad word and things like that you know, and every time
> he did it, my mum would sort of get angry [...] I just used to get so
> embarrassed. [1999, aged 18]

> **I was always** frightened as well as being embarrassed because my
> dad never sort of – here's an example. When it comes to football, my
> dad never sort of took us over the park – and to play football with me
> – with the boys erm, things like that, so I never really played that and
> then my classmates would say: 'Do you wanna play football?' Because

> I had actually no idea how to just to kick a ball, that's about it. Erm,
> so I always used to be frightened of embarrassing myself. So I used to
> just sit out and that just – that never really went away even now. If I
> go to somewhere new. [1999, aged 18]

In these examples we can also see how embarrassment marks boundaries: between the private and the public, the actual and the conventional, the normal and the perverse. The coincidence of Devon's coming out as gay and his 'outing' of his father's unacceptable masculinity not only involves a breaching of the public and private, but also challenges the ownership of 'normality'. It appears that for Devon, at this point, one of the costs of forging a 'normal' gay identity (as opposed to that of the 'sex-crazed pervert') is a rejection of the working-class masculinity of his father (Bell, 1995).

In his second interview, conducted over a year later, Devon was back living with his parents, having struggled to maintain his own flat. In retrospect he expresses regret at leaving the shared gay household, finding living independently lonely and expensive. Returning to the family home did not represent a retreat from gay identity, although the coinciding unemployment that he experienced had taken a toll on his social life. By the time of the interview Devon was working, earning good money and enjoying himself on the gay scene, while also being a supportive and dutiful son at home. In this interview I invited him to complete the lifeline exercise, predicting his situation in a range of areas of life in three years' time, at the age of 25 and at 35. In general, he found this a difficult exercise, explaining that he lives in the present and does not plan ahead. When asked to predict his future home life, he says that in three years' time he will be 'back in the flat share, definitely, I can't see myself at home'. Asked to look further forward, Devon is unable to respond, explaining:

> **I'm trying to** draw from what I'm going through now (...). What
> I'm feeling now and that sort of path that I'm on (...) that I'm already
> on (...) where it could lead to, to how things have changed over the
> past three years and the past 16 years (...). Can't even remember that
> far back (...) but yeah I'm just trying to think of how I've got to this
> stage and where it can lead me on to. [2000, aged 19]

The absence of a normative 'blueprint' for the future was also evident in his discussion of the 'Relationships' strand of the lifeline. His initial response to this question was to emphasise the continuing centrality of friendships in his life:

> **True friends, they'll** always be there and that's what I'm more
> concentrating on and that's what I would like more than to go out and
> meet Mr Right tomorrow and be with him until I'm 60. It's wonderful,
> but it's not a part of the plan (...) no. [2000, aged 19]

Although falling in love and settling down are attractive, Devon doubts that 'people can stay with one person for that long, before someone wanders or they fall out of love'. When asked if he could imagine himself having a relationship as long as that of his parents he replies:

> **Even now I** still think two men together is errrr, so I'm quite happy to have sex with men but the idea of you know setting up home with another man, bringing up kids with another man, having pets with another man, going shopping with another man (...) you know as far as I am concerned that is what straight people do, that's not what we do (...) that's definitely not what I do.
>
> INT: But then again, some of those things are part of what you want, aren't they, having kids.
>
> Yeah, it is a complete and utter contradiction. [2000, aged 19]

Consistent with Devon's strong identification with family life, his mother and sisters, Devon repeatedly asserts his desire to be a father. Although he could imagine parenting as a single man, he could not imagine co-parenting with a lover. He recognises the inconsistencies within his own account:

> **This is going** to sound so selfish, I see them for me as something that I wanna do (...) and it will be great, it will be a huge help to have someone else to go through that with (...) the whole bringing kids up thing (...) it's not just a couple of months of changing smelly nappies, it's the rest of your life. (...) It would be great to have someone there to go through that, but as far as I'm concerned, it's not necessary, kids are what I want.
>
> INT: So what, are you going to see yourself as a single parent?
>
> I can, I don't want to, but I can. And I know that again, because of the relationship thing, the sexual relationship, I don't think it's possible, with or without kids. [...] Am I making sense? I've got a real bad headache just trying trying to work it all out, I feel like I'm going round in circles. [2000, aged 19]

Over the course of the successive interviews Devon struggles to square his ongoing identification with his own family, his growing familiarity with urban lesbian and gay cultures and the available narratives through which it is possible to imagine family life. If his first interview is characterised by a claiming of normality, his second interview is characterised by a pleasure in difference. Living at home demands that he draw lines between his social life and family life, so while he is very close to his sister, he nevertheless feels that he 'can't tell her what I'm up to on the weekend'. By his third interview Devon has moved towards integrating his family life and gay identity. At the time of this interview he is 'living in' at his new job, but visits his parents regularly. He appreciates the ease with which he can go 'home', compared to his co-workers who are mostly far from their parents. Living away from his parents also means that he can invite his family into his world. He explained that he had been sitting with his mother in a gay bar when I had telephoned him to arrange the interview: 'If we'd still been living together that would never have happened [...] I can show her bits of what I'd always tried to keep separate from her' [2001, aged 21]. This reworking of public and private boundaries was also evident in Devon's revisiting of Majorca – the site of an earlier (rare) family holiday where as a 'new born' he had his first sexual experience – and to which he returned this time as an economically independent young gay man.

If we understand 'home' as involving a sense of belonging as well as physical and emotional security (Rutherford, 1998), it is possible to see a dynamic relationship between Devon's family of origin, his emergent identity as a gay man and the beginnings of his own 'family of choice' (Weston, 1991; Weeks et al, 2001). Despite a traumatic exit from the home, family continues to play an important role, providing security and authorising the value of relationships. Over time the friendships that Devon forges with other young gay men and lesbians become increasingly important. It is tempting to draw distinctions between family-of-origin relationships that are based on obligations, dependence and hierarchy, and family-of-choice relationships based on equality, reciprocity and contingency. Clearly, both sets of relationship are more complex and exist in conversation with each other. While non-heterosexual identities and positionings may disrupt hetero-normative categories of age, the lifecourse and 'family life', they do not entirely displace them. Ideals may come apart from practices, so while it is difficult for Devon to imagine himself as both a father and a (sexualised) gay man, he nevertheless has practical experience that comes very close to parenthood and defines maturity and adulthood primarily in terms of care.

> **I think, the** only thing that will ever make me feel like a grown-up is the day that I become responsible for someone else. At the moment I'm still responsible for me, the same as my little brother. He's responsible for himself. A few years ago, I don't know whether I said about this, there was a lot of trouble with my parents and my sisters and I sort of took on the responsibility of, how can I put this, of caring too much, of taking over my parents' place in the family. And, it nearly drove me to a nervous breakdown and I had to take a few months out of the family home. And sort of since then I've learnt that I don't have to be responsible. There's a line between being responsible, feeling responsible for everybody and being concerned about everybody, which is what I always will be. That's just me, so I will always be bothered about my

little sister. Will she get the job that she wanted? Or my big sister, gets pregnant whatever. She's not but – so things like that would always concern. But they don't feel like they're my responsibility anymore. And sort of really since then I've felt that when I do become responsible for someone, someone will look to lean on me, then I'll feel like a grown-up. At least I hope I do. [2001, aged 21]

In a discussion of the relationship between intimacy, citizenship and public space, Phil Hubbard (2001) argues that for 'sexual dissidents' the ultimate aim of intimate citizenship is to forge public legitimacy for their own privacy. In practice this initially demands a form of politics in which private practices are made public as the first stage of winning the status of social inclusion. Yet the ultimate aim is not public visibility per se, but rather a form of socially included privacy. In terms posed by Jeffrey Weeks, this is the dynamic relationship between successive moments of transgression and citizenship that punctuate the narrative of sexual progress. In Devon's changing account of family life it is possible to see this dynamic in play. Although he begins by claiming normality, it is necessary for him to occupy an excluded identity in order to forge the kind of practices and relationships that he needs so as to re-engage with the meaning of family and home. So although Devon is never only located in the closet – always keeping a foot outside – he nevertheless is able to creatively use the space symbolised as the closet to gain resources, skills and support. This process can be seen operating explicitly in relation to the world of work.

Work: 'six months is about all I can give you'

Work, identity and dependency

Throughout the period of our conversations, Devon's attitude towards work was deeply ambivalent. Over the four years he reports walking out of a number of jobs because he was bored, felt uncomfortable, and was going on holiday. In contrast to Stan, he deliberately avoids engaging in a relationship with work where his identity is implicated within notions of 'career' or 'craft'. Work is treated primarily as a means to an end rather than an end in itself, and at this point in his life it is secondary to his social life and personal relationships. Devon's gender identity depends on employment and unemployment in quite a different way – the devaluation of work plays a role in privileging investments in other arenas.

At 18 Devon actively seeks to distance himself from the masculinity of his father. Central to his disidentification is his father's identity as a non-worker:

How do I put it nicely – he was always out of work and taking it out on one of us [...] I'm never going to be like my dad [...] laying about the house, not even looking for a job [...] What sort of person can do that for that amount of time? [1999, aged 18]

At the time of this first interview Devon was working as an office junior. He explains that 'at this point in my life I've got pretty much everything I've wanted: family, my own place, I haven't got a great job but I've got a job.' Flexibility in work is more important to Devon than responsibility or career development.

> **I'm one of** these weird people that really doesn't mind being at the beck and call of people. I find I like the er, repetitive jobs like the faxing and the filing and they really don't get to me. Erm, just things like that. But yeah, as I say, where I am at the moment, although it's everything I've always wanted I can't stay still. I don't like the idea of 'okay, I've got everything now, I'm just gonna live with it'. I like the idea of moving on and getting more and doing different things. [1999, aged 18]

In this interview he describes himself as busy and 'self-sufficient', explaining, 'six weeks in all, I was unemployed and they had to be the longest six weeks of my life. I absolutely hated every minute and how my dad managed to do it for 18 years, no idea.'

At this point Devon was about to leave his travel agency job to sign on at several temping agencies, to maximise his choices in relation to work. This coincided with his move out of his foster placement into his own flat, which was located at the other side of the city. At his subsequent interview he explained that he was initially excited by his new-found independence, and optimistic about finding work. In practice, he was absorbed by the demands of a new flat and neighbourhood and reports finding the travelling difficult. After a few weeks of temping he gave up on work and was then unemployed for his first five months in the new flat.

> **Between sort of** getting over the initial great feeling of independence and starting my new job, it was very lonely, it was quite horrible in fact, things like when I'd leave my parents' house to go home, doing that long journey by myself, if there were times when I weren't anywhere, I was just in the flat, sort of thinking well I can't really go anywhere cause my mum's at work and my dad's at work, my carer's at work so, there's nowhere I can really go to, now I'm just stuck here, which from what I've heard most people go through when they're out of a job in that situation. [2000, aged 19]

In order to fill his time Devon accepted a very low-paid job, which did not enable him to pay his bills. Eventually he felt compelled to go back into unemployment in order to survive financially. Luckily he did not lose his benefits, which he then supplemented with occasional temping for an agency. He describes this as a 'very low period' in which the flat became a burden and a symbol of his failure to be self-sufficient. He avoided the flat, fearing letters from his landlord demanding rent arrears.

Returning to his parents' home was 'strange, I mean I left home in May '97, after nearly three years being back there, every single day, going to sleep there every night, waking every morning, it's been very weird'. Devon's attempts to minimise the burden of his dependency on his parents reflect his sensitivity in this area:

> **Yeah, if I** dirty the plate, I make a cup of tea and still, whatever, I just clean it up so, my mum's quite pleased about that. [...] I was paying her an awful low amount of money, but that is what she asked for and it was what I could cope with [...] but I always felt guilty that I wasn't giving her enough. [1999, aged 18]

His experience of independent living had made him aware of the labour that had formerly been invisible to him, and the extent of his dependency:

> **I'd catch myself** buying sort of six lamb chop things, whatever, putting them away. I noticed doing that way, which is the way that my mum does it. You can't go out for four people and buy ready meals every night. So I noticed doing it that way is a lot more expensive. I mean in the long run I suppose it does work out cheaper, but to go out in any one go to buy that sort of stuff, it's expensive. Which is how – 'cause I pay my mum once a month – it's how I still think of it. She'll go out and do a month's shopping in one go [...] So that's why I'm still sort of stuck in this idea that the money I give her isn't enough. So I mean I've stuck to it. [2000, aged 19]

Subsequently Devon secured a much better-paid job, and continued to live at home, contributing to the family budget. He explains that 'although I am on this great job and I'm earning nice money – it doesn't actually feel like I am a grown-up still. And for me, I think, the only thing that will ever make me feel like a grown-up is the day that I become responsible for someone else.'

Work as a (hetero-)normative space

As a working-class young man with relatively few qualifications, it is hardly surprising that Devon is ambivalent about work as a source of identity. From his perspective, temping was an ideal solution in that variety compensates for work with few prospects. Yet, as a space, work may not be entirely welcoming to a young man coming to terms with being gay. Having first explained that he left a job because of the low pay, he subsequently describes a situation in which he was bullied by a senior colleague who was consistently unpleasant to him. During the long period that Devon was subsequently unemployed and living at home, he became very active in the lesbian and gay youth group, taking up the position of Chair of the young people's steering group.

> **When I was** out of a job, basically it became pretty much a full-time job, I put in say roughly 50 to 60 hours a week [...] pretty much a full-time job, but I loved it. I loved just having the feeling of going in making a difference even if it's just filling out an application form, going to the bank to pay in a cheque. It's one of those things I'm so used to doing, it's hard to put into words to describe how it is. I'm enjoying it and I still get to do it now as well. It doesn't affect my work and my work doesn't affect it. [2000, aged 19]

The role of Chair demanded high levels of responsibility and Devon's achievements were recognised by a youth work award. Yet, although these activities were very important to him, he does not count them as part of the world of work, nor as aspects of his identity as a worker. This again contrasts with Stan, who deliberately blurs the boundaries between paid and unpaid work and leisure. By the time of his second interview Devon had found himself in a job with prospects, as administrator in a small voluntary sector organisation. He began the job as a temp, but the organisation invited him to stay on, offering training, decent wages and career development. In this second interview Devon was still feeling his way in the office environment. He recounts his suspicions that his boss might be gay, citing the way in which he had been impressed by Devon's voluntary activities with the youth group: 'he's sort of said quite a few times and he sort of makes connections between what I do there to what I do at the steering group, so I think it's helped'. However, Devon was not yet confident that he could, should or even wanted to be 'out' in the office. He reflects back on the episode at his previous job:

> **I'm not out** completely yet. I think 'cause I was so comfortable being out with my last job, just sort of get a bit paranoid that was why that woman picked on me. She was a very Catholic woman, strong Irish Catholic woman. So I made an effort not to be quite so out. I drop hints and say things like, I'm single, I go out to a place which is a gay place, if you're gay you'd know about it, if you weren't, it's just a bar. So dropping hints, not completely out still, and I'm not sure if I wanna be now. Maybe they think that one is enough in the office. [2000, aged 19]

Although Devon is very enthusiastic about this job he is uncertain as to whether he wants his sexuality to be visible in the office. As I have suggested before, Devon actively disinvests his identity from work. While this may be a response to a lack of opportunity, it also facilitates his investments in other areas. So, for example, he makes links between his carefulness in relation to his intimate relationships and his carelessness in relation to his career:

> **I'm not a** big risk taker. Usually I'd have someone as back up, someone out with me. So I do usually spot when something could turn risky or there is an element of risk involved and I tend not to go for that physically. So I'm not really frightened of anything in that way because I know that there's no way I could get myself into that sort of situation where I could be scared of something [...] Around work and other aspects of my life, I do take risks. But I only realise that they are risks after I've already taken them. 'Cause I'm the sort of person that will just act on a feeling and then afterwards thinking, that was a big risk [...] My last job, leaving that without another job to go into. That was a big risk and it was one that I failed, I ended up back on benefits. So in that way, yeah, I am a risk taker, it's only because I don't tend to really weigh up, I go for gut feeling. [1999, aged 18]

At this point in his life it may be that Devon positively welcomes work as a space in which his sexuality is, to a certain extent, excluded, in that it enables him to experience the dissonance between the 'straight world' and the values and dynamics of the gay scene. In this second interview Devon repeatedly reflects on the boundaries between work and play, embodied in his delight in feeling the ring in his navel piercing beneath his austere work clothes. Work then comes to symbolise forms of authority and hierarchy which are turned on their head in his night-time world. On the gay scene, Devon's youth and ethnicity give him value, at work they locate him at the bottom of a hierarchy constructed in relation to age and status. At this point, the mismatch between the two is a source of pleasure.

> **I'm 19 years** old, I've got blonde hair, blue eyes, I earn a good wage now. I can go out, I can do what I wanna do. People will always be attracted to that and [...] you know. Look at me, I could have you, I could turn you away. You know, feeling that, if you go through a whole night of feeling like that, for a while after it will still affect you. And I've noticed that when I go into work the day after, the day after that sometimes, that I do still feel like that. And the work goes easier and I feel better and I have a much better time at work than I would even normally. Because I still feel confident. [2000, aged 19]

Devon talks a lot about the absence of generational boundaries within the gay scene, and is excited by the way in which the rules of straight society do not seem to apply. Examples that he offers include middle-aged people clubbing and the explicit articulation of eroticism irrespective of age differences. Devon attributes this 'freedom' to an absence of family obligation meaning that lesbian and gay adults can socialise without having 'anyone to answer to'.

> **The way I** look at it is, it's purely a night-time thing. During the day there's regular jobs just like everyone else. I'm an administrative

assistant, Noel works in a department store, every job where there are gay people there are straight people doing exactly the same jobs and exactly the same pay, but it's really on the social side that I see more gay people as just teenagers. [2000, aged 19]

In fact, Devon is very conservative about age hierarchies at work:

> **I know for** a fact if I went into a job and I found out that my manager was the same age as me, wouldn't be seen as a manager, and God forbid, I got to my thirties and my manager was 19, there wouldn't be a manager, there would be the kid, you know. [2000, aged 19]

Devon does not accept his employer's offer of recognition and career development. When asked to predict his work life in the future, Devon imagines himself working in administration for the foreseeable future, explaining that he likes 'the routine, I like the stability'. He expresses no burning ambitions for greater responsibility, noting that he is 'confident in my work place, but in my work the confidence I have isn't lasting, it's not strong enough'.

The job with prospects did not last very long. When I met Devon for his third interview, the following year, he looked back wistfully, commenting 'that was the best job I ever had. Best pay too.' He explains that 'I could never get to grips with their filing system.' It is not entirely clear from his account whether he walked or was pushed, but he left the job to go on a much-anticipated holiday to Ibiza and never came back.

> **Yeah, I finished** work on Friday I think it was. I actually left early Friday. I went in, had a meeting for my probationary review at 11 o'clock. And I sort of said, I'm very sorry but six months is about all I can give you and I can't do this any more. They said, 'Thank you,' and y'know, 'We had noticed that your work had started to sort of slip,' just through boredom basically. They said, 'We was hoping that it was something else but, y'know, it happens' [...] I think they knew in advance that I would be going away. And so I said, y'know, 'I don't know what to do.' And they said, 'Oh forget it. You're going away next week, there's no point in us paying you. We'll pay you up to today, which is officially the end of the month, and then you can go.' So me, not really thinking about it, I haven't got a job to come back to, 'OK bye'. And I went back to my desk, and I sort of stayed in for a bit longer, and um I was sort of carrying on typing a letter that had been given to me. And the boss came out and he said um, 'You don't have to finish that if you don't want to. Your heart's not gonna be in it for the rest of the day, is it?' And I said, 'Well no to be honest it ain't.' So he said, 'Well pack up. Off you go'. [2001, aged 21]

Devon explains that he returned from holiday desperate for money. Rather than taking another temping job, he answered an advertisement in the *Gay Times*, and worked for a time as an erotic model. For the first time, Devon's paid employment was located within the 'gay world'. His account of the experience draws attention to this distinction. For example, he points out that the images were made only for 'private collectors' and were not 'publicly available'. Although he was very frightened at the start, the older gay men who ran the business were kind to him, and he described them as 'like my dads'. In his account of this episode he places himself within the categories generated within this commercial niche, talking about how his body fitted into the market – smooth, hairless and boyish 'goes down really well'. There were a number of occasions when things could have 'gone too far' and in which he would have been in physical danger, and he asserts that the experience helped him to be more confident and a better judge of risk. Previously important boundaries between private self and public work appear to have dissolved.

By his third interview Devon had moved into yet another job, working as butler in a Gentlemen's Club. He describes the job as being badly paid and with no career progression, yet he is also very excited by the status of 'the establishment' and the many famous members. Devon presents the job as a quasi-gay environment, noting that 30% of the staff are gay and the existence of a thriving gay life-style 'below stairs'. Devon was enjoying introducing work mates to the gay scene of the city. His plans for the job were to 'stay as long as – till it stops being fun'. He reflects that when he gets to the age of 25 he may think again, but at the moment he is still young enough 'to get away with [...] trying on these different jobs'. 'Living in' had allowed him some independence from his family without the costs of independent living. He was now budgeting successfully and avoiding debt, observing that 'I have worked hard to sort out my life as easy and comfortable as this'.

Devon is relatively unusual for someone of his generation in that he has been working (on and off) since the age of 16. Work is not seen as a supplement to education, as for most young people of his age. Nor is work seen as a primary source of identity, as is the case with Stan. Rather, work is a financial and moral necessity, guarding against the passivity and depression that he associates with unemployment. Living in the city gives Devon access to a buoyant market in temporary administrative jobs which enable him to work without having to make an emotional commitment to a career. Sexuality also plays an important part in the way in which he orients towards work and the forms of authority that it symbolises for him. Over the course of the three interviews it is possible to see Devon negotiating work as a hetero-normative space that exists alongside his emergent gay identity. Initially, the prospect of a gay work space is not comfortable for him, and he engages with a number of different versions, including that symbolised by the 'out gay boss', the hard-core end of the gay economy and the traditional gay subculture of the establishment. Even though work is crucial to his material and emotional survival, at this point in his life it is marginal to his identity.

Play: 'cheap, tacky and very me'

Devon invests considerable energy in making boundaries between the fields of his existence and the different modes of interaction that characterise each. It may be that the rule-bound mode of interaction of the workplace enhances the mode of interaction that characterises the night-time gay scene, which in turn gains meaning through its difference from the responsibilities and identifications of family life. In this third part of Devon's case history I will explore the biographical realm of his life that I categorise as 'play', which includes his friendships, his sexual relationships and the environments within which these relationships occur. The environment is important, in that these relationships are for the most part kept separate from family and the workplace. Moreover, it is worth considering that the strong lines that are drawn between fields may, following McNay (2000), be productive of reflexivity. This perspective, while supporting some aspects of the argument that lesbian and gay communities may be the vanguard of detraditionalisation, certainly questions the assumptions behind the notion of there being a 'post gay' generation. It appears from Devon's case that the closet may not be a metaphorical place that is simply passed through, but rather refers to a practice of boundaried living in which the dissonance between fields and their associated habitus is experienced productively.

Although Devon had made contact with a lesbian and gay youth group at the time of his first interview, his account is dominated by an identification with his family. Much of his discussion concentrates on mediating the boundary of his 'old life', in which he was 'petrified of the idea of being gay. Petrified that I'd get AIDS. Er, things like that or dirty old men, you know, things like that,' and his new life in which he 'can totally be myself'. It is in the context of a perverse model of gay sexuality that Devon postpones sexual intimacy for the meantime.

> INT: We haven't mentioned love and romance?
>
> **Erm, oh well,** it's not really that important to me to be honest. It's – I mean it'd be nice to have somebody to come home to and to say, oh I've had a really lousy day. No – but it's (...) see though I'm comfortable with myself, I still do have low self-esteem. Erm, so I just can't help thinking that it's – it's not likely to be happening soon. [1999, aged 18]

By his second interview Devon had been through an intensive learning curve, although his ability to socialise had been severely curtailed by his periods of unemployment and poverty. He finds low-cost ways of participating in the scene, which rely on inside knowledge. Clubs are chosen carefully in order to stretch limited resources – 'it's a matter of choosing your night'. He describes his favourite club at the time of the interview as being 'cheap and it's tacky, it's wonderful, very me'. Since his last interview he had discovered the pleasures of dancing. He steers clear of drugs, preferring alcohol, which he uses strategically, drinking 'till I'm drunk and then I can stop [...] I still remain just on the right side of happy'. During this period Devon socialised with a core group of friends that he made at the lesbian and gay youth group. These young people, as well the other tenants in his shared house, provided him with an introduction to a gay life-style. He describes his first experience of a gay venue, accompanied by a housemate:

> **I was absolutely** petrified, I'll never forget it. I was in there 10 minutes, had a Coke, Diet Coke even, and then I was out the door. It was something like 10 to 10 and I was absolutely paranoid if I stayed there any longer, I'm gonna miss my last train. I knew for a fact that that wasn't true but that was what I told him and that was what I actually believed in order to get myself out. If I'd admitted to myself I just don't wanna be here, there's all gay people here, and scary, yeah. [2000, aged 19]

Devon distinguishes between the experience of the gay teenager who must be mobile, moving out of his locality in order to meet others like him, and the heterosexual teenager who has the choice to socialise within their locality. While Devon recognises this as a burden, he views it as a productive burden that forces greater resourcefulness:

> **With a straight** teenager, they don't really feel that so much. It's just a pub, there's friends in there, I'll go in and meet them sort of thing. They don't really think you know, oh God, there's gay people in there! Or they don't think there's other straight people in there. So building up your confidence that way, I think gay people do have an advantage 'cause basically it's just, from what I've heard, it's just something that straight people don't really experience, or have to do. [2000, aged 19]

In order to become competent in this respect, Devon was taken in hand by a housemate:

> **He's exactly 15** days younger than me, but he'd been out on the scene for years before I even met him. So it was having his confidence out on the scene, me tagging along, which I only ever felt I did. I tagged along, being with him though it helped me a lot. And sort of, after a while, I got confident that I didn't have to go out with him. You know, I could go out by myself, which I've never been a big fan of doing anyway. Or I could go out with other friends, meet friends in places like. When I first started, if I made arrangements to meet with someone – like I'd been out somewhere else or with my parents and I'd arranged to meet them and they'd be waiting inside for me – it'd take me about

10 minutes just to get inside to meet them, even though there was people in there. Horrible. But now, yeah, I'm confident enough to go out and spend the evening on my own. [2000, aged 19]

The process of acquiring 'confidence' is labour intensive, and involves the construction of a demeanour and the acquisition of new modes of interaction. Devon describes this process in terms of losing inhibition and becoming more himself: 'I mean I remember when I first started on the scene, I was very nervous, very very nervous, but spending more time in it, you do get more relaxed and it's like that relaxedness never goes.' This is also a process of the construction of artifice, central to which is the embodiment of camp:

> **Sometimes I can** think of certain things I say, the way I see it, head movements, hand movements, things like that – and I will recognise a part of somebody that I know [...] Very scary. Don't suppose it's their influence rubbing off on me, I think it's more me just trying to be as confident as they are. [1999, aged 18]

Devon distinguishes the support that he gets from his friends like Noel and Shane and the support of adults such as his middle-class youth workers, who, while they may be gay, are nevertheless authority figures. The key to Devon's friendships at this point is lack of hierarchy, and a shared age and class habitus:

> **Gordon is the** youth worker, he's been pretty much the same. I've been able to talk more freely with Noel about certain things and also, in my sort of, the style that I talk, which is I'm ashamed to say, is a bit more vulgar, shall I put it, it's just a bit more relaxed. My language and Noel's is exactly the same so, I can say things to him or describe certain people in certain ways – in a way that I would never dream of saying in front of Gordon, let alone to him. Gordon is more there as the support, a friend, but also someone that can help me. Whereas Noel is someone I can lean on. Gordon is there to help me as well. I don't ever expect Noel to help me, it's nice when he does, he offers to but I never really expect it from Noel. Gordon I do usually. [2000, aged 19]

Devon's description of his first sexual experience with a man 10 years his senior suggests some of the ways in which he struggles to negotiate age boundaries within the gay scene. His initial account stresses his feelings of immaturity, explaining that he 'felt like I'd done something wrong and that I was waiting to get in trouble'. Yet with the help of friends he is able to rework the account, giving himself a sense of value and agency – occupying the position of the object of desire.

At the time I felt it was bad, that I'd done something really really bad. Looking back on it, I felt that it was great, but I would still think of ways that it could have been better. If I'd have bought him a drink, or if I decided to talk about this. Or if you know, and a million and one things about how the evening could have been better. And I mean I never, as I said before, I'm not one to think like that, what if, what I just couldn't help it you know, just try and find a way to turn it around so I would be more in the lead [...] since Noel said this to me, you know, you're 19, you've got blond hair, blue eyes, you can do anything. Since then, yeah. Really most of well, yeah, pretty much every time it's, it's either I've been in control, or I've agreed really. Or absolute closest it could get to them being in control, is that I've agreed and I felt comfortable and confident doing that. [2000, aged 19]

However, being in control is not an entirely comfortable experience. Here again Devon experiences dissonance between the fields of his existence. He describes an episode where he spent time talking to a man at a club, but had no desire to then have sex with him. He struggles with the dilemma of whether he has led the guy on:

When I came out of there I felt fine really, didn't really bother me at all 'cause I'd been in control and I was feeling pretty confident from the night. But it was only really the day after that I thought about it and I thought I'd probably seemed like such a cold bitch you know. And you do what I say, you don't get anything, you only get what I want to give you.

INT: Is that sort of unfamiliar territory for you, isn't it?

Yeah, definitely, 'cause I'm usually quite happy, how can I put this, being a sort of a lesser role, my work, my social life, my family life, I don't mind tagging along behind people. That's when I feel most comfortable. But around things like sex, then usually yeah, I'm a lot more confident and I like to be more in control. [2000, aged 19]

By his third interview Devon had gained in confidence in relation to the commercial gay scene, and had moved from the position of the 'apprentice' to that of the 'teacher'. His memory book included a page devoted to Gaydar – a gay dating website that he uses to search out newcomers to the city whom he might take in hand. Devon tells the story of guiding Jamie (a work colleague) through the scene, taking up the role of the young expert, teaching him to cruise as he in his turn had been taught by others. Devon's language here also suggests the extent to which he has come to consider his value within a wider market in instrumental terms. What he calls 'knowledgism' then compensates for what he feels he may lack in looks:

> **Things like getting** to know the scene, getting to feel comfortable with other gay people and things like that. He was still learning about that and it wasn't something that he did feel comfortable. [...] And I've sort of been, at his request, introducing him more to the scene and how to cruise people and things like that. [...] It is nice. It's the same with sort of when there's new people. It's just having that little bit more knowledge. I suppose in a way it sort of compensates, I know that I'm not the most attractive person, I know that when I walk into a room it doesn't light up, sort of thing. I know of people that, friends of mine that do, and I hate them for it (*laughs*). Yeah so just the sort of knowledgism is my way of sort of compensating. I love learning about new things anyway, so if it's something that I can actually use to sort of teach another person, I just love that – to sort of learn about the scene and learn about the city or how to pick up people. [2001, aged 21]

Devon makes direct links between his experience as a model, his own sexual confidence and his ability to take on the role of the teacher:

> **Yeah it sort** of comes with the confidence thing. Y'know I could walk into a complete stranger's house and take my clothes off, it doesn't worry me. Sort of it carries on into other parts as well. So it's all a bit of that and then introducing Jamie to the scene, helping him sort of thing, when you take on the sort of 'teachery' role, your confidence is accelerated anyway. You think, well, if he has a problem he'll come to me about it. [2001, aged 21]

Learning how to operate in this way had been a struggle for Devon and he tells several stories marked by the pain of rejection and the difficulty of balancing the sociability demanded by the scene and feelings of jealousy. Devon also reports conflict with his closest friends as they attempt to live by the ethics of erotic friendship (Blasius, 1995; Nardi, 1999). He and best friend Noel fell out over a boy to whom they were both attracted. In the end both had had a short sexual relationship with him, and finally all became friends. But although Devon is now more proficient in negotiating casual sex, he also continues to desire but disbelieve in the possibility of a more committed partnership.

> **Yeah, I'm a** lot easier with the idea of – I go and pick someone up, have fun, then I'll go home. But the idea of sort of, trying not to, and trying to think, yeah this could be someone I could have a lot of fun with, and sticking to one person, sort of thing – it scares me. The idea

of having to try to do it, sort of, I can't. But it is something that I do want to try. [2001, aged 21]

A source of great sadness for Devon in his third interview was the troubles that had come to dominate the life of his best friend, Noel. In earlier interviews Devon pinpointed Noel as vital support. Along with other close friends such as Shane, he associated Noel with a bravado attitude, characterised by living in the present and showing a disregard for both the past and the future. He describes Noel as 'one of those people that is a bit out there anyway. But he's not, in any way harmful [...] But y'know, he's like me, he's one of those people that say, "Well no I don't wanna do that. I wanna do something else".' Nevertheless, Devon himself is wary of taking certain kinds of risks, particularly in relation to his physical and sexual safety. 'He takes much bigger risks. Ones that I could never dream about. And y'know, it just scares me.' Devon tells a painful story of visiting Noel in a youth detention centre, where camp was not enough to bridge the divide:

> **But I did** get down to see him and it was horrible just seeing him sitting there and knowing that I couldn't go and sit next to him and have a laugh, or couldn't just turn around and say, 'Oh I'm bored with this place now, come on, let's go down to the pub'. Nothing like that – it was horrible. [2001, aged 21]

Devon explains that the risks that he had taken while working as a model had been important in helping him define boundaries and manage complexity in a way that defended him from the dangers associated with living in the present. He also comments on the importance now of being able to begin to draw aspects of the different fields of his world together, most significantly, being able to share some of his gay existence with his mother:

> **Yeah, yeah that's** the biggest one. Um being able to feel comfortable around my mother and I sort of (...) It's like I feel that all these different little aspects of my life, so that I can just (...) It's like um, stepping stones, sort of thing, I suppose. So I've placed stepping stones in certain places so I know that if I wanna go this way, I will be carried that way and I will still be safe and dry. [2001, aged 21]

In drawing strong boundaries between the different spheres of his life it seems that Devon creates space for identity work to take place. These are the stepping stones that make movement possible. When I ask Devon how he is placing the stones for the next bit of his life, his response reflects this compartmentalised yet incremental methodology:

> **So the next** way will be concentrating on career more. I have my family and I have my friends to be able to come to me and me to go

to them whenever I want. Social life will always be behind me [...] I'm not concentrating on that so much any more. It'll always be with me in whatever aspect like clubbing or anything like that, or if I wanna sit in and go out once a week or spend every night sitting in.

INT: And sexuality, you've kind of got that one worked through?

Yeah that's another one that's behind me. That's, I know what I am and I know what I'm doing (*laugh*) maybe. [2001, aged 21]

Conclusions

Forging an identity as a gay man demands that Devon depart from the models offered by his neighbourhood and former school friends. But he does find models of how to be among gay adults and teenagers. Devon's biography is not dominated by the demands of the extended dependency associated with higher education in the way that Sherleen's and Stan's accounts are. Yet, like them, he struggles to balance security and risk taking, immediate and deferred gratification. In this chapter I have traced three fields of Devon's biography over three interviews: family, work and play. In doing so I have explored the relationship between a particular social and historical location and the production of a reflexive subjectivity, including the part played within this by the mediation of boundaries between private and public, heterosexual and homosexual. I am intrigued by whether Devon's experience illustrates something of what Scott Lash (1994) calls a 'mobile being in the world', given his highly boundaried approach to living and the centrality of class, age and sexuality to the choices available to him. In unfolding the case history I have noted Lois McNay's argument that reflexivity may be produced by dissonance between the habitus of different social fields, drawing attention to the significance of boundary drawing as a biographical practice. The strategies employed by Devon suggest that mobility may be tempered, or even anchored by continuities between social fields relating to class and gender, and movement between fields may be held off until resources are secured sufficiently to make such interconnections safe.

Devon's case history also draws attention to the different ways in which 'disembedding' and 're-embedding' may take place. Although Devon is relatively disembedded from the physical locality of his community of origin, he nevertheless continues to be embedded in a particular generational class culture, expressed in part through the camp practices of his gay peer group, his experiences of work and his enduring connections with his family of origin. It is also possible to see a process of re-embedding taking place as Devon learns and conforms to the rules of the scene, adopting new modes of interaction and investing in particular technologies of the self. Yet within each of the social fields of his life there is movement between modes of interaction, invoking corresponding identities, motivations and styles. Devon's case history points to the importance of stylised performances of self as one of the media through which new ways of being are improvised. In the next chapter we explore the potential and limits of the improvised self in a very different setting.

SEVEN

Acting out: rebellion with a cause

Karin is a white Catholic young woman from a working-class background, living in a city in Northern Ireland. This chapter draws on data generated by a series of four interviews with her between the ages of 16 and 19 as well as a memory book. The interviews were conducted by Sheena McGrellis, and initially took place at school and subsequently at the university. Karin had also been involved in a focus group and pair interview when she was 14, as part of the earlier Youth Values study.

Through Karin's successive narratives it is possible to gain a sense of gendered self-in-the-making, yet one that is situated in a particular historical context and underwritten both by a cast of intimates and by a wider backdrop of social and cultural possibilities. Questions of resistance and innovation are central motifs, as are struggles to secure recognition from others. The case history is structured by an exploration of change and continuity within the different fields of existence that structure Karin's biography: education, play and family life. Over this period Karin moved from school to college. Shortly after her third interview she participated in an Operation Raleigh initiative in India, which effectively meant taking a year out of college, which she made up on her return. By the time of her fourth interview she was making applications for university. Over the whole research period she was living at home with her parents, her siblings having left for university and, subsequently, jobs elsewhere.

Education: hanging in and hanging out

We first met Karin at school, an integrated comprehensive that sought to transcend the sectarian divides of a large Northern Irish city. As an integrated school it also transcended the demarcation between grammar and secondary modern schooling, holding an ambiguous place within the wider educational landscape. Karin explained that the school was seen as 'snobby' by many and she took delight in disrupting its liberal ethic of integration. At 14 she described herself as a 'wee Fenian', yet also insisted on being interviewed as a pair with her best friend Gina, a working-class Protestant girl. By the following year Karin had developed a searing critique of the techniques employed by the school to promote integration, in particular resisting their censorship of visual expressions of working-class religious difference, such as the Celtic and Ranger football club insignia. In her view, the repression of these symbols, and exhortations that 'you should be integrating' were 'wile patronising'. Yet at the same time she expressed frustration at the difficulties that her mixed-religion friendship group had in meeting up outside school, finding taxi drivers unwilling to drive between Catholic and Protestant neighbourhoods, and having few spaces outside of the school grounds where they could spend time together.

Although the school endeavoured to instil a commitment to integration, in practice it was unable to make the conditions for such relationships available to students. Moreover, its attempts to repress the expression of religious and class difference through a control over style and fashion flew in the face of the very strategies that students such as Karin were employing to work through difference (McGrellis, 2005b). Yet Karin had sought out a number of settings in which it was possible to access a non-sectarian youth culture, most notably the Skater scene and the Basement, a city-centre youth club. At the Basement a mixed group of young people cultivated 'freak' identities in which difference was elaborated and celebrated. Her excitement about Skater culture focused both on the opportunities it presented to meet new people and on its global, non-local character.

The considerable investments of time, energy and creativity that Karin was making in order to break into these scenes existed in tension with her schooling. She described herself as 'switched off' from school work, asserting that 'I've got other things going on'. Yet, paradoxically, she also made it clear that she was very committed to an educational path, asserting that she would 'stay at school as long as possible' as part of a strategy that got her out of Northern Ireland, to university and a more cosmopolitan life-style.

> **I had this** big long talk with my sister a couple of weeks ago and she was all – the longer you stay at school it does kind of open your mind on other prospects. And if you go to university and things like that you meet different types of people. You travel, right, it was all in perfect context when she said it. But you don't hear of someone who's working in this city thinking right I'll go to the kibbutz for the next couple of months, go to Israel like. But if you're a student in university that's the kind of things you do and that. So I want to stay for as long as possible. [1999, aged 16]

Education is understood primarily as route into new social worlds: 'when I think about university I don't think about the courses, I think about the nightlife (…) the atmosphere'. In her lifeline exercise Karin revealed detailed plans about an educational route from school, to Tech (further education college) and ultimately to university in a big city, studying fashion design. These plans were resourced by conversations with her siblings – the first generation in her family to go to university. Decisions about subject choice were driven by a notion of the 'sort of person' that she wanted to become rather than any particular commitment to a course of study. In contrast to Sherleen, who sought to master the subject positions made available by the educational regime, Karin only did what was absolutely necessary – her emotional investments being somewhere else entirely.

At the time of her second interview Karin only had two more weeks of school before revision and GCSE examinations. During the intervening eight months her excursions into non-school-based friendship networks had left her badly bruised. In the face of her effective exclusion from the 'Basement crowd' she again relied on her old school friends for company. Karin regretted that she had failed to keep contact with her best friend Gina over the summer holiday, and expressed concern that their friendship might not survive school. Karin continued to present herself as emotionally disengaged from her school work, yet clear about what she had to do in order to make the next stage of her planned transition.

> INT: So how's the rest of your course going then? The GCSEs and that?
>
> Pants. Absolutely pants. I'm doing awful all over the place. I have like two more weeks at school and I have three course works to hand in and I have to start them. Not just finish them. I'm like I have to start them. Oh my God! [...] There's no way I'll get it done. [...]
>
> INT: So are you revising yet or (...)
>
> Oh no. A wee bit like the night before as usual.
>
> INT: And how many are you doing?
>
> Um, eight.
>
> INT: Eight and how do you expect to do?
>
> Och I don't think I'll do that bad but I'm not gonna come out wi' As and Bs. Bs and Cs maybe. [2000, aged 17]

Karin struggled with *being* in school, portraying herself as a thorn in the side of the educational establishment. She resisted the authority of teachers, yet also self-consciously avoided falling into the well-worn traps of educational resistance. While she wanted to rebel, she was also determined not to fail:

> **They don't like** me but I don't get in trouble. I don't get in trouble to spite them. 'Cause they don't like me.
>
> INT: And why do you think they don't like you?
>
> Um (...) too independent for them. I think all teachers just want to make little models of themselves, don't they? Like all the secondary school teachers want you tae look well and just, they want you to be this proper image for their school. They don't want you to be yourselves

and I can't be someone else's (...) I'm just not the right person for that. [2000, aged 17]

One of the consequences of her refusal of authority is that Karin must deal with not being liked. At this point she can bear the disapproval of her teachers because she has friends and she can anticipate another, more sympathetic environment. She imagines Tech as a place where 'I just think I'll fit in with that. I think I'll have come home when I get that.'

Karin's predictions of her GCSE results proved to be conservative – she gained two As, three Bs and three Cs, which she judged as 'not bad, considering that I didn't do a tap of work'. Her results had been good enough to get her into Tech and her Foundation Art course, something she 'really needed, really wanted'. In her third interview it became apparent that she still experienced herself in opposition to the teachers in this new setting, describing with considerable pleasure how she 'tested how much' her head tutor 'would take':

> **Oh they do** put pressure on you, but a lot more relaxed than in school, a lot more. But they do still put pressure on you. See the head tutor, Brendan, I hate that man with a passion. And um I started getting really nasty with him and he's taking it, I can't believe it. If um (...) he tells me to do something I go, 'No I don't wanna do it.' And he starts trying to explain and I go, 'No I think my way's better,' and then just ignore him, and he takes it. [2001, aged 18]

She contrasts the liberal stance adopted by Brendan with the more assertive behaviour of another, female teacher, whom she accords authority as a mother:

> **See even other** teachers now, this wee one Pauline, she's well on her way in as well, but you can just see she's (...) she's just a mummy. And she acts like a mummy when she's a teacher as well. And um what was it? She went in and he started at her with something and instead of her going, 'Yeah Brendan that's OK,' she stuck up for herself. [2001, aged 18]

Karin tests out the limits of the more relaxed teaching style of the Tech, and ridicules the idea (that she herself had previously voiced) that being a college student positions her in a fundamentally different way than being a school student. She stands out among her friends by refusing to use the new terminology of college life:

> **No we're totally** *pupil* that way, totally the wee 'uns (*laugh*). But we're fighting it, we're fighting it now. We're trying to act more as equals, but we're not.

INT: Are you surprised by that? Were you expecting it to be different at the Tech?

No, I expected it to be the way it was. I knew it would be a bit more lenient than school, but I knew I was still gonna be the pupil. I still call them teachers and everyone goes, 'Oh you know you're just out of school calling them teachers, they're tutor.' They're teachers, they teach us. [2001, aged 18]

Even at her fourth interview Karin insisted on calling her college 'school' – to the confusion of the interviewer. Yet by this point she had repositioned herself significantly in relation to education, having taken several months out of her course to participate in an Operation Raleigh initiative in India shortly after her third interview. Karin expressed contradictory feelings about this episode. In keeping with her resistance to educational techniques she was cynical about a request that she had received from the organisers to write an account of how the experience had changed her, observing: '[It] hasn't changed me one bit. It opened my eyes more than they were beforehand. Building toilets for a primary school. It really got me seeing the kids and the sheer poverty they were living in.' She goes on to make scathing comments about 'Americans with cream shorts and baseball caps' who had had paid thousands of dollars 'to help the wee lamas', then remarking, 'we weren't really helping either'. Towards the end of the same interview she also revealed that on returning from the trip she had had a serious bout of depression, struggling to find ways back into her old life, having lived outside 'closer to the ground'. On reflection, she observes: 'I've been thinking about this. Going to India. I did learn from it. I know now that I can do things, not *how* to do things, but that I can.'

It is possible to understand the time out of her normal life as an individualising experience. The trip took Karin out of the trajectory of her age cohort and by the time that she was ready to go back to college her classmates had moved on. When interviewed for the fourth time in 2003 she was repeating the second year of her Foundation course. This had meant joining a new class, who were a year younger than her, and mostly from a different town. In this interview she revealed that she was much happier, having escaped what she described as a 'very bitchy' year group, and that she was relieved that she had the opportunity to 'fix up her grades', expressing regret that she had not worked hard enough before. She reflects that if she had not had the time out, she would probably have dropped out of the course.

For the first time, in this interview Karin presents an identity that is more invested in education. Rather than ridiculing the educational system, she presents herself as a vulnerable student, confused by the flexibility offered by the curriculum and teaching styles. She explains that she struggled to find a way through the course, abandoning her plan of becoming a fashion designer and opting for a specialisation in interior design. This was made on the basis of finding a teacher and a study environment that she felt comfortable with, explaining that 'I really like it in here', 'the teacher is key, it's really sad but that's the way it works like'.

What was initially expressed as a resistance to the authority of teachers now is expressed as an awareness of her dependence on them. Karin acknowledged that she didn't really decide to change courses, but went 'with the flow whatever that is', adding, 'I really like structure, something where you can't go wrong if you do what you are told'. The freedom to manage her own study time had not been a comfortable experience: 'I'm not good at this half teaching you half not'. Nor had the shift in the role of teachers from enforcers of rules to arbiters of style. In her words: 'One teacher will hate it and another will like it. You are permanently changing your style and it takes you so long to find your style.' The decision to take a pragmatic route involves letting go of an identification of self as an artist: in her words, 'I'm not a completely artistic person, if I was really mad and dark I would just *have* to, but I'm not.'

The shift between Karin's third and fourth interviews marks a change in her narrative around education, revealing her ability to reorient her identity from an oppositional to a more dependent stance. The life plans laid out so clearly at 16 were still relatively intact. She would apply to university – in Scotland, the Republic of Ireland or Wales – to study interior design rather than fashion. The changes were subtle yet significant. For example, she no longer countenanced England as a possibility, citing the experience of friends becoming estranged after attending university there. Karin explains that hardly anyone comes back to the city after leaving for university – except for those who fail to stick out the course. Those people return and don't leave again.

In this discussion of university Karin expressed more complicated feelings about leaving her home town than she had previously. Where in the past she had focused herself entirely on 'escape' she now felt torn, in terms both of having a long-term boyfriend and of being the last of her siblings to leave home. Her choice of universities reflects a desire for 'moving away but not really moving away', and she observes: 'I never had anything to keep me here – now I do it's scary.' In this interview Karin also talked at length about her mother's desire for her children to gain a university education. Her mother had left school at 13 without taking the 11-plus, even though she had been told that she would pass it. Karin reports a family story that includes her grandmother's fear that she would never 'afford' to send her daughter to the grammar school and a teacher's view that there was no reason for her to sit the 11-plus as girls like her 'were only being educated to work in factories'. In Karin's words, 'mum didn't have any options [...] She couldn't do more than shop and bar. I already have more than her.' She also recounts how her father had failed to realise his prospects. Despite the benefit of a grammar school education, when faced with the choice between university and work he had chosen the latter, and then followed his own father into alcoholism.

These intimate stories give a sense of the powerful and conflicting emotions involved in intergenerational projects of social mobility (Lawler, 2000, 2002). By sharing them Karin reveals the obligations that she feels to fulfil the thwarted ambitions of her parents, who, unlike their own parents, made sacrifices to give her and her siblings 'more'. She is conscious that not all of her parents' generation made that same decision.

Both of Karin's siblings had already made the journey through higher education, to England and into the middle classes. This demarcates her family within their community, where they (like the integrated school) are perceived as 'a bit snobby'. Karin is the youngest and the last at home. It is a privileged yet difficult position – from where she simultaneously anticipates feelings of guilt about leaving her mother and her own educational failure, explaining that if she doesn't see through a university education it would 'break my mother's heart'. The costs of going and staying are both high, each demanding sacrifices. She is able to appreciate the different cultural understandings of success, reflected in this statement:

> **I can do** anything I want to do and my mum couldn't. I could go and
> get married now and settle down. I could go to university. I could leave
> it a couple of years and pack a back-pack and go on travels. There's
> nothing I can't do. [2003, aged 19]

By opting for a local identity as an art student, Karin is able to distinguish herself in the immediate present from a local future. The next stage of leaving for university will demand another round of separation from her most intimate sources of support and security. In the following comments the extent to which Karin has to engage with an intergenerational narrative as part of her own project of self becomes evident. In the terms outlined by Bjerrum Nielsen and Rudberg (1994), while her gender identity is of an independent and cosmopolitan woman, her gender subjectivity continues to be bound up with the frustration and desires of her mother's biography. Echoing the dynamics between Sherleen and her mother, it is far from clear who is leaving whom, with the separation of daughter and mother mediated and displaced through commitments to men and local destinies. Of her mother she says:

> **I feel a** bit guilty about leaving my mum. She knew it was coming.
> She'll sort it out. She made her decision, if she wants to change her
> mind she can. She can leave him [Karin's father], or she can stay with
> him. Maybe she would rather stay with him and argue a lot than be
> on her own, if that's what she wants to do that's grand (...) But I still
> have to do what I want to do. She would still even feel guilty if I stayed
> at home for her. I know she would. [2003, aged 19]

Of her boyfriend she says:

> **I'm going. I** have offered him he can come with me if he wants,
> even as a friend. He's not going to hold me back, 'cause if he did I
> would hate him. It might take a while 'cause I'd be happy to stay with

him now, but come 15 years' time I would *hate* him for taking away my chance. 'Cause I would see it as me giving up my chance, I would see it as him taking away my chance (...) I've tried to work out ways I could stay and still do what I want to do. And I've never done that before, because this town is the most unattractive place I can think of, there isn't a way. [2003, aged 19]

The movement that takes place over the course of these four years is striking, and the shift in Karin's orientation towards educational authority, from resistance to dependency, coincides with a growing recognition of the costs of social mobility. We leave Karin at her final interview as determined yet uncertain about what she wants, why she wants what she wants, and where her loyalties lie. In the next section I will explore in detail the 'extracurricular activities' that provide a buffer and refuge from schooling, exploring the ways in which Karin creatively confronts and negotiates her fears.

Play: style, sexuality and trying men on

At 16 Karin was beginning to make forays into non-school social spaces, which were separate from the religiously and class defined spaces of her neighbourhood. As mentioned previously, she struggled to find ways to socialise with her mixed-religion friendship group outside of school. However, with a female best friend in tow, Karin located and sought to gain access to the Basement, a city-centre youth club. The young people frequenting this youth club placed themselves outside the dominant cultural divide between working-class Catholic and Protestant youth culture. While the label of 'freaks' was seen by most as a term of abuse, Karin is attracted to the distinction that it provides. Breaking in did not prove entirely easy, creating new and ambiguous lines between 'us' and 'them'.

> **It's kind of** like a bar without the alcohol and you can just talk to anyone. They're all totally friendly except for the GOTHS (*whispers*), I don't like them. You see my friend Avril, she's a bit of a Goth right, but she wears dog collars and things like that right. They all give her dirty looks, see since she started wearing the dog collars they all give her dirty looks. Because I think they think it's like she's trying to be one of us but she's not, but she's not, that's just her style. But I don't like it, that's the only thing I don't like about in there. [1999, aged 16]

Karin explained that she tried to get more of her friends from school to hang out with her at the Basement, including Sonja, who she reports ran into the building 'wearing her Kappa outfit and shouts "you bloody freaks!" and runs out again'. Asked to explain the different youth cultures of the city, Karin describes a classificatory system where style operates as a signifier of classed identity, through which individuals can place themselves (and be placed) within a sectarian landscape. Her description reveals the tensions and dynamics of her school-based friendship group:

> **Sonja's a Kap,** member of the Kappa crew, Kappa kids.
>
> INT: So there's the Goths, Kappa kids and the freaks and what else?
>
> There's Majellas, Gina's a Majella.
>
> INT: Majellas, what are they?
>
> I've explained this in school and there's people ready to kick my head in 'cause I've called people Majellas, not meaning it. 'Cause I call Gina Majella, but everyone takes it as a really bad thing to call somebody. It's pure [name of town] woman, it's pure mad [name of town] woman, going to the Station or Intercept [clubs], high heels, skirt, loads of make-up, big hair, it's kind of like a tart or something like that, but see I would call my friends that 'cause that's just their style, you know. [...] I think Skaters are different, everything because Skater blokes fancy Majellas whereas freak blokes don't fancy Majellas, right. But some of them are into like really freaky music and some of them would be into like hip-hop. [1999, aged 16]

Over time Karin became increasingly involved in public representations of youth culture, initially as a consumer, but subsequently as a producer. In this first interview she had recently discovered the Skater scene:

> **I think, I** went to a skateboarding jam-up and seeing the talent up there made me want to start skating and I think that is something's going to change my life, skating, 'cause it's like once you're a Skater, no matter where you go in the world if you meet other Skaters you've got a link with them. [...] Skateboarders are really laid back, they don't care about nothing but their sport and things like that. Most of the ones I met anyway. I really love that kind of chilled out, it's like pure, they're not neds anyway, they're not lads out there to get into fights and things like that, to drink and get into fights. Most of them just seem really laid back and cool things like that. To get in with all those people I think is changing my life. [1999, aged 16]

She quickly encountered exclusions, finding that the preferred role for girls was as spectators and girlfriends. Nevertheless, Karin bought herself a skateboard and was practising. She was also on the look-out for a boyfriend and fun. Her first sexual relationship had been with a boy from school, a year previously. He was now away on an exchange trip and she was determined that she would not 'spend my whole summer pining after him, this is the summer I turned 16, for God's sake'. Rather, she was hanging out at skateboard jams, busily fancying people.

At her second interview Karin brought with her a memory book that she had kept for the previous nine months. In it she had a picture of her 'dead skateboard' that had been destroyed by baggage handlers on a trip to London. The 'skateboarding phase' was now over, superseded by 'a new little phase' – graffiti. Her identifying tag was a symbol generated from highly personal resources, reflecting her identification with her sister. In characteristically pioneering style Karin had taken the first steps herself, buying paints from a Skate shop in a neighbouring city while on work experience. She then invited a girlfriend to join her in the game.

> **One day I** was walking home through the subways with a friend and um, like I didn't tell anybody about it 'cause I didn't want, I didn't want everyone knowing, everyone like saying – 'cause I think it's illegal, you know what I mean? And um, I go 'Look at that, isn't that cool?' and she's all 'Oh my God! Who done that?' and I go 'I did!' And she was all proud of me and all, so then I got her into it [...] and I bought my friend spray cans for Christmas 'cause she was all really – she thought it was just so cool. So me and her go out all the time now and do it. [2000, aged 17]

The first two tags were completely pink, and then she acquired purple and blue cans, saving the pink for highlights. Kevin McDonald describes tagging in terms of entry into a social world of signs and movement 'centred on visibility and intensity, the search for recognition' (1999: 149). Through her tag Karin achieves an audacious yet anonymous insertion of a feminine self into the public sphere. Elsewhere in the interview she also talks about how she identifies with a particular Pokemon character, observing that 'they're furry and they're cute and I can be furry and cute'. Both examples can be understood as ways of extending the self through a prosthesis, through which a self-identity is constituted in the relation 'I can, therefore I am' (Lury, 1998: 3).

> INT: So what's the thrill of it?

> Aww it's – if you're able to walk around town and you walk past your stuff in town and you've got this big massive smile on your face and you're like 'Everyone knows that was me!', I'm smiling away too much. Either that or they think I'm mad like, and I was like, you see people walking past and you know they see it [...] and I like the idea that people don't know who it is either. Like I can be stood there right beside it and they – they might know. They might not. [2000, aged 17]

In order to make sense of the appeal of this paradoxical combination of display and invisibility I need to explore the context within which such representations of the self could be understood as challenging (or talking back to) representations of the self constructed by others (Gordon and Kay, 1993). As the following section shows, the absence of female solidarity (as a result of friendship breakdown) makes Karin vulnerable to being constructed by others as 'a bitch' and 'a slag' within a highly gendered and sexist regime of signification. It is in this context that we need to understand her attempts to represent herself, and to control how others might read her.

Falling out, falling over and falling in love

A large part of Karin's second interview was taken up by the story of falling out with her best friend Avril (whom she had brought with her into the Basement social set). Karin discovered that Avril had been talking behind her back: 'Like she called me a fucking exhibitionist. The wee girl is a Goth and she thinks she can call someone else an exhibitionist!' As a result Karin had withdrawn from the group and was now socialising primarily with school friends. But she was also determined to keep a foot in the door, explaining: 'I just like pop in every now and then, just to show face, 'cause [...] if these people are ever gonna like accept me again and forget about what she said, it's not gonna happen if I'm not there.'

Karin explains that she had never entirely trusted Avril, and describes events that may have fuelled difficult feelings between them, including competition over a boy (Connie) who was central to the Basement clique. Sexual reputation and jealousy appear to lie at the root of their troubles, illustrated by several stories that Karin tells in the interview. One of the highlights of her year had been a trip to London to stay with Avril's brother. (This was the trip where her skateboard had met its untimely end.) Her memory book was full of memorabilia from the trip, including a ticket representing her first ride on the London underground unaccompanied by an adult. She provides a vivid but confusing description of a night of drinking in which Avril's brother behaved badly, getting drunk, picking fights and kissing Karin in front of his girlfriend. At the end of the night Karin 'got off' with the bar man, whom she describes as 'covered in tattoos, big shavey head and old enough to be my father'.

In a subsequent discussion, Karin explained her particular sexual ethic, in which she resisted notions of feminine propriety, explaining that 'I take a pure wee fella attitude to the lot of it'. After her first sexual experience, with a boy from school who subsequently refused to talk to her, Karin had decided to take the initiative, establishing a competition with her friends (both girls and boys) as to who could be the first to lose their virginity. The following extract reflects the complexities involved for a young woman such as Karin to position herself as sexual, powerful and respected (if not respectable).

Like there's my wee fellas from my school, they would be the only other people I would consider going with 'cause I just love them to bits but um I know what they're like. They're all assholes and then so am I so.

INT: Right. Do you think it would change your relationship with them or your friendship if you went out with them? [...]

Um (...) they would talk about me. They would talk about me way too much. Like if I went with any of them, they would all find out all the details 'cause I find out all the details about their wee girls like, so that's about the only thing that really stops me I think [...] Me and the girls are trying to get someone to go with um this wee fella Jo. He's like trying to lose his virginity. We're trying to get someone to go with him. Right, I would love to find out myself except it would be just too weird kinda, but um, he's really skinny. He's like really, really skinny so everyone will find out if he's tall and skinny, we wanna find out if his cock's like long and skinny because we think it should be. Just like – just so he'll look right naked. [2000, aged 17]

Here we see Karin operating simultaneously as 'one of the boys' and 'one of the girls'. She positions herself both as a sexual object – that can be desired or rejected – and as a sexual agent who desires and rejects others. In a playful and capricious way, she moves between identifications and loyalties, detaching sexual acts from gendered discourses of loss and gain by treating them as gifts that can be bestowed at her whim. Karin's willingness to transgress conventions and expectations can be understood as strategies to claim authority within the context of her peer group. It is a high-risk strategy that demands the support of others if it is to be successful. Her falling-out with Avril and subsequent retreat from the Basement clique suggests what may happen when such support is withdrawn. At her third interview, 14 months later, she reflects on the break-up, explaining that they had been the two 'freaky ones' from school, both interested in breaking out into new spaces and networks. In her view, their troubles could be put down to a mismatch in the timing of their wild behaviour. Since their falling-out Avril had been drinking and indulging in the kind of behaviour for which she had exposed Karin. Karin notes that at the time Avril 'stayed sober and watched everything I did'. Now they maintained the appearance of civility, talking to each other 'as we don't want to look bad to everyone else'.

Although Karin had some success in cultivating new friendships, she was disappointed that she had been unable to keep a relationship alive with her best school friend, Gina, whom she 'always wanted to stay really good friends with'. She reports a painful moment when she texted her mobile: 'I was sending "happy Halloween" messages to everyone. And I sent one to her and she phoned me and goes, "Who's this?" "Oh it's Karin. Happy Halloween." And she goes, "Oh right,

I didn't know it was you, 'cause I've taken your phone number off my phone."
And I cried that night'. She made sense of her disappointment by reporting a
fellow school friend's verdict that 'she's turned into a loyalist little bitch (*laugh*)
basically. And to be honest, I would believe it wholeheartedly, because she's seen
me in the street and just not even seen me, looked me straight in the eye and just
walked on.' Karin recalls their last meeting, the previous summer, where their
difference had become too difficult for either to overcome:

> **'Cause the last** time we met up during the summer [...] I said to
> her and her cousin, 'Come for a pint with me' [...] Gina was all, 'No I
> don't wanna go in there with all those freaks'. And I was like, alright,
> I know what she's like, there is times that she would be more like us.
> But I think OK. Then she said something to me like um, 'You could
> have wore some nice clothes seeing as you knew you were coming
> out to meet me.' And I was like, 'OK right, I'm not ringing you again.
> If you wanna see me you can ring me.' I think that's kinda where it
> ended. [2001, aged 18]

The moment of rejection cited in this story centres again on style, and the line
of distinction drawn between working-class 'neighbourhood' styles and the more
cosmopolitan identity of the freak. Although Karin presents the Basement as a place
for the excluded ('freaky little bastards, anyone who doesn't fit in'), it could also
be understood as a very exclusive group of young people, distancing themselves
from working-class styles and positioning themselves for geographic and social
mobility. While Karin moves easily between a range of scenes, she appears to avoid
those that tie her in to local working-class identifications. Preferring to move
around pubs and clubs in the centre of the city, she is comfortable around Goth,
Metal and rock scenes – all of which centre on drinking and smoking rather
than what Karin sees as more serious drug taking (Ecstasy), which she associates
with a loss of self control.

In this third interview Karin reports a life-style phase in which dressing up and
acting out a part is displacing the graffiti art of the previous year. Also competing
for Karin's time and creativity was her increasing interest in having a relationship.
Where in earlier interviews she described an archly instrumental attitude towards
men and sex, she was now fixated on one particular man. Karin had first mentioned
Connie in her second interview; in this interview she describes how she 'finally
got him':

> **He's mad about,** y'know, the film *The Matrix*, so am I [...] Somebody
> said Connie even thought I looked like your woman Trinity. So it was
> like, 'Hey he must like me' (*laugh*), y'know. So I went like all dressed
> up and um (...) went over to a friend's house. And um I spent the
> whole night getting really annoyed because Connie didn't seem to be
> taking me on. And I was like, 'I'm dressed like this and he's not even

noticed me. What is the craik?' [...] And we tried to talk to each other, we knew exactly that everyone was trying to set us up, we knew why they wanted us to talk to each other, we knew why we wanted to talk to each other, but we couldn't, it just wasn't happening [...] I went out in the kitchen and started talking to someone else there. So Connie came barging into the kitchen, lifted his coat, nearly knocked me off the chair grabbing the coat from under me and walked out the door. And I walked round the kitchen for a while saying, 'I'm gonna have to go after him aren't I?' Like – chuh – I knew I did. So I went out in the rain, raging rain and PVC don't go well together like. I went out anyway, 'Connie, Connie, come back'. He goes, 'Why?' I go, 'I want you to.' And then that was it, all happy now, from there for about three weeks. [2001, aged 18]

In pursuing Connie, Karin was engaging with the epicentre of the power relations of the Basement clique, Connie being the most popular and longest-serving member. She talks gleefully of his physicality – a big, hard man with tattoos, piercings, sexist attitudes and hints of physical violence. The relationship ended after a month, when Karin began to demand more from him than the 'weekly shag'. Although Connie was the one that ended it, the subsequent dance that Karin recounts between the two suggests that they were wrangling over power that was both intimate and public. The 'relationship' was the culmination of three years of obsession on Karin's part, 'daydreaming [...] dressed up in case he was there'. And while she was clearly disappointed by his rejection, she also asserted her own agency, noting 'word is he is still in love with me' and 'I'm just bored, I've got no one to think about'.

The falling-out took a familiar form of social exclusion. The story that Karin reports suggests that Connie himself took no active part. The agents were 'bitchy girls', including Connie's new girlfriend. Karin reports a series of slanderous email messages being sent around her social group signed 'Trinity'. Her mobile phone then disappeared and was used to send similar text messages to her address book. The outcome was another major bust-up with the Basement clique, with none of her erstwhile friends talking to her. So although Karin is highly adept at cultivating prosthetic versions of the self, she is not always able to control how these selves are read, and in the case of Trinity she lost control of the 'self' completely. But, despite concerted ostracism, Karin continued to attend the Basement, eventually gaining a place on the management committee – in her words, 'I persevered, and I didn't lose face either'.

Karin has since had another relationship with 'Jamie the sap'. Her description of this relationship suggests that she did not emerge from the confrontation with Connie unscathed. She explains that she became frustrated with Jamie's lack of agency in their sexual encounters and she finished with him after finding herself becoming physically aggressive. She comments: 'I'm the wee girl, fellas should try and get it off me and I'll tell them if they can or can't, just because I can.' Karin reflects that she was 'no longer comfortable with one-night stands':

> **I started putting** thought into it now 'cause there was a time when I just would have gone out and just had tried it on. I would have gone for it, no matter who they were. That was stupid, that was really bad. I don't know why I wised up [...] I want to *go* with someone now, I want a relationship *(laugh)*. Like that was experimenting and I want a relationship. [2001, aged 18]

At the very end of her third interview Karin announced an important shift in allegiance:

> **Oh, oh I** should have told you this at the start. I just realised last week I'm bisexual. *(laugh)* Yeah it just came to me all like that. Aye 'cause I've spent ages, I've even said to my mum, 'Right if I turn around to you and say I'm a lesbian, don't die of shock', right. But I didn't know. I've seen people ask me what I was and I was like, 'I'm nothing, I'm none of your business, that's what I am.' 'Cause I've always like gone off with girls, I've always liked girls. But like imagine giving up wee fellas like, that's just not gonna happen y'know. I wanna get married, I wanna have kids.

> INT: So when did that (...)?

> D'you know what it was? It's 'cause this wee girl, this wee girl Caitlin was at school with me too, and I didn't realise she was bisexual. But I'd snogged her before but there's a wile lot of people who just snog their friends when they're out and it'd just be a bit of craik right. But she just turned round to me on Monday and goes, 'I'm bisexual'. I'm like, 'God that's nice'. But people who say they're bisexual. It's like wee girls who want to impress wee fellas and go, 'Oh God me and my friend's bisexual and we'll snog in front of you.' To be honest I hate it. If I'm getting off with a wee girl when I'm out, you get this little circle of fellas round you and it's really annoying, I don't like it. I'm not doing it for their pleasure, I'm doing it for mine. But I've never wanted to be a lesbian either. I've never wanted to say I'm bisexual 'cause that's just like a cop-out or something, but I am. So *(laugh)* there's nothing I can do about that. I'll have to find a new name for it if that's what I am. [2001, aged 18]

Yet again, Karin brings into play the themes of sexual play, female solidarity and a battle over meaning. The rules of the public sphere in which she moves denote female eroticism as a source of pleasure for men. Being a good girl in this context means not being sexual. Being a bad girl either means being sexualised (and vulnerable to the kind of punishment that Karin has endured on several occasions) or inhabiting a category that is denigrated and which appears (to Karin at this point in time) to cut her off from other aspects of female identity that she values – in particular, notions of relationship and motherhood.

In her final interview, almost two years later, Karin tells the story of how she came to finally escape the Basement clique. After returning from her trip to India she was pursued by Seamus. Initially she did not trust him, as he was one of the crowd involved in the 'horrible email/phone situation'. In time, the two moved into new social networks of older people, frequenters of a local pub scene. Karin now socialises in the same pub where her parents had first met. She reflects that she was pleased to escape the Basement crowd, 'my freaky friends, I hated them, horrible people'. She explains that the escape was only possible because she did it as part of a couple, observing that it is hard to leave a friendship group other than when you leave school. Karin talks romantically about being in a couple:

> **I know you** shouldn't say this as a wee girl but you feel more whole when you're with a wee fella. You feel like, even if it is a bad relationship, you still feel like you have what you're meant to have. Every person is meant to be with another person. And when you are you feel like you can do more, take on more. I would hate to say that. In a couple of months if I'm still single I'll be 'Jesus, I'm a complete person the way I am!' You are, but you don't really feel it. If you did you wouldn't keep looking for people. [2003, aged 19]

For the past year the relationship had provided support, intimacy and a catalyst in various areas of her life. For example, Seamus had been a 'wee ray of light' within her family, being the 'first one of my friends my dad has even spoke to'. When asked in this interview as to whether there had been any critical moments in the last two years, Karin identified the trip to India and being with Seamus. However, she adds:

> **I know I** am going to uni so I know it's not important, not THAT important, not the relationship of my life like. He's just great, so special. Makes me want to mother him, I want to look after him all the time. [2003, aged 19]

Karin had recently ended the relationship, ostensibly because it had become 'too familiar', with Seamus 'taking her for granted' (and suspicions that he had been unfaithful), but perhaps also because of the dangers it posed to her dreams of escape. She had asked Seamus to accompany her to university as a friend, but was determined not to give up her chance of leaving for the relationship. When asked whether she still saw herself as bisexual, Karin replies:

I still think that. I have gone with girls since, haven't had proper relationships with girls, never have. There's this kind of thing, you can go with girls but as soon as you have a proper relationship that makes you lesbian like, completely lesbian, if you go with a wee fella it's like stigma on him and on everything. Maybe it's narrow-mindedness in this town, I'll see what happens. A friend said to me you don't know till you fall in love 'with the person'. If it's a he then you're straight, if it's a she then you're gay. And that one person, what they are makes you what you are. The person rather than the guy. [2003, aged 19]

Karin's presentation of self is highly playful – and she provides a dramatic and entertaining account for her interviewer, in which she plays the part of a feminist trickster – experimenting with herself and with others – desiring and rejecting. Yet it is an account that also provokes anxiety in its audience, revealing the potential cruelty of the peer group. While Karin presents herself as a creative agent in the world, the subtext of this part of her account is the communication of an acute sense of vulnerability.

Family life: the baby, the sister and the mother

In constructing this chapter, I struggled to locate Karin's intimate relationships within the different fields of her biography. Initially, her sexual experiments and friendships seemed to be part of her social life and the field I have denoted as 'play'. By her final interview things had changed and the couple relationship with Seamus was much more part of her family story. Aspects of family life have arisen throughout this chapter, and in this final section I will tie these threads together, charting the key changes that take place in her relationships with siblings, parents and the idea of family.

From the outset Karin was negative about living in Northern Ireland. As we have seen, she resents the ways that everyday threats of violence circumscribe her ability to move around the city and socialise freely. But she also asserts that 'I don't want to bring kids up here'. This identification of herself as a mother, in the distant future and a distant place, was an enduring theme throughout the successive conversations. Articulated initially as part of her first lifeline exercise, Karin sketched out a version of motherhood delayed to the last possible moment: 'I don't want kids till I'm really old. Last minute kind of thing. Then my whole life will be for them.' This deferment enables her to imagine an extended education, travel and career path, and facilitates an identification with childishness in the here and now. Karin is in no hurry to grow up. She describes herself as 'a big wain' who is domestically useless, and cared for entirely by her mother. And although Karin is very negative about her home town, she is careful not to reject her mother, noting that she wants to parent in the same selfless way, but just 'much later'.

Karin happily accepts her position as the baby of the family, who is nevertheless able to sample the life-style of a student by visiting her two elder siblings (a brother and a sister) who are away at university. She reported some conflict with her brother (focusing on instances where he tried to protect her in a heavy-handed manner), but she was in awe of her glamorous older sister, whom she describes as having 'presence'. The extent to which she observes her sibling is revealed in comments such as: 'I can see my sister getting older. Dressing like a 22-year-old. I don't think she realises what's happening.' Nine months later Karin recalls smiling all day after being told by a taxi driver, 'I think you're even worse than your sister', whom she describes as 'a dizzy bitch' for whom 'everything works out in her life' – stylish, academically able and always with good-looking boyfriends. Yet, by her third interview Karin's sister's magic was beginning to wane and one of the power shifts that characterises sibling relationships over time appeared to be in process (Mauthner, 2002). Karin explains, 'she's a mess at the minute, as much a mess as I am', going on to describe unfulfilled career aspirations and her over-dependency on her boyfriend.

Until her visit to India Karin's orientation towards family can be characterised in terms of idealised womanhood (her mother and sister), problematised manhood (her father) and determined childhood (herself) – positions that she acts out in other areas of her life. Her mother remains a source of authority throughout, able to respond flexibly to Karin's assertions of agency. Karin's memory book includes a drawing of her pierced belly with the by-line 'the first time I had done something without her permission'. At 17 she describes how her mother was treating her more as an adult, allowing her to share a drink in the house and to come home later. She describes their relationship as 'pretty damn good', adding ironically, 'I come from a one-parent family'. In contrast, Karin is extremely negative about her father, whom she describes as 'a loser', 'alcoholic' and a drain on her mother. Yet from the outset she also asserts that she 'can see a wile lot [of him] in myself'. The memory book that she shares with researchers at 17 includes a page devoted to a family holiday in which she wrote: 'I pray I don't have kids in case I hurt them like he hurt me.' Again she explains: 'I know I am so like him. He's everything I hate about myself. It's so much easier to hate him than me.' When reflecting on her parents' relationship in her third interview, aged 18, a more complex picture begins to emerge with her observation that it might have been different 'if she had let him be involved', but 'it's made me who I am' but 'I don't know what a father is supposed to do'.

Almost two years later Karin's relationship with her father had substantially improved, something that she attributes to Seamus's 'wee ray of sunshine'. She explains that while she had enormous admiration for her parents, not least bringing up three children who loved them, she would nevertheless do things differently herself. She would like to be the same kind of mum to her kids but she would not want 'to take all the responsibility'. Getting 'the dad to play a bigger role' was important. Again she observes that while she was 'made' by her mother, having a father too would have made her 'a fuller person'. In her first three interviews she expressed rage at her father and exasperation at her mother for not leaving him – at the same time she was pursuing a pathway of challenging men and 'trying them on'. The point where she makes a commitment to a man coincides with an improvement in her relationship with her father. And when Karin talks about leaving home and going to university, she also talks in terms of the two relationships, that between her mother and father and that between herself and Seamus.

In this final interview Karin also describes the emergence of a less-dependent role in relation to her mother, who had recently suffered a minor stroke. She now appeared to recognise that she herself might have a role in supporting her and provides a detailed inventory of all the care duties that her mother performed for an extended family network. Several times she asserts that she wants 'to be the helper and not the helpee'. This is cited as a lesson that she draws from her experience in India, yet it might also be understood as an effect of her appreciation of her mother's role as she comes closer to the point of leaving. She was particularly proud that she and her siblings had organised and paid for a holiday for her mother's birthday.

One of the most illuminating sections of this last interview arose through a discussion on community, in which Karin talks about her responsibilities for the religious identity of the family. The discussion was prompted by a question about the communities that Karin felt that she belonged to. Her reply began with the expected catalogue of 'art student', 'freak' and 'drinker'. She then explained that in taking up these identities she had sought to escape more local, community-based identifications:

> **There is a** local community – the parents. But children no. I've chosen to be part of the art student and freaky community that they aren't. Where I come from it's kind of 16, get a job, get a husband. I'm not like that. Religious – God I don't feel part of it but if anyone slagged off my church I'd rip them apart. I'm not practising but I know at some stage I will be. 'Cause my mum was never big on her religion but since her mum died she's taken over the role as the kind of – there's always, especially in Catholic families, the granny is the really religious one, and then it goes down from the daughters, and the gran kids even less. And then as soon as my granny went my mum just stepped into her role and I think that when my mum goes I'll just step into her role. Because my sister is not an atheist, she would believe in energies and karmas but not God or Buddha. My brother doesn't care. I know at some stage I will be part of that there. I'm gonna have a parish that I'm going to belong to and I will know the name of a priest and things like that. I don't now. Haven't been to mass in 6 years. At some point. [2003, aged 19]

Conclusions

In this chapter I have constructed intersecting narratives from the raw material of successive interviews. These narratives reflect the three key fields of Karin's biography: education, play and family. Each of these stories has its own temporal flow, constructed through the talk of interviews. The temporality of each story is also punctuated by a common critical moment from which point narratives and identities take a different direction. I have described the time that Karin spent in India as 'individualising', in that she stepped out of the collectivities, practices and routines of her normal life, some of which in turn moved on in her absence. On return, she appears to have reoriented herself significantly. Educationally she moves from the position of the rebel to a recognition of vulnerability and dependence. In terms of her social and personal life she moves from being part of a scene to being part of a couple, withdrawing from experimentation and distantiation as techniques of self. This also coincides with shifts in her relationships with her family, including a growing recognition of her mother's vulnerability and mortality and a revised appraisal of her father's absence from parenting.

Karin responds to a highly complex social world with a high degree of agency. In seeking to escape classification within the dominant local terms of social class-inflected religious sectarianism, she throws herself into a frenzy of aesthetic activity that takes in clothes, music, art, friendships and sex. Yet her rebellion can also be understood in terms of practices of distinction necessary to defend against the pulls of a local working-class future (Bourdieu, 1986; Lawler, 2008). Beneath her experiments with gender identity lies a family project of social and geographical mobility that makes contradictory demands on the youngest daughter. Rebellion, a refusal of authority and dealing with not being liked are all motifs of Karin's different stories and identities. Perhaps we can also understand these in terms of the generation of personal resources, necessary for what lies ahead. That so much is mediated via the aesthetic realm does not mean that Karin is not embedded within particular embodied, familiar and historical circumstances. Everything and anything may not be possible, yet aesthetic play may be an important medium through which innovations can be forged and thwarted.

As for Sherleen and Stan, the prospect of university education provides a scaffold for an imagined future, and economic dependence is offset by performances of agency and autonomy. Over time we can see Karin's recognition of the pleasures as well as the dangers of security and belonging. Karin is able to look to her sister for a model of how to escape a local destiny, yet, as with the other young lives in this book, the passage of time demonstrates how plans for who we want to be can be disrupted by competing moral claims and intergenerational obligations. Karin's case history was constructed with the benefit of a fourth interview, after an interval of almost two years. Important changes had taken place over this period, and in telling her story from this position in time, earlier material was brought into a new perspective. In the following chapter I introduce two new interviews with Sherleen and Devon that were not available at the time of writing their case histories. In forging a new perspective from which to understand their narratives I will also reflect on the neglect of temporality within sociological paradigms.

EIGHT

Interruption: from explanation to understanding

Despite a growing interest in temporality as an aspect of social life, it is still unusual to find explicit discussions of the passage of time and the generation of hindsight as aspects of sociological production (Kemper and Peterson Royce, 2002; Mauthner and Doucet, 2003; McLeod and Thomson, 2009). And while there has been a move towards making the silent academic author a more explicit presence within texts (Coffey, 2002: 324), the academic self is by definition compelled to display a command over the 'data' and the temporality of the production process (Skeggs, 2002: 351). In practice things are messier, recursive and incremental (Law, 2004). We evolve, change our minds, read and discover as we go. Yet the composition of an academic text demands that we reconstruct this process, situating our labours within a narrative that obscures the temporal dynamics of production and, with it, the mobility and uncertainty that characterise our deliberations. Exceptions to this include the deconstructive turn in ethnographic writing (Clifford and Marcus, 1986; Davies, 2008).

A longitudinal data set disrupts the smooth narrativity in which 'the past is always remade in the light of the present' (Lawler, 2002: 251). Finding ways of managing such data draws attention to the hidden codes of a sociological discourse within which research subjects are isolated from the temporal flow. It is by eliminating the future from the picture that it becomes possible to focus on the relationship between the data and the social. This continues to be the case even when we have a sequence of data, as with the preceding chapters. The moment at which the analysis is undertaken is a moment of analytic closure. Explanation is achieved retrospectively – the past is condensed, enabling us to see how the individual has come to be where they are, with the quality of explanation being measured by a sense of inevitability. Although destinies may make sense in hindsight, it is impossible to know how futures will evolve and it is important to map the possible destinies which fall away, as the ghosts of 'unachieved possibilities are an effective part of reality' (Bertaux and Bertaux-Wiame, 1993: 82).

Julie McCleod suggests that a series of interviews conducted over time constitutes a longitudinal archive that 'is not exhausted by any one explanation' (2003: 204). Time does not stand still, research subjects keep living and changing, and longitudinal methods demand that we keep looking. The arrival of new data reconfigures the archive, revealing the provisional character of analytic accounts while testing the validity of earlier interpretations. The overall structure of this book reflects the sequence of my analysis. Chapters are presented in the order in which they were written, and they include the data that was available at that time.

As it was written last, the data from all of Karin's interviews are captured within her case history. Since then a further interview has been undertaken with each of Sherleen and Devon. What is missing is the continuing story of Stan, whom we struggled to recontact, discovering only that he was away snowboarding, nursing a broken heart. His parents explained that they had sold the family home and were returning to missionary work abroad. The existence of the two additional interviews with Sherleen and Devon posed a challenge for me. I could have ignored them, or I could have incorporated them, reconstructing my original analyses from a new position. One of my aims in this book is to demonstrate a method-in-practice, making the temporal dimension of the qualitative longitudinal methodology explicit. So in this chapter I reveal 'what happened next' to Sherleen and Devon, reflecting on how this new data resonates with and complicates my original interpretations.

Sherleen: renegotiating allegiance

Twenty months had elapsed between Sherleen's fourth and fifth interviews, the latter taking place in December 2002 when she was 17 years old. Sherleen was still 'on track' educationally and had successfully managed the transition between school and college, gaining As and Bs in her GCSEs. Although the school had offered incentives to stay on to the sixth form (including a scholarship for an elite university), she had been determined to leave, explaining 'I just had to get out [...] Meet new people.' Not only did a further education college offer a wider range of A level courses, but it also meant being in 'a completely different area where no one knows me'.

In her previous interview Sherleen had explained that she was applying for a college some distance from her home, in a suburban middle-class part of the city. It was not until the new term had started that she turned down her place at the suburban college, choosing to go to one a few miles from her home. In her words, 'I just decided to stay local really.' In practice the local college had been 'a lot better than I had expected', given that she had 'heard it had a bad reputation and the grades weren't that good'. Although the timetable did not allow her to pursue her chosen combination of subjects, she had no regrets about the move. Sherleen makes it clear that school culture posed significant dangers to her project of educational progress. She explains: 'I was picked as one of the populars and I didn't really want to be [...] that's probably why I just had to get out of there really.'

Initially she found college to be anonymous, with people just coming for lessons and then leaving. Gradually 'people began to relax' and she got to know fellow students. One of these students, Paulo, became her boyfriend. Sherleen describes him as a 'typical nice guy' and a 'hard-working' student. She met him in the classroom and they quickly became established as a couple. At school she discovered that a boyfriend was a dangerous distraction, at odds with achievement. At college she can be popular without being public property and a boyfriend can offer privacy as well as a study partner. She and Paulo work together in the library, revising, and pushing each other to achieve.

> **He is very** smart, and that makes me work harder (*laugh*), he is really intelligent.

> INT: Do you think he is smarter than you?

> That's what makes me angry (*laugh*) but I actually do better than him in the AS grades, he got like a lower grade than me in practically every subject except for English – 'cause we both got Ds in that. We were working so hard as well, and he got just a grade lower than me in all these subjects, so it's made him work harder.

Although Sherleen talked in the past about relationships taking up too much time, she nevertheless sees herself as someone who always has a boyfriend. Previously her mother had intervened in order to ensure that boyfriends did not disrupt her work, and Sherleen complied with her advice: 'it was just like freezing boys while I'm at school'. She initially thought that her mother would disapprove of Paulo, but is pleased that she likes him 'because he's in the same kind of lessons as me, and he does get the same kind of grades, so she's OK with that. So she sees that he's hard working, so it's alright'.

Although Paulo is two years older than Sherleen they are at the same stage of their studies, and are both applying for university within their city. On the advice of college tutors, she is focusing on prestigious universities:

> **We've been looking** at the best universities for our courses really. We've just said if we end up going to the same one, that's fine. But if we don't that's OK [...] even though everyone says 'don't know how we're going to manage it' because we're mostly joined at the hip.

Sherleen and Paulo have established great intimacy in the year of their relationship. The relationship is sexual and she reports that he accompanied her to the clinic when she decided to go on the pill. Paulo is easy to talk to and she finds that 'we say the same things at the same time, we think the same things at the same time'. Asked whether being in a couple has changed her sense of security, she expresses more ambivalent feelings: 'sometimes I feel like I'm less independent, 'cause every time I want to go somewhere, I'll ring him, "What are you doing today?". It's like I can't, I just don't get up and go somewhere and just forget about him all day'.

Negotiating dependency

The context for this relationship is provided by an understanding of changes that have taken place in Sherleen's family life. In my original analysis I observed boundaries within her family. The more 'private' realm was between her and her mother in their flat – this was where studying took place, as well as the coaching and emotional support that was so central to her academic project. The more public dimension of family life was with the extended family, the grandparents, aunts and cousins. A crisis between Sherleen and her mother was evident at her third interview, when her mother withdrew into depression, at which time she invested more in friendships and the locality. By the fourth interview the intimate couple of mother and daughter was re-established and Sherleen was, in her words, 'back on track'. But in this fifth interview it becomes evident that her mother is again unavailable. She refers to their 'chats' in the past tense – 'we did talk a lot' – adding, 'I don't see much of her anymore, but we do have the odd girly chat'. Sherleen explains that her mother is working nights again, and merely comes home to sleep. Sherleen rarely eats at home any more, preferring to go to her grandparents' house, which is half way between college and home. By the time her mum comes in from work she is 'just like a zombie, she makes her breakfast and goes to bed, so anything that is left out, I'll just do it for her 'cause I know she's tired. But erm, other than that I'm hardly ever in the house [...] its like a (...) that house is so empty its just dead.' Asked about the meaning of home she explains:

> **Home's changed (...)** Home was (...) home is now my nan's. 'Cause like, everyone's there at weekends anyway, so it's like, that is the place I, I really do identify as home. 'Cause Paulo as well comes there and everyone, well most of my friends are welcome there. I can take them all to my nan's whenever I want, so (...) there's like always a plate of food laid out and things. So that is home for me now.
>
> INT: So your, like your mum's home is sort of less of a (...)?
>
> But my mum is at my nan's all the time. So when she's not working she's there (*laugh*) so that's OK.

Sherleen visits her grandparents' house most days on her way home from college, as well as spending her weekends with her extended family. Her best friend is her cousin, whom she has match-made with Paulo's best friend. The two boys love coming to her grandmother's house and have been welcomed into the close family group. The talking and studying that had formerly taken place within the flat seem to have moved into Sherleen's relationship with Paulo and her cousin.

Unlike many of her friends, Sherleen does not work. She is still economically dependent on her mother, and expects to continue to be so at least until she has left university, when she may consider leaving home. This dependence is part of their personal pact in which Sherleen continues to achieve and to pursue a professional future. But she is also economically dependent on her boyfriend, who, though studious, has his own business promoting dances and clubs in the UK and abroad. At one point she jokingly describes herself as a 'kept woman', explaining that it 'took me a long time to get used to 'cause I was so used to paying things for myself'. Interestingly, the money that Sherleen made during her time working in the summer is not available for paying her way, being earmarked exclusively for the future.

If we look also at her relationship with her wider family it is possible to see some of the wider consequences of Sherleen's 'debt' to her family, in terms of being drawn into relationships of care. While Sherleen willingly helps her grandparents, the 'consideration' that she describes could be seen as a way of reciprocating to those supporting her, as well as confirming her commitment to her family within a collective project of social mobility. So, for example, when asked about how she has changed since her last interview, she replies:

> **It's like I've** got more consideration. I think I've become more considerate about other people's feelings as well. Things like that. So I do try and help out with other people a little bit more. I do help my nan and my aunts when I can. 'Cause I'm not working anyway I may as well do something to fill my time.

Intergenerational conversations

Paulo and Sherleen have been together for over a year. Both have spent time in each other's family, which on Sherleen's part has entailed beginning to learn Portuguese (his family are from Mozambique). She explains: 'He's like, if we're gonna get married then you have to know it (*laugh*) and he's trying to teach me bit by bit'. When asked if they were *really* talking of marriage Sherleen responds ambiguously, 'He's messing about. But he's serious if you know what I mean [...] it's his way of saying it's a good relationship really.' Sherleen's grandparents like him: 'I think they trust me now, cause I'm growing up and I go and help my nan out a lot'. Her grandparents' approval of the relationship is not only a product of Sherleen's decision to share in the care of the older generation, but is also underwritten by an acknowledgement of her educational success to date. In a sense, she has survived the critical period in which finishing compulsory schooling could be derailed by pregnancy or disaffection.

> **And I've got** all my grades behind me and everything, like the GCSEs and everything. And I got my AS behind me. Now it's just like, people just accepted me more as an adult, that I've made a decision to get

good grades and whatever, of my own accord. So I've got a lot more respect from my family, and other adults that I meet as well.

In her seeking to gain recognition from her grandparents, the relationship with Paulo moves into the more collective arena of the intergenerational family. While this may offer securities for Sherleen, one of the prices is that her grandparents feel they have the right to construct the nature of the relationship. So, for example, Sherleen explains that her grandfather is now teaching her to cook, in the belief that she must feed Paulo – even though this flies in the face of her grandparents' own division of labour.

> **He's like, you** have to learn to cook this and you have to learn to cook that. And then they expect me to cook for Paulo. And I'm 'NO!' I'm just like 'no, it's not going to happen, he can cook for himself thank you very much' [...] I know he can cook for himself, he doesn't mind doing it either so (...) when they was telling me you must cook for him, you must cook for him, I'm like, I just do the big eye roll and 'yeah I will'.

> INT: Just quietly agree sort of thing and carry on?

> It's true, because my nan's very (...) it's like she expects the – I don't know. She never did it herself which is why it makes me laugh. She expects the woman to cook and stay home and she was always working. That's all my aunts ever tell me – that my nan worked, she worked two jobs at one stage, 'cause she had so many kids she had to. It was like she worked so many jobs and she didn't do it herself, so when she tells me to do it I have to laugh. [...] I'm a lot like my nan, so more than, more than I know. So sometimes, even though I'm helping there we argue a lot (*laugh*), sometimes we really do. We argue, but we're making the same point.

The motif of cooking is highly loaded within the context of Sherleen's biography. Her mother cooks all day to make a living, exhausting herself to the extent that she no longer cooks at home. Sherleen likes to go to her nan's house because there is always a plate of food 'laid on'. Cooking is both a positive signifier of home and a career trap:

> **When my mum** was young, they were trying to push her towards catering. And even though it wasn't what she wanted to do, everyone was trying to push her towards catering anyway, or nursing. That's what most of my family have got like. Like my aunt, she's done nursing for ages, and my other aunt was at college training to be a nurse. So I

think that's what it is, they're either nurses or caterers. Or they taught them to be secretaries.

INT: Which doesn't sound like what you wanted?

No. Neither of the things, none of them. I've never even considered being any of those (...) professions. But, now, 'cause I've always wanted to do law really.

The thwarted ambition that fuels Sherleen's educational project also implicates her grandparents. What might be understood sociologically as historical and structural shifts can also be seen in terms of interpersonal investments and betrayals. Between Sherleen and her grandmother 'tradition' (as represented by cooking for a man) is treated playfully – with the recognition on both sides that it stands in some tension with practice. Between Sherleen and her mother, recognition of these tensions was potentially painful. Such intergenerational conversations may be easier over three generations than two, revealing the logic of the shift that takes place between the fourth and fifth interviews as to the location of Sherleen's 'home' (from her mother's house to her grandmother's). By negotiating her grandparents' approval for her relationship with Paulo she further forges solidarity between the three generations.

Remaking the local

One of the interesting changes in this final interview is the fading of Jamaica from Sherleen's imagined future. This may in part be connected with her relationship with Paulo, who, although also second-generation black British, has a different heritage. When asked whether she still plans to live in Jamaica, she replies that 'anywhere hot is fine by me', and goes on to describe a recent holiday that she and Paulo had taken together to Spain as 'probably the best holiday I've had of my life yet'.

Sherleen continues to be strongly identified with her family, but at the same time family is a looser configuration within which she has more autonomy. She explains that she has little to do with people living in her street or neighbourhood; 'staying local' means being in connection with her family, to be near to aunts and cousins. Although Paulo has suggested that when they are at university she and he may get a flat together, she is uncertain about his offer, explaining, 'I'd rather be near my family. It depends on where he moves to, 'cause if it's in the area then I might move in with him, but it depends on how the relationship goes between now and then.' When asked whether she could make her home anywhere, she replies, 'as long as it was somewhere I am comfortable with and I could get to, it's local then'.

At the end of her fourth interview Sherleen was poised somewhat fearfully on the edge of her familiar world of school and the flat with her mum. She was ready to throw herself into the world beyond, in search of opportunities – to a college in a distant suburb, and into work experience in barrister's chambers. Twenty months later she has reinvented 'home' and the 'local', forging versions that she can inhabit and draw sustenance from. She continues to express concern that she may not have sufficient resources (economic and social) to achieve the ends that she has set herself.

> **Yeah, 'cause I** don't know many barristers, on a good level. And I need those kind of connections if I'm really gonna get through. But, erm, I do know a few solicitors, well my aunt knows a few solicitors, my aunt's friends, she's got two friends that are solicitors, so that can help me get my foot in the door. But erm, just to er really, just to really go to university and learn it all first.

She is aware that she must learn 'it all from scratch' and understands that she must pace herself in this incremental project. Her family has been a vital resource in this process so far. Maintaining her security in the face of the tensions that are inherent in the project of mobility in which she is engaged is no small feat.

In drawing Sherleen's ongoing story to another provisional close I am aware that I am retelling the story from a new perspective. Where previously her account was of educational endeavour, my interpretation deliberately kept open the space for a range of outcomes. In seeking to show both the serious and fragile character of her educational project I had posed the question of whether she would in fact 'make it' in the terms that she was pursuing. In the light of her subsequent success in her GCSEs, her story moves into the terrain of educational success against the odds. If she had not passed her GCSEs a very different story would have been told, but one for which the groundwork had been laid out, in terms of tensions between social mobility and identification with family, and between deferred and a more immediate and local gratification.

In Chapter Three I established my commitment to the pursuit of *understanding* rather than *explanation*, my goal being the production of a 'thick' description in which the actions and accounts of an individual make sense within a wider understanding of the social, yet are not reduced to manifestations of that social. Yet my anxiety in taking on another round of data was that in some way my earlier analysis would be invalidated by subsequent developments. Although I was content to be judged by narrative criteria of validity (breadth, coherence, aesthetic appeal, insightfulness and parsimony), I was all too aware that there was another test of validity posed by the life that is subsequently lived and the story that is subsequently told. In fact, I have been reassured by the felicity between my earlier and more recent analyses. This does not mean that nothing much has changed in Sherleen's life and narrative. I suggest that the shift of home to her grandmother's house and the relationship with Paulo are significant. But, by and large, familiar biographical resources are deployed in new circumstances and for different ends. Many of the tensions and contradictions are enduring, as are the resources on which she draws.

The metaphor of the 'magic writing pad' (Bjerrum Nielsen, 1996) provides a compelling representation of this dynamic interplay of continuity and change. Sherleen draws from a constrained set of calligraphies and, in comparison to others (such as Karin), does not deliberately experiment with new fonts. Yet, as time goes by, these calligraphies do new work for her, enabling her to forge provisional identities which themselves may sediment over time. Timing is crucial, allowing the 'boyfriend' to move from threat to resource over the course of the two interviews. So far from acting as either positive or negative 'proof', this fifth interview provides further 'evidence' in a project of understanding, consistent with Stanley's 'kaleidoscope' approach to validity in which 'each time you look you see something rather different, composed mainly of the same elements but in a new configuration' (Stanley, 1992: 158).

Devon: 'playing it as best I can'

The anxieties that I describe above did not characterise my feelings about Devon's most recent interview – drawing attention to the subtle but significant differences between primary and secondary analysis of data within this project. Shortly before I conducted this fourth interview I had drafted a case history based on Devon's first three interviews. The fact that I had written about him had no impact on what took place in Devon's life. Yet the experience of writing and making interpretations did make a difference to me and to the research relationship. The vantage point provided by the analysis influenced the interview, both implicitly and explicitly – allowing me to check out whether my interpretations were consistent with the story that Devon was currently telling about himself.

Walking out and coming home

At the time of the interview Devon was working in a well-established gay pub and it was from a tumultuous work history, which he recounted in detail. After a year at the Gentlemen's Club he decided that he wanted 'more variety'. Failing to secure a move within the institution, he looked outside. He found a job that looked perfect, but it did not live up to his expectations. He left on his second day, after his new boss made sexual advances to him. Devon 'told him where to go and walked out' – adding that such behaviour was so 'typically' him; 'I make a decision thinking I am doing the right thing – like with the flat – and then fall flat on my face'. After several part-time and short-term jobs in hotels (during which time he lived at home) Devon got a job at a well-known restaurant which turned out to be much less salubrious than its famous name. Yet again, he found himself walking out with nothing but his pride. He then went to the gay pub in which he had been working part time and asked whether there was a chance that he might increase his hours. They 'took a big chance on me', and in time he was promoted from barman to bar supervisor. More recently, the manager had suggested that he might become assistant manager.

At our previous meeting Devon had outlined his 'stepping stone' approach to life. This demanded that he create and maintain strong boundaries between different areas of his life until he felt sufficiently 'confident' to move on, or to draw aspects of the different fields of his world together. A key moment for him had been the process of sharing aspects of his gay world with his mother. At the end of his third interview he acknowledged that, having come to terms with family, his sexuality and the gay scene, he was likely to begin the process of investing more in work. In my analysis of his succeeding accounts (Chapter Six) I drew attention to the importance of boundary making between Devon's emerging gay identity and straight spaces of work and family. The one exception to this was Devon's brief experience of working as a model. His current job at the heart of London's gay community can be understood as a resolution of this ongoing tension between a working and a gay identity. Moreover, I will argue that there are particular characteristics of this job that facilitate biographical movement for Devon in relation to belonging within a 'familiar' working-class environment.

Management: a new technique of the self

Previously, Devon had avoided responsibility at work. The exception to this was his volunteering for the lesbian and gay youth group, which he refused to see in these terms. In his job at the pub Devon was learning how to enjoy responsibility. His account of learning to manage others suggests his willingness to allow work to change him – something that he previously defended against. Learning to become a manager can be understood as a new technique of the self in which responsibility and power are internalised and naturalised.

> **I've had some** shitty managers in my professional life so I just remember how they'd done, how they made me feel and try my absolute hardest [...] Not to emulate them. But then also to try and remember to take their good points and try and think how can I use that.

Taking on responsibility is a slow and tentative process. He explains that he likes being a bar supervisor because 'I still have someone to answer to', enabling him to be in 'both camps', maintaining friends with everyone. Slowly he is moving away from an earlier identity in which his youth and inexperience were valued, towards a position of being respected for his competence and professionalism:

> **Before I would** just be you know (...) little Devon stands behind bar and pulls a pint [...] I interact with the other staff now, I have to take them aside and either tell them off or praise them or (...) so I think er (...) more confidence I've had with how I've spoken to customers.

Er (...) even down to silly things like having to kick people out which is a horrible thing to do […] I'd like to think that they do have a bit more respect. At least not think of me as just oh campy Devon all the time […] rather than someone who's hard or someone who's a bitch, I would like to get the reputation of somebody who's competent and can do their job […] I don't know if that is likely to happen. At times I am still just silly campy Devon, blond hair blue eyes you know, stands behind a bar and smiles.

Kenny – the manager of the pub – is an important new figure in Devon's life. He reports Kenny's 'big plans' for him, which include one day having a pub of his own. Devon was flattered by, but wary of taking up, Kenny's offer of promotion to assistant manager:

I came to him as a complete clean sheet, and he's sort of, he's made me (...) even down to the way I talk to the boys, it's like (...) that is how Kenny would talk as well. I try not to do it. I try to be my own (...) sort of, have my own style. But Kenny just gets on so well with everyone that it's just, you see him and you think that is the right way to do it. So it's not too bad if I nick his sayings now and again.

Previously, Devon had talked about taking on the style of friends as part of a process of gaining in confidence and learning to walk, talk and feel like a gay man. Here we can see him engaging in a similar process with a man who is older and more established than himself.

Working long hours at the pub left Devon little time for his voluntary work. However, he describes an easy and positive relationship between the pub and the lesbian and gay youth project. Friends from the project regularly come and hang out in the pub, and customers express interest in the activities and security of the youth project. Devon also acknowledges that he is no longer young enough to be a user of the project and will in the future have to think about making a contribution as an adult.

The pub also provided Devon with a home in a very practical way. Before he got the job he had been living with his family, sleeping on the sofa (his older sister having taken his room). The post of bar supervisor brought with it live-in accommodation. By the time of the interview he had one of three bedrooms above the pub and described the set-up as 'like a shared house'. He explains that 'my room *feels* like my bedroom', 'the pub feels like a front room'. If he wants to use the PlayStation he goes into the assistant manager's room, 'all the way up it feels like home'.

Towards the end of the interview I asked Devon about his relationship with his mum and whether he had continued the process of sharing aspects of his gay world with her that he had talked about so positively in his previous interview. He replied enigmatically, 'for her it's gone really really well, for me it's gone wrong'. I asked him to explain.

> **One afternoon, we'd** gone out shopping and I said 'oh seeing as we're so close, shall we go to my pub and you know see where I work?' So she said 'Oh alright then', so we've gone down and we sat there and got really pissed, all afternoon we were sitting there. Kenny absolutely loved her [...] he bought her a little present, these two little teddy bears but they were all dressed up in bondage gear [...] Before I knew it she was just showing up. I'd be standing behind the bar, serving people and all of a sudden there's my mum in the bar with her friends. It's a really mad thing. [...] Then Kenny came up with this great idea er (...) because he'd been talking to me about me having my own pub for months, I sort of said to my mum, as a joke you know, 'oh it's fine you can be my assistant manager – so I always know where you are'. And she said (...) 'It's something that I've always wanted to do is to get in to the pub' [...] Kenny was like, 'Right OK, well come and work in the pub'. And she was like 'Oh no I don't want to leave my job', and he said 'Well just come and work one night a week'. And she does, she's been doing it now for about three months.

INT: And loves it?

Loves it absolutely loves it.

INT: Everyone loves her?

Yeah.

INT: And how do you feel about it?

> Sort of mixed, I like the idea of her doing something different and it's something that does make her very very happy. She really loves working there, so, in a way I like support her through that, because I think that's great. I just – not in a gay pub (...) although to the customers she's like a novelty (...) 'oooh that's Devon's mum, it's a mum' (...) and in fact she's only ever known as 'mum' – but on the other hand it's er (...) not in a gay pub, and also not in *my* pub.

I have quoted this passage at length to capture the complexity of the transgression. On one hand, Kenny is mischievously transgressing the line between the 'family of choice' (Weeks et al, 2001) represented by the pub and Devon's 'family of origin'. The fact that Devon's mum has become everyone's mum behind the bar is clearly good for business and both attracts and repels Devon. It seems that the price of having Kenny as a father figure is to let go of any boundary making between these two versions of family. Devon is not entirely comfortable with this. He neither wants his mum to work in a *gay* pub, nor in *his* pub. While there are clearly issues about autonomy and privacy at play, it is also possible to discern echoes of Devon's earlier defence of the boundary between his gay world and other hetero-normative spaces of his life. His mother's decision to work in the pub can also be seen as an intervention in the micro-politics of the family. I ask Devon what his father thinks about it all:

He doesn't like it.

INT: Was he angry?

He is with her, he's not with me. And when he comes down, he comes down every now and again to take her home, er (...) and when he's down here he's not rude to any of the staff. You know, him and Kenny would have a joke and a laugh with him. But he'll do things like give her really dirty looks across the bar. He's not happy with the fact that she's working there. I've had a go at him about it, she's had a go at him about it as well. And (...) my argument is, alright, so I'm not particularly happy with her working there either. But if she wants to, fucking let her. There's no way I could stand there and say I don't want you working in my pub.

Devon manages his mother's presence by ensuring that she only works on his night off, commenting, 'I can't stand behind the bar and be your supervisor, you're my mum.' Although he jokes about the dissonance caused by having her in his working environment – 'I just say "No you're using the wrong tote glasses, give that beer more head, you know your vodka's behind you", you know stupid things like that just to keep her on her toes' – the experience has also enabled him to distance himself from his mother in new ways. Looking at her as a 'manager' has facilitated distance and reflection.

Professionally my mum is not great in her job, because she has taken a route [...] where the people that she works with are her friends. And this is why me and my sister are the toughest ones in the family, because we both know that no they're not just your friends, they're still your staff, under you. You're responsible for them, if they do something wrong the blame will come to you because they will say well what sort of manager are you? [...] You can't be soft. So professionally, no I don't tend to go to my mum for advice. I give my mum advice but I don't tend to go to my mum.

Later in the interview, when asked whether he anticipates that his life will be very different to his parents' generation, he expands on this process of dis-identification:

> **To be honest** a couple of months ago I probably would have given a different answer to what I'm thinking, I probably would have said er (…) yeah I can see myself as having a similar life-style. But now the past few months where things have changed […] the way it feels for me is that I'm at the (…) more or less the same level as my mum – I'm just 24 years behind. And it sounds awful, and I know mum is having a great time, but what's going to happen to me in the next 24 years? By the time I reach her stage what will I be doing, you know? But I think at the moment though me and my mum are pretty much on par with each other.

Getting behind the bar

Working in the pub has not only had an impact on Devon's work identity and family relationships, but has also transformed the way he engages with the gay scene. He is no longer a 'punter' and appears to have abandoned the 'knowledgism' described in earlier interviews. As the comments above suggest, Devon has not abandoned the forms of identification in which value is calculated in terms of an erotic economy. Yet he increasingly calculates his value within different terms – being 'known' and being in 'role' as a supervisor and a worker while others are at their leisure. This movement from in front of to behind the bar involves the adoption of a new 'technique of self'. His account is redolent with the practices of distinction that set the producer apart from the consumer within the context of the pub. Although friends and family come and see him, when he is working he is 'on', he cannot completely join in. For Devon 'having a fag' and being able to kiss your boyfriend are all markers of not working. And although he expresses frustration about this, it is nevertheless a source of pride that he is working while others are playing.

Devon's understanding of what the scene consists of has also changed. Where previously he thought in terms of pubs and clubs, he now thinks in terms of businesses: 'shops, bookshops, restaurants, even down to just the people you see walking between these places'. Paradoxically, now that a gay identity is the centre of his life, it takes up less time and space. By living within a gay space, sexuality becomes normalised and other things grow in importance. Devon now very rarely goes to clubs, the exception being the occasional 'bender' with his old friend Shane. Otherwise he participates in an extended family of gay businesses, including a couple of 'sister pubs' that are spaces for 'private' leisure, breaks and after-hours socialising. A similar crowd moves between the three pubs, and Devon remarks that he often bumps into people he recognises from his own – 'it's very strange,

I'm not where I'm working, but I still know you from work'. When I ask Devon about his sense of 'belonging' he talks about how both living and working on the scene have changed his relationship to the gay community:

> **I understand more** of what it means by gay community [...] whereas before it was just like a bunch of blokes going out and getting drunk. I was one of those blokes, but it didn't feel like a community, it just felt like a night out.

He observes that few of his regular customers actually live in the neighbourhood (reasserting the line between the punters and the workers), but that 'it's that familiarity that I really like, that I've not really noticed before, don't have that actually in different jobs'. When I suggest that some people have that sense of familiarity in the neighbourhood that they grow up in, he replies:

> **I must admit** I didn't, I think that's why I've been able to move about so much, er (...) it's now about the eighth or ninth place I've lived in since I was born – always been in the city. Yeah. You know this does definitely now feel, I feel like I am part of something outside my family.

In Chapter Six I commented on the extent to which Devon disassociated himself from the working-class masculinity represented by his father. Nevertheless, class differences have been in play in the ways that Devon has chosen to identify or dis-identify with particular people or practices. At a number of points in this interview there are suggestions that Devon is reclaiming aspects of working-class masculinity that he had previously distanced himself from. For example, he talks proudly about how he was able to get rid of unruly customers and the word 'tough' peppers his account in a way that it did not before. In moving away from his identity as 'camp, blond and blue eyed' it appears that he is beginning to forge a new gender identity in which he is able to incorporate aspects of his gender subjectivity (which involved less-conscious identifications relating to family) which previously had been excluded (Bjerrum Nielsen, 1996). The following extract suggests this movement as Devon reflects on a new form of solidarity that has grown up between him and his older sister – a form of 'fighting talk' that could be understood as a response to this new sense of belonging:

> **Because we've got,** this sounds really awful but we've got the arrogance that is (...) literally is throughout my dad's side of the family every single one of us has it [...] we take care of ourselves and we take care of our own, very East End thing, I'm not (...) a real butch person and if I got into a fight, I more than likely would lose but that doesn't mean that I would just roll over and let them. You know (...)

I'd give as much as I could in the meantime, probably still get my arse kicked but I wouldn't.

Mobile intimacies

Devon explained that since we last met he'd had three boyfriends. The first, Damien, coincided with his time working at the Gentlemen's Club and involved highly complicated arrangements to enable them to share a bed together on a single evening. In Devon's account of the relationship Damien is positioned as a beautiful yet inexperienced boy living in the suburbs and unfamiliar with the scene that Devon took such pride in knowing. Although they were the same age, Devon describes him as 'vulnerable' and 'oblivious', recalling that on their first date Damien had waited outside the pub for 20 minutes, too nervous to meet him by the bar as arranged. The relationship was short lived, yet Devon describes himself as heartbroken after it was over. He had been able to 'talk' to Damien and this had unsettled his categorisation of relationships into men for sex ('they're playthings to me. I don't do relationships') and friends for the disclosure of intimacies ('I have my friends, I don't need a boyfriend').

After a period without a steady boyfriend, Devon met Peter, who had come for a drink in his pub. They began by 'dating', but as Peter lived outside London with his parents and Devon did not yet have his own room, they had nowhere to spend time alone together. In his account of the relationship Devon expressed annoyance at Peter's habit of hanging out in his pub while he was working, talking to his friends and 'holding court'. The relationship faltered after three weeks, when a drunken Peter declared his love for Devon on the telephone. Devon talks of him as a 'sweet boy', but the declaration was 'way too soon. I knew for a fact that he didn't love me. He had a crush on me. Saying it (a) pissed me off and (b) freaked me out.' Devon's response was to end the relationship, leaving Peter 'broken hearted'. Subsequently Devon felt some regret, but the practical problems of fitting intimate work around working schedules meant that the relationship did not continue.

At the time of his fourth interview Devon describes himself as being 'in a couple' for the first time with Sergio – a barman at a sister pub. This coincides with many of his friends also being in couples, and in several cases living with their 'other halves'. The relationship began with a crush on Devon's part, and invented excuses in order to visit the pub. One of the bar staff had given the relationship a helping hand – 'she literally pushed me upstairs'. He and Sergio talked all afternoon, and started seeing each other on a daily basis:

> **It was like** normal, that's how it's supposed to go. Met up, have a chat, go for a drink (...) walked him down to the bus stop then I'd go home. Then a couple of days later, pop in say hello – it became a very familiar thing.

Just as Devon was beginning to get over his crush and to see Sergio 'as a friend', a play fight turned intimate (in Devon's words 'just like a porn movie') and they moved into a sexual relationship. Devon explains that previous partners had felt 'like friends' that he 'happened to have sex with'. However, with Sergio 'it actually feels like a boyfriend'. Central to this new kind of commitment is an obligation of sexual exclusivity and a sharing of time. Devon was already struggling to balance power within the relationship, the most recent problem being Sergio's resentment when Devon spends his 'time off' with his family. As Sergio's family live in Spain he does not have the same option.

Over the course of these three relationships it is possible to see changes in the way in which Devon 'does' intimacy. With Damien he was still practising the 'knowledgism' that had previously helped him navigate the scene – where looks, money and experience were all currencies that could be exchanged. The sharp division between friend and sexual partner that this strategy presumed was a struggle for Devon to maintain. His relationships with Damien and Peter point to the importance of a private physical space for the building of intimacy. Devon was clearly frustrated that his relationship with Peter was played out in such a public and demonstrative manner – with love declared before they had been able to get to know each other. I would also suggest that, with a change of job, tensions arose from their different positionings vis-à-vis the scene. The relationship with Sergio appears to transcend many of these barriers – they have a private space to be in. They do similar jobs, both working long hours and are part of the same extended 'family of choice'. Although Devon mourns his loss of freedom he also seems to be enthusiastic about what he can learn from being in a relationship. If family, sexuality and work have been the successive 'part projects' (Du Bois-Reymond, 1998) of Devon's wider project of self, then I would expect that intimacy and the couple relationship will be the central themes of the next episode.

Although there is a clear sense of movement and resolution in this most recent account, there continue to be areas of moral density and connection that are relatively uninspected. For me, these continue to centre on Devon's relationship with his father, including both an active dis-identification and alternative attachments. When I asked Devon directly as to whether he was able to identify with his father, he is both dismissive and poetic:

INT: And you don't compare yourself to your dad at all?

I would never want to, I love my dad, in a way, but (...) there are definite things about him that I couldn't do, myself [...] Especially around work, so er (...) I just couldn't imagine being bored for 15 years like he's been (...) so no [...] But he's (...) sort of, he's like this view from this window. If this window is my life, that window there it's always been there, you can look out the window a thousand times a day that window will always be there (...) That's my dad.

Devon's hopes and fears for the future suggest the salience of this relationship and the extent to which it is not always possible to bring gender identity (who you want to be) and gender subjectivity (how you feel about yourself) into line. Having expressed the desire that his present situation endures, that his mum leaves the pub and that his dad is 'happy for her', Devon reveals his fear:

> **Em, professionally, I** don't know. I just hope that I don't disappoint anyone, that Kenny doesn't take this huge chance on me (...) even just supervising and I don't disappoint. And that's sort of related to the fears as well, because I do (...) I can stand someone being angry at me, I can tolerate that, not tolerate that, I can handle it you know. But disappointment, I've never been able to. Not many people can, it's a tough one to deal with. But er (...) that's one thing I've always hated, just can't stand the idea of disappointing someone.

> INT: Who've you disappointed?

> My dad I suppose, I know I've disappointed him but then (...) that doesn't (...)

> INT: He's disappointed you too hasn't he?

> Yeah yeah, I suppose (...) nenenenene so er (...) yeah. But I'm at the stage now where I've stopped feeling that oh I wish I hadn't disappointed dad. I'm now like 'Tough, it's the hand I've been dealt and I'm going to play it as best as I can.'

Conclusions: time the revelator

Interviews are like 'snapshots' of lives in particular times and places and are characterised by a sense of openness and possibility as to what comes next. The analysis of one-off accounts tends to locate the individual within their wider social landscape, mapping positions and relationships. Multiple interviews enable these snapshots to be articulated, providing a timescape that accentuates agency, serendipity and processes that enables us to see the relationship between discernment, deliberation and dedication (Archer, 2007: 20–1). In this book I have tried to capture the dynamic interplay of the temporal and the spatial. In earlier chapters I did this by tracing a series of partial narratives into an overall account through the analytic lens of biographical field. By employing 'field of existence' and 'interview round' as structuring devices, there is an explicit sense of movement, but the accounts are also fixed in a moment in time, effecting a kind of analytic closure. In this chapter the cases are opened up again, with new material both enriching and destabilising these interpretations.

There should be no single method for qualitative longitudinal analysis, but there is much to be gained by approaches which reveal the interplay of diachronic and synchronic dimensions of the data. I have found Doreen Massey's argument for the 'inseparability' of time and space useful in making sense of the potential of longitudinal qualitative data. Massey does not seek to counterpose or differently privilege time and space as dimensions. In her words, 'temporal movement is also spatial, the moving elements have spatial relations to one another. And the spatial interconnections which flash across can only be constituted temporally as well' (1994: 264). In practice this means accepting that the synchronic is not simply determined: there can be synchronic outcomes (such as unintended consequences, happenstance juxtapositions and accidental separations) that give rise to 'emergent powers which can have effects on subsequent events' (1994: 268). Likewise, the diachronic dimension is not simply dislocated (or undetermined): agency is bounded, and both narratives and pathway fall into well-worn patterns.

Yet, finding forms of representation that capture this interplay can be challenging. For Massey, 'it is not the "slice through time" which should be the dominant mode of representation, but the simultaneous co-existence of social relations that cannot be represented as other than dynamic' (1994: 265). Over the course of this book I hope to have captured something of this dynamic, creating thick yet animated descriptions. The case histories show *how* four young people have moved through time and space, tracing both continuities and movements in narrative and resources. Yet, in Bertaux and Delacroix's (2000) terms they may still remain four unrelated 'gems'. In the final chapter I will bring the case histories into conversation, exploring whether and how it may be possible to move from these empirically grounded examples to the generation of a broader conceptual framework.

NINE

Conversation: reading between the lines

Integrating the individual and the social, agency and structure, the temporal and the spatial has been a central yet thwarted project in contemporary social theory. Approaches that focus on the individual, such as Anthony Giddens' (1991) notion of the 'reflexive project of self', or even Foucault's later work on the practices of existence, have been criticised for failing to relate the self to their social horizons (McNay, 2000), for downplaying the embeddedness of the subject (Scott and Scott, 2001; Plumridge and Thomson, 2003) and for universalising cultural forms available to some but not others (Skeggs, 2004). Conversely, accounts which emphasise the social and the structural tend to foreclose the temporal or aspects of it (Massey, 1994). For example, the classic criticism that has been levelled against the work of Bourdieu is that it portrays an overly synchronic (and thus static and determined) view of social relations (May, 1996: 126). It may be that a generous reading of all these authors would acknowledge that their perspectives privilege different elements of spatiality/temporality and individual/social, yet still recognise these elements as indivisible and mutually constitutive. Nevertheless, the challenge continues to be to find theories, methodologies and methods that *represent* this dynamic mutuality.

Margaret Archer has attempted to transcend these binaries by conceptualising the reflexive subject through the lens of critical realism. She argues that, in order to 'accord reflexivity its due', sociological accounts must acknowledge the following points about how we make our way in the world:

1. That our unique personal identities, which derive from our singular constellations of concerns, mean that we are radically heterogeneous as subject. Even though we may share objective social positions, we may also seek very different ends from within them.
2. That our subjectivity is dynamic, it is not psychologically static nor is it psychologically reducible, because we modify our own goals in terms of their contextual feasibility, as we see it. As always we are fallible, can get it wrong and have to pay the objective price for doing so.
3. That, for the most part, we are active rather than passive subjects because we adjust our projects to those practices that we believe we can realise. Subjects regularly evaluate their social situations in the light of their personal concerns and assess their projects in the light of their situations. (Archer, 2007: 22)

The qualitative longitudinal approach that I have taken provides the evidence of these dynamic processes, showing how individual lives are implicated and constrained, yet also agentic and undetermined. Through an engagement with the detail of ordinary lives I have tried to capture something of 'the universal singular' which enables us to read the social from the personal and vice versa. These accounts are animated through an analysis of repeat interview accounts, demanding an engagement with fields of existence that change and interact over time. My approach has privileged the individual and the unfolding temporal, yet in doing so reveals the extent to which that individual is located in relationship to dynamic configurations of family, community, class and generation.

In this chapter I reposition myself, stepping back from the case studies, asking what I can learn from juxtaposing the accounts of Sherleen, Stan, Karin and Devon. The case histories capture some of the microprocesses and practices of personal and social change that make up individual biographies. Although the cases cannot be understood as representative in any direct way, in Chapter One I suggest that they might be seen to be emblematic of certain patterns in youth transitions, expressing hotspots in the emergence of new biographical forms. But is it possible to move between these accounts in a way that not only speaks to the relationship between an individual and the wider social context, but which also locates these four individuals within a web of relationality?

The approach that I will take in this chapter is to bring the four case histories into *conversation*. I approach this in two stages. First I concentrate on the temporal dimension, focusing on the biographical *methods of living* through which these young people's biographies are animated in narrative. Here I suggest a set of conceptual tools that can be employed across the case histories, including biographical motifs, methods, impasses and solutions. In this section I employ the notion of the reflexive project of self as an umbrella term, and the section concludes with some critical reflections on the concept. In the second part of the chapter, I move from a focus on projects of self to a focus on the wider gender order within which these projects are situated and to which they contribute. Here I seek to identify *mediums* within and through which these young people's unfolding biographies are played out, privileging a focus on structural elements that emerge from the case histories. This involves distinguishing and relating the fields of existence that characterise their accounts, the technologies of self made available therein, the investments and identifications that constrain their adoption, and the social and spatial horizons that frame their biographies.

There is no convention for this kind of project, which seeks to capture and account for lives as they unfold, and this chapter reflects my search for 'unfolding theory' – conceptual tools that realise the dynamic character of the data as a work between case histories. Over the course of the chapter I move from a focus on temporality and the connected individual to a focus on the spatial and the social. In doing so I take seriously the flux and fluidity of the process of growing up, drawing on a range of disciplinary traditions to generate an eclectic analytic vocabulary through which to capture commonalities between young people without obscuring the generative legacy of social location in shaping distinctive and unequal lives.

Temporality: methods of living

A longitudinal methodology provides a privileged insight into the ways in which lives are storied over time. Although the methodology does not release us from the constraints of the interview account, we can access the way in which it is described, observing shifts and continuities in this. At the most general level, Giddens' (1991) notion of the 'reflexive project of self' offers a framework for capturing these changing narratives. In Table 9.1 I have juxtaposed the projects of self of the four young people and, in doing so, distinguish some conceptual tools that may facilitate a conversation between them.

Table 9.1 Tools in the reflexive project of self: biographical motifs, methods, impasses, solutions

Tool	Sherleen	Stan	Devon	Karin
Biographical method	Deferred gratification	Immediate gratification	Boundary drawing/erosion	Incursion/ transgression
	Shifting allegiance	Experimentation	Knowledgism	Prosthetic self
	Family project	Shape shifting	Mimesis	Burning bridges
Biographical motifs	Loyalty	Transformation	Confidence	Escape
	Determination	Worry	Walking out	Rebellion
	Mirroring	Money		
Biographical impasse/ 'magical' solution	Mother's depression/ reworking 'home'	Dropping out/ reworking masculinity	Social exclusion/ transcending boundaries	Social isolation/ reworking dependencies on the local

Each of the case histories is characterised by particular biographical motifs. For example, Sherleen's successive accounts each featured discussions of loyalty towards her family, being 'like' particular members of her family and being 'determined', an implicit and explicit recognition of the labour involved in achieving her professional ambitions, located as she is as a black, British, working-class woman. Within the project of self these motifs can be seen to be associated with particular methods – biographical practices that can be detected through the repeat interview form – through which projects of self are animated. Methods can be understood as characterised both by repeat performances, habitual ways of being and dispositions that have grown up over time in response to a particular environment – and in this sense can be seen to bear some resemblance to Bourdieu's understanding of the habitus of the 'player'. But biographical methods also include the serendipitous and agentic responses of individuals to their environment – ways of playing that are not simply determined by or complicit with the 'rules of the game' (Lovell, 2000).

Sherleen's attention appears to be simultaneously focused on an imagined future of success and on a past that is defined through identification with family narratives of migration and frustrated ambition. The 'determination' that she speaks of so often can be understood as part of a method in which the seductions of the present are rejected, and with them the various forms of immediate gratification that could threaten the long educational haul. Where she is drawn into forms of investment that are at odds with her project (such as the perils of popularity), she shows herself willing to withdraw from that arena. Sherleen is remarkably self-resourcing and avoids overextending herself or assuming support when it is not there. Clearly, there are moments in which the pressures brought about by her project become intense and where there is no clear way forward. I have called these 'biographical impasses' – points at which it may be necessary to metaphorically 'backtrack' and seek a new pathway in order to maintain biographical momentum. I suggest that it is at these moments that we can see a shift in the shape of Sherleen's interdependencies (Irwin, 2003), marked by realignment of allegiance and reworking the meaning of both 'home' and 'locality' in the face of feelings of dependency, belonging and vulnerability.

In contrast, Stan's accounts are characterised by an 'extended present' (Brannen and Nilsen, 2002) in which one is 'perpetually "on", ready at a moment to take advantage and spring into action' (Tronto, 2003: 123). Although Stan is also embedded within a wider family narrative and draws on different aspects of this narrative over time, his accounts privilege spontaneity and immediate gratification, reflected in his rejection of the educational grind. His narratives also suggest the fragility of this orientation, with a willingness to engage in self-transformation, accompanied by expressions of anxiety and worry. That Stan is open to change can be seen in the impact that love, religion, work and exposure to new people have on him. I suggest that his biographical method can be understood in terms of experimentation, through which he 'tries on' different lives and identities. These small explosions of agency are associated with moments of explicit dependency (such as his account of falling into debt), as well as a willingness to embrace the certainties offered by tradition (such as his investment in a traditional couple relationship and the identity of a family man). I would argue that Stan's biographical impasse should be seen as arising from his decision to drop out of education. His three interviews suggest that he experiments with a range of solutions all of which entail reworkings of masculinity and related notions of success, conducted in conversation with those available in his immediate and extended family. I have come to see him as a 'shape shifter' – searching for new possibilities and life-styles, yet often finding himself without the requisite resources to support his experiments. That he eventually abandons (or is abandoned by) these experiments to go travelling and snowboarding suggests the fragility of his methods, as well as indicating something of the fluidity of the family resources on which he draws.

There is a similar sense of exuberance in Karin's interviews; she also looks to popular culture as a medium for experimentation and exploration of the self. However, Karin begins from a rather different place, an explicit desire to escape her origins, both physically and metaphorically. Throughout her interviews, rebellion is a recurring motif, expressed both as criticism of the educational institutions within which she finds herself and through her attempts to break into arenas of practice and representation that are coded as male. The methods which most characterise her biography are incursion and transgression. Her involvement in graffiti and skateboarding can clearly be seen as examples of incursion in which she attempts to insert herself as an active agent into spaces in which women (while present) are supposed to act as either audience or object. Sometimes this involves simply being there (with skateboard in hand), but in other cases she projects herself through various prostheses such as her graffiti tag and fictional characters. Her transgressions tend to involve a disruption of femininity and an assertion of female sexual agency – a willingness to be seen to see sex from 'a wee fella point of view'. Yet where I characterised Stan's biographical method in terms of experimentation, I am drawn to seeing what Karin does more in terms of rejection – or a deliberate process of burning bridges in which, by 'spoiling' her chances of achieving a respectable feminine identity, she is propelling herself away from the local into a more cosmopolitan future.

I would also suggest that Karin's method is unsustainable in the absence of solidarity from her female friends and acquaintances. Again and again, she finds herself socially isolated and subject to disciplinary measures from her peers. The expectations of geographical and social mobility that frame her project of self give rise to complicated emotions, investments and disinvestments. Although she rejects the local, she is also deeply invested in it through her connection with her parents and notions of motherhood. I would identify her biographical impasse as arising from these tensions, brought to a head by travelling abroad. Becoming part of a couple on her return can be seen as a partial solution in that it provides a bridge between her rebel identity and her family, as well as containing her transgressions vis-à-vis more public arenas of representation. But being part of a couple also poses a problem to her project of escape, for the first time giving her something to stay for.

Where the accounts of Stan and Sherleen both lend themselves to temporal metaphors (extended present, deferred/immediate gratification), in making sense of Karin's accounts I have been drawn toward metaphors of spatiality (local, cosmopolitan, incursion, transgression). Spatial metaphors are also central to Devon's series of interviews, but in a different way. There are two motifs that I feel characterise his series of accounts. The first is the 'leaving' or 'walking out', that always seemed to be part of the interview story – whether it be leaving home, his flat, another job. In leaving situations in which he is unhappy or uncomfortable he expresses agency, and he tends to do this when he does not feel ready or able to deal with the demands of the situation. The second motif that characterises his account is 'confidence'. Over the course of interviews Devon often reflects on his need to build up confidence before taking the next step. Like Sherleen, he is careful not to extend himself, not to run before he can walk. Yet, unlike Sherleen, Devon has been forced into the world away from his family and his neighbourhood. And it is through his compartmentalised and incremental methodology that he seeks to maintain some boundaries for the acquisition and accrual of personal resources. Boundary drawing is an important method within his project of self. He deliberately keeps areas of his life separate until he has built up sufficient 'confidence' to protect aspects of his emergent identity from the expectations, meanings and demands of different areas of his life such as work and family. The transgression of boundaries is not always in his control (as shown by the appearance of his mother in his pub), and as he gains in confidence he is more able to survive and even enjoy an increasingly 'joined up' life. From his accounts, it appears that the key method through which he accrues confidence is a combination of what he terms 'knowledgism' (knowing the unwritten rules of how a particular social field works) and a form of imitation.

Michael Taussig (1993) has written that 'the mimetic faculty carries out its honest labour suturing nature to artifice [...] granting the copy the character and power of the original, the representation the power of the represented' (xviii). For Taussig, the mimetic faculty plays an increasingly important part in modernity, operating at two levels: as a copy or imitation, and as a connection between the perceiver and the perceived. It is possible to identify elements of a mimetic method in the accounts of most of these young people: Sherleen's assertions that she is just 'like' her mother and grandmother; Karin's possession of the identity of fictional characters; Stan's projection into the role of the breadwinner. Yet it is in Devon's accounts of learning to be camp and learning to be a manager that we find the clearest expression of mimesis as a process through which power is acquired, as well as the 'active yielding' (Taussig, 1993: 65) that Taussig believes is central to the mimetic faculty.

There is a sense in which the incremental and compartmentalised methodology pursued by Devon makes this active yielding possible and safe. By letting go of an imagined future – and thus too acute an awareness of the consequentiality of his actions – he is able to build in the present the resources necessary to move himself one more step along. Each of the biographical compartments that Devon enters can be understood as a biographical impasse. His response is not marked by narrative assertion, but rather by absorption into the regimes (knowledge and practices) of a social field. Such responses do not necessarily look like 'solutions' but, as Taussig observes, 'turning points cannot be mastered by contemplation alone but are mastered gradually by habit under the guidance of tactility' (Taussig, 1993: 35).

Reflections on the reflexive project of self

In Anthony Giddens' terms the reflexive project of self is 'the process whereby self–identity is constituted by the reflexive ordering of self narratives' (Giddens,

1991: 244). Sherleen, Stan, Karin and Devon each have a project of self, which is reflexive – even if only as a result of being involved in a study that demands the performance and sharing of these narratives. Yet Giddens does not offer us many tools for dissecting or comparing these projects of self. Elsewhere I have explored the value, for example, of Giddens' notion of the 'fateful moment' as a tool for comparing narratives (Thomson et al, 2002), as well as how this is complicated by a longitudinal method (Plumridge and Thomson, 2003; Holland and Thomson, 2009). Yet there is a tendency for Giddens' approach to overstate the rationality and autonomy of the subject at the heart of the reflexive project of self. For example, fateful moments are supposed to be associated with processes of risk assessment and personal reskilling. As others have also observed, the overly intellectualist idea of a 'project of self' needs to be tempered with an understanding of practices that are embedded within social fields.

By employing here the notion of the biographical impasse and associated 'solutions' I hope to show that these are not simply 'moments' but coincidences of events or pressures, expressing the culminations of the biographical contradictions. Such contradictions are not simply resolved or left behind. In coining the phrase 'magical solution' in 1972, Phil Cohen sought to show how oppositional youth cultures seek 'to express and resolve, albeit magically the contradictions which remain hidden or unresolved in the parent culture' (1972: 23). Although I am using the term in relation to the practices of individuals rather than youth cultures, I want to hold on to the insight captured by Cohen, that the contradictions that young people grapple with will often be encountered indirectly, and because these contradictions are bound up with the lives of earlier generations, they are unlikely to be within the power of young people to resolve. What, then, is magical about the solution is that it is engaged with symbolically and that, as a result, some kind of movement (if not resolution) is achieved. In biographical terms this may translate into a form of biographical momentum, even though the underlying contradictions remain and are likely to resurface again in a different way. The impossibility of the 'magical solution' can be seen to enrich the metaphor of the 'magic writing pad', which is drawn from the rich reserve of clinically derived psychoanalytic concepts. While the idea of the palimpsest preserves a sense of the presence of the past within the present (as traces of earlier inscriptions), it does not provide a sense of how collective, conflictual, unresolved and dynamic that past may be. Symbolic solutions may be improvised by individuals but they also connect individuals to each other and to particular times and spaces.

I have used the terms 'biographical motif' and 'biographical method' in order to capture the particularities of individual lives as well as the kinds of insights that arise from a longitudinal method. It is only over time that motifs emerge as a result of repetition. These repetitions provide a thread through which narrative continuity can be traced, even where such continuity is explicitly rejected as part of an individual's self-narrative. Tracing the motifs of the *life as told* enables us to generalise from the formal features of the narrative and to maintain the integrity of the case. This contrasts with the approach to generalisation used in the creation of typologies which proceeds from an aggregation of substantive features of the *life as lived*. Motifs and methods can be distinguished from techniques of the self which, by definition, arise from discursive regimes. Individuals engage in and with techniques of the self, and such techniques can become part of an individual's biographical method. In this way the individual is saturated but not obscured by the social.

Spatiality: mediums for living

In this section I shift analytic attention from methods of individuals towards a focus on the mediums of the gender order, identifying conceptual tools that speak to more structural and spatial dimensions of the case histories. I will begin by exploring the 'fields of existence' that characterise the young people's biographies, those physical and social spaces within which they engage in identity work. In coining the term 'field of existence' I have combined elements of Foucault's notion of 'aesthetics of existence' and Bourdieu's notion of the 'social field' – arenas of social practice characterised by a set of explicit and implicit rules governing behaviour. Within Bourdieu's schema, a social field is associated with particular forms of authority and regimes of knowledge and practice. Within Foucault's schema an aesthetic of existence is associated with formations of knowledge (such as dietics and erotics) which concern the relationship of the self with the self (Foucault, 1994). Because my analysis has been led by a focus on biography, I am drawn into the biographical significance of the different fields of their lives. A different method (such as participant observation) would have resulted in a very different engagement with the notion of the field. By using the term 'field of existence' I am seeking to engage with the rules, roles and forms of authority that characterise the different arenas of a life, how these resources are accessed and how the self is maintained across fields.

Having identified the biographically important fields of existence, I also seek to identify the technologies of the self that young people engage with that arise specifically from these fields. It is important to note that individuals do not simply take on those technologies that are available; these may be resisted, ignored and disrupted as well as adopted. The notion of investment/identification (and disinvestment/disidentification) is adopted as a means by which to consider when, where and why individuals engage with socially and discursively available resources and when, where and why they do not (Hollway, 1984; Skeggs, 1997; Hollway and Jefferson, 2001; Walkerdine et al, 2002). Finally, I move on to an exploration of spatial and social horizons as the backdrops for individual biographies, exploring how positions within a gender order are structured by relations of power and hierarchy. In the spirit of decentring the individual, Table 9.2 reverses the relationship between concepts and cases followed in the previous section, and my commentary will follow this structure accordingly. Although I revisit themes discussed above, complementary insights are generated by changing the direction of analysis.

Table 9.2 Mediums of the gender order: fields, techniques, investments, horizons

	Fields of existence	Technologies of the self	Investments/ identifications	Spatial horizons	Social horizons
Sherleen	School Home Martial arts	Pedagogy	Student Black woman Daughter	Migration Home/family Keeping local	Upward social mobility as a family project over generations
Stan	Work Pub Holidays Church	Consumption	Craftsman Consumer Lover Leader	Travel International horizons vs local plans	Individualised downward social mobility?
Devon	Foster care Youth project Workplaces Home The scene	Erotics	Friend Son Desirable Expert	Exclusion Gay/straight Insider/ outsider Producer/ consumer	Social stasis, but mobile being in the world?
Karin	City centre School Home Away Work	Aesthetics	Child Sexual Rebel Mother Cosmopolitan	Exile University Rejection of the local International	Upward social and geographical mobility

By identifying fields of existence I draw attention to the *situated* nature of identity work. The fields identified here reflect their relative importance within biographical terms. So, although most of the young people spent significant amounts of time at school (or other educational establishments), as a field of existence education was only central to the accounts of two of the young people: Sherleen and Karin. Where Sherleen drew heavily on the technologies of the self offered by the educational institutions that she was within, Karin was (at least initially) more concerned to resist and subvert the values and authority that she encountered. Clearly, individuals are situated within fields differently, and access to fields may be the result of serendipity, happenstance, or more often as a consequence of the interests and resources of family members. For example, Sherleen's participation in martial arts and Stan's involvement in the church can be understood as a result of family connection, even though these young people translated these activities into independent aspects of their biographies. Access to other fields may be seen more as a consequence of the actions of individuals – for example, Karin's pursuit of city-centre non-sectarian leisure spaces and Devon's identification with and immersion in the lesbian and gay youth project and the commercial gay scene that eventually provide him with a 'sexual community' (Weeks 1996).

The range and kinds of fields that young people have access to are constrained by a configuration of many factors including age, gender and material resources. Young people of a certain age have little choice but to go to school. Depending on how old they look, they may or may not be able to access more adult leisure environments. Fields are highly gendered and it may require formidable agency for girls to break into spaces such as martial arts and skateboarding. Fields are also marked by sexuality. Thus, Devon is aware that his neighbourhood and initial workplaces are implicitly coded as heterosexual. Being 'out' in these spaces is potentially dangerous. Fields are also marked by 'race' and by class, as reflected in Sherleen's pursuit of comfort and belonging in her choice of school and college. The fields that young people have access to can be seen as a barometer of their geographical and social location at any particular moment in time. The fields that they actually do access and which take on biographical significance can be understood in terms of the animation of that social location within time: reflecting a sense of competence, the recognition of that competence by others and continued investment of time and energy (Thomson et al, 2004).

The notion of 'fields of existence' is useful for making sense of the different spaces, institutions and practices through which young people move. Yet, what the term fails to do is to communicate a sense of how those different fields of existence might be related. A common feature of all the young people's biographies is the home. I feel rather uneasy about identifying home and family life as a field alongside others, in that it fails to reflect the very different nature of this space. In a sense, 'home' is the default space through which all others gain a sense of meaning. School becomes meaningful as a space that is different from, but related to home, as do non-domestic forms of leisure and work. But I do not want to leave the home out of this model. The different ways in which young people orient themselves to the home are interesting. Of all the young people Sherleen is probably the most invested in home. Yet, as I have said before, the way in which home is constructed changes over the course of her five interviews, from herself and her mother in their flat to an extended family in the house of her grandmother. Like Sherleen, Stan lived at home throughout the study, yet, unlike her, put much of his energy into imagining a home of his own in the future. At the same time his pursuit of travel as a life-style implicitly assumes a home to return to. From the little that I know of recent events in his life, it appears that this family home may no longer exist for him in the same form. Karin's intrepid forays within the public spaces of the city were supported by a notion of home in which she played the part of the dependent child, and the project of 'leaving' was complicated by her being the last child to be still living in the family home. Although Devon moved out of his family home at a relatively young age, his family and their home never stopped being an important part of his world.

Home is more than a physical place, and the meanings and practices associated with this arena of life vary enormously. There is ample evidence in the data presented here that for these young people 'home' is the most significant field of their existence, with greatest moral density and complexity. In Bjerrum Nielsen and Ruberg's terms, home may be the primary site of gender subjectivity (a sense of me), while the other fields may be the sites of gender identity (a sense of who I want to be). Yet home is also a dynamic field of existence, in which relationships, roles and identifications are reworked and through which the material and symbolic responsibility for creating and maintaining a home are passed between generations. The ways in which these young people engage with other fields can be understood as taking place in conversation with identities and obligations formed within the domestic field. As young people negotiate between their family of origin and other kinds of relationships (with friends, partners, colleagues and teachers), they are forging new gender identities, informed by the past but created in the present and framed by unique historical and social conditions.

Technologies of the self

One way of identifying the biographical significance of a particular field is through the way in which individuals do or do not take up the technologies of the self that arise from that field. Foucault's discussions of technologies of self were concerned primarily with the ethical substance, methods and models through which the 'individual acts upon himself [sic]' (Martin et al, 1988: 19). As I have said earlier, these are different from but implicated in the biographical methods that emerge from an analysis of an individual's accounts of themself over time. The virtue of identifying the particular technologies of self that take on biographical significance for individual young people is that it provides a way of embedding biographies within specific fields. In doing so it may be possible to relate the individual to their social horizon rather than simply juxtaposing them – a criticism that Lois McNay lays against Foucault's work (2000: 155). In Table 9.2 I have noted the technology of self that I feel most strongly characterises the accounts of the four young people. This has meant leaving some important examples out, for example the form of charismatic leadership that Stan adopted in the context of church and the therapeutic discourses that Devon accessed through his encounters with social workers. As before, I have concentrated on those technologies of the self that I believe have biographical significance for young people and, perhaps most importantly, that young people 'made their own', transposing them into other fields of their lives and, through these technologies, engaging in personal change.

Sherleen's case history is characterised by an ongoing engagement with a pedagogical technology of self, accessed initially through her acute sensitivity to the implicit rules, values and expectations of the formal curriculum. Over time she developed and explored the various positions available within the medium, moving from the subject position of the good student, to that of the teacher and back again. Through her experience of martial arts she experimented with the boundaries of the fields of her existence, exploring the potential of pedagogical relations with family members and boyfriends. By performing the roles of both teacher and pupil Sherleen developed a disciplined relationship of self-with-self that helped her to concentrate on long-term goals. The technology of self that most characterises Stan's successive accounts is that of consumption. The privileging of the present, of pleasure, immediacy and freedom are all consistent with an ethic of consumption, as are the feelings of disappointment and dependency that follow. As a relationship of the self-with-the-self consumption has side effects, including what Bauman calls '"social deskilling", a neglect to learn the skills of discussing and negotiating the ways out of trouble with others' (Bauman and Tester, 2001: 114). Consumption is far from the only way of being and relating available to Stan, yet I suggest that the immediate gratification offered by consumption was particularly attractive to him in the light of his attempts to forge and give value to a kind of masculinity different from the corporate masculinity that seemed to be his destiny.

I have characterised the technology of self adopted by Karin as aesthetic. Her conclusion in her final interview, that she is 'not an artist', gives insights into the relationship of self-with-self that she had been pursuing. We can make sense of the ways in which she seeks to make visual and performative representations of herself to particular audiences by conceptualising her project as cultural producer. Central to this is a stylisation in which the self is 'performed' to others. As a technology of the self, this is highly individualised and, by definition, exposing, in that she is open to the evaluation of others. The way in which her biography unfolds suggests that, at this point of her life at least, an artistic technology of the self is not sustainable. It is interesting here to compare Karin's parodying of gender with that engaged with by Devon. While we might understand both as examples of 'camp', Karin is more isolated in her experiments, but also less vulnerable, in that she has more options available to her. The refusal of others to perform with her means that, within a wider context (such as that provided by the interview), her performances operate as forms of cultural distinction, marking how she is different from others (Bourdieu, 1986; Mock, 2003).

There are two moments in Devon's biography when we can see him engaging explicitly (and reflexively) with technologies of the self: his engagement in camp as part of the process of learning to be gay, and the process of acquiring the practices and identities of a manager. As a field of existence, the gay scene offers Devon new ways of envisaging himself, one of which is as a commodity within an erotic economy in which his youthfulness and looks are valuable resources. Experiencing himself as an object provides Devon with an empowerment that is also inflected with pathos, echoed in his acknowledgement that he is 'not the best looker in the bunch'. His repeated identification of himself as 'blond, blue eyed and gorgeous' can be seen as a serviceable identity that places him within the gay scene with access to new forms of solidarity available to him as a young, white working-class gay man. Over time he also explores the alternative subject position of the sexual agent and it is here that we see what he describes as 'knowledgism' coming into play. Not only does knowledge of the unwritten rules of the erotic economy of the scene enable him to shift subject positions, it also enables him to act as a teacher and guide to those who are new to the scene. His subsequent movement from punter to producer as he moves 'behind the scene' suggests that technologies of the self can provide stepping stones towards new identities and experiences. By his last interview he is able to engage with a relationship with himself that is predicated on a confident exercise of responsibility, something that he had previously shied away from. Here we see the significance of the interplay of fields of existence and technologies of the self, where forms of identity that are uninhabitable within hetero-normative spaces can be comfortable and accessible within a gay environment.

Investments and identifications

Each of these cases suggests that technologies of self are not simply chosen. There are processes involved that make some attractive and viable, and others difficult or impossible. It is here that notions of investment and identification become important. A number of scholars have looked to notions of investment in order to flesh out a conceptual framework in which individuals are understood as constituted in discourse (Hollway, 1984; Connell, 1995; Skeggs, 1997; Lucey and Reay, 2000; Walkerdine et al, 2002). Investment, it is argued, provides a means of understanding why particular subject positions may be taken up and defended rather than others. By and large, investments have been explained in psychological or psychic terms. Walkerdine and colleagues argue that an exploration of these more psychic aspects of identity is consistent with a Foucauldian approach to the social, suggesting that defences and fantasies are crucial in preventing spillage (or slippage) between the 'fictions' that are discursive subject positions (2002: 180). My interest here is to explore the potential to make sense of investments within both biographical and sociological terms. Individuals are connected, and they learn, as a result of their social locations, what kinds of investments are reasonable (if not rational) for them to make. There is not a simple relationship between making an investment and reaping a reward, as our energies 'may not always be captured by the category in which investments are made' (Skeggs, 1997: 101). The notion of investment is critical in making sense of why particular technologies of the self become central to young people's identities, pointing to the influence of less-conscious forms of subjectivity (and the search for what Bourdieu calls ontological complicity between habitus and field).

A focus on investments alerts us to the underlying contradictions and complementarities of a biography. Investments in one area may be associated with disinvestments in others (for example, the incompatibility that Devon experienced in his second interview between investing in career and in a gay identity). However, combinations of investment may also be complementary and mutually reinforcing (for example, Sherleen's investments in family and education). Investments may also complicate and undermine a project of self, as may be the case with the lack of critical reflection that Stan gives to 'settling down' and that Karin gives to motherhood. A focus on investments also sensitises us to the importance of what Skeggs calls 'disidentifications' and 'dissumulations' and what Butt and Landridge (2003) call 'disavowals'. These should not be seen simply in terms of absence, but can be understood as expressions of agency. Butt and Landridge describe this in terms of a 'refusal to achieve particular perception' (2003: 487) and Skeggs in terms of 'how the dialogical judgemental other is central to their productions' (1997: 13). It is tempting to see the disidentifications of both Karin and Devon with their fathers in this light. I hope that the case histories furnish the biographical detail that facilitate an understanding of why the young people are invested in particular identities. Although a structural account of the gender order may provide a sense of the way in which resources are distributed, it is only with a dynamic concept of investment that is biographically grounded that we are able to make sense of why people act as they do.

Spatial and social horizons

The conceptual tools – 'field of existence', 'technology of the self' and 'investment' – can be understood as providing a rubric for understanding the relationship between the self and its spatial and social horizon, or what McNay terms the positions and the possibilities that are available to the individual (2003: 144). I now want to explore how and where these horizons are drawn and the relationship between them. There has been a long-standing interest in the relationship between geographical and social mobility within sociology, and in particular the notion that working-class and rural young people may have to 'get out' in order to 'get on' (Jones, 1999; Jamieson, 2000; Lawler, 2000; Pilkington and Johnson, 2003). Commentators have begun to explore the powerful emotions that are part and parcel of such mobility, what Doreen Massey (1998) has called 'the politics of rejection', which may be experienced by young people in terms of 'conflicting feelings of longing, belonging and abhorrence' (Reay and Lucey, 2000). Mobility and 'a mobile being in the world' (Lash, 1994) are increasingly being looked to as an axis of inequality within a late-modern world (Bauman, 2000; Urry, 2000), with the categories of the cosmopolitan, the local, the exile and the tourist as reflecting positions within an economy of movement (Urry, 1995; Bauman, 1996; Hannerz, 1996). Feminist commentators such as Lisa Adkins (2002a), Beverley Skeggs (2004) and Doreen Massey (1993, 1994, 1998) have complicated this picture by pointing out that gender, sexuality and race play an important part in structuring the flows of these new forms of privilege.

In order to explore the interplay of spatial and social horizons, I will begin with Devon, whose spatial horizons I have characterised in terms of exclusion. Over the course of his interviews Devon was highly mobile, yet within a small geographical area of a single city. His movement between spaces was generally prompted by some form of exclusion. Some of these exclusions were beyond his control – for example, his departure from school, home, his neighbourhood, his flat and his job as a clerk. Others, such as his leaving a number of jobs, were the result of his own decisions. The spatial motif of insider/outsider becomes a creative element in his project of self as he learns to relish his sexual difference, having previously struggled with notions of perversion and normality. He rejected opportunities for social inclusion on a number of occasions, positively asserting boundaries between gay and straight worlds. By his last interview, some of these boundaries were beginning to dissolve, although we might see new boundaries being constructed between the roles of punter and producer.

In spatial terms, Devon's world is highly differentiated, yet in terms of social mobility it is relatively static. It was only in his last interview that Devon began to reflect on how his ambitions distinguished him from his parents. Up to this point, he rejected any consideration of career. Although he distanced himself from the radical version of living in the present that he associated with certain friends, he did not seek to occupy the future, concentrating on the immediate demands of each biographical compartment. His attention was absorbed with questions of how he might reconcile the 'normality' that he associates with family life with the life-style of an urban gay man. As these spatial boundaries began to break down, the potential of upward social mobility appears to form a new social horizon.

For Karin, geographical and social mobility are inextricably linked. She deliberately rejects the local (as defined in terms of religiously segregated neighbourhoods) in favour of spaces that are integrated and cosmopolitan. This strategy is fuelled by a project of upward social mobility that is predicated on an escape from her home town. Within her current horizons this movement is symbolised by university and the trajectories of her siblings before her, although her trip to India gave her a glimpse of a much larger canvas. I have characterised her spatial horizons in terms of exile, reflecting her highly ambivalent feelings about these different forms of mobility. On the one hand, she rejects any sense of belonging in her own home town and engages in practices that will propel her away. On the other hand, her final interview suggests that she remains deeply invested in a matriarchal family narrative of obligation, duty and place. Where Karin's spatial horizons are the product of her own choices and creativity, her social horizons are much more bound up with an intergenerational project of upward social mobility within which she is more an actor than an agent. This is a point that I will elaborate later in the final chapter.

A matriarchal and intergenerational project of social mobility also operates within Sherleen's family. However, their project of migration does not demand a physical or symbolic dispersal of the family. In contrast to Karin's and Devon's accounts, Sherleen presents a highly constrained spatial world confined primarily to school, college and home. Although Jamaica features as a real and imagined home, in practice the family operates within a small space within a city. Sherleen has no intention to leave home or to attend university in another town. Yet, at the same time, she also rejects the local, as represented by the neighbourhood. Like Karin, she recognises that for a working-class woman, an investment in neighbourhood can be inconsistent with social mobility. In her last interview we see Sherleen reworking the local into the space that exists around her extended family, and she is determined that the resources and obligations represented by the family will accompany her in a family project of achievement.

Stan is the only one of these four young people who seems to be facing the prospect of downward social mobility. In dropping out of higher education he must forge a much more individualised route to the kind of material success than has been mapped out for him. He identifies travel and an international worldview as part of the family resources on which he draws, and one of the experiments in masculinity that he engages with is that of the 'traveller' who harvests life experiences on his journeys. This vision bears similarities to Ulf Hannerz's definition of the cosmopolitan who is defined in opposition to the local and whose 'surrender to the alien culture implies personal autonomy *vis a vis* the culture where he originated. He has obvious competence with regard to it, but he can choose to disengage from it. He possesses it, it does not possess him' (Hannerz, 1996: 104). Yet Stan's confidence is fragile, and we see him move between investments in cosmopolitanism and a more local future. I would suggest that the relative instability of Stan's spatial horizons may in part be explained by the uncertainty of his social horizons. Although downward social mobility appears to be an increasingly common feature of middle-class cultures, with the extended dependency of young people and the evaporation of universal welfare (Attias-Dufont and Wolff, 2001; Dwyer et al, 2003), there are few comfortable narratives available for making sense of such experiences. His parents were socially mobile themselves, and continue to be geographically mobile still. It is not clear that Stan's fate is so closely tied to that of his family in the way that we see in some others of the case histories.

By exploring the mediums within and through which young people construct their projects of self it is possible to gain a sense of their very different and particular social locations. Gender, class, race, sexuality (and an articulation of these differences) frame the kinds of projects that are possible and desirable. Yet other dimensions of difference also become apparent, for example the shape of families, the position of children within these and changes in family dynamics over time and between generations. If we add to this the specificity of localities and the interplay between physical and social mobility over time, we begin to gain a sense of the range of coordinates that may be involved in mapping positions within a three-dimensional web of relationality. In order to map trajectories we also need to mobilise these coordinates within vectors of magnitude and direction, understanding personal and social change in terms of a reconfiguration of difference, interdependence and hierarchy (Irwin, 2003). Documenting and interrogating the concrete unfolding of a life provides a way into seeing the world in this kind of connected and dynamic way – using depth as a way into breadth.

Conclusion

This chapter has involved a conversation between the four case histories, exploring whether it is possible to generate higher-level interpretations and representations in which spatial and temporal dimensions are mutually constitutive. By alternating the direction of analysis, I capture the relationship between the individual and the social from different starting points. Privileging the temporal facilitates the identification of a range of biographical *methods* that characterise the four young people's projects of self: motifs; methods; impasses and magical solutions. Privileging the spatial by mapping the *mediums* through which these projects of self are realised enables an understanding of the interplay between fields of existence, technologies of self, investments/identifications, and the spatial and social horizons that frame biographies. By observing and plotting the narrative threads of unfolding biographies I hope to have demonstrated a distinctive approach to the study of youth transitions, one which articulates the relationship between personal and social change. In the final chapter I bring the methodological, empirical and theoretical threads of this book together in order to focus on the making and remaking of gender identities. I enquire whether the qualitative longitudinal method employed can provide new insights concerning the practice and meaning of reflexivity, and how this might contribute to a wider theoretical debate about the changing shape of gendered biographies and the transition to adulthood.

TEN

Youth, gender and change

The four case histories that lie at the heart of this book represent singular lives, formed through the articulation of social location through time, and in relationship with the lives of others. Each presents a different combination of gender identity, subjectivity, and social and cultural possibility – giving rise to distinct narrative themes. For example, in Sherleen's case history (Chapter Four) we see the importance of the intergenerational family in a project of upward social mobility. In Stan's case history (Chapter Five) we encounter how downward social mobility may be mediated through shifting masculinities. In Chapter Six, Devon's transition from a bullied teenager to a competent and confident gay man highlights the importance of boundary drawing to this process. In Chapter Seven we followed Karin's project of rebellion, within which the disruption of conventional gender identities is implicated in a wider family story of social class and migration. Each case history details the microprocesses of gender detraditionalisation, the ways in which young people construct their own gender projects over time, and how these are constrained by and disrupt wider formations of class, gender, sexuality and ethnicity. This has entailed exploring the operations of agency, the factors that contribute to the ability of young people to innovate in the construction of gendered identities, and the extent to which these innovations are recognised by others.

In this final chapter I ask some questions about the role of young people as agents of social change. In doing so I revisit the debates concerning the detraditionalisation of gender that I touched on in Chapter Three, in order to understand the different forms of innovation encountered in these four lives. I do this through a focus on reflexivity – a concept that appears to transcend the conceptual boundaries between the individual/social, temporal/spatial, public/private. In the final discussion of reflexivity and heresy I attempt to capture something of a four-dimensional sociology in which the young person and the social, the temporal and the spatial are all simultaneously in play.

Reflexivity?

Reflexivity plays a central role in theories of social change. It is argued that, in the move from fate to choice biographies, conscious reflection on previously unthought categories is the central mechanism through which detraditionalisation takes place (Beck, 1992). There are a number of ways in which such reflexivity can be imagined. Diane Reay cites Bourdieu's view that the 'practical analyst' is born when 'individuals situated at the point where contradictions in social structure are most apparent' 'practise a kind of self analysis' in order to survive (cited in Reay, 2002:225). Reay draws on this definition to explain the emotional intelligence of a young working-class man struggling to maintain his loyalties to his single mother and female teachers while also 'passing' within the demands of an anti-academic working-class masculinity. A complementary understanding of reflexivity is developed by Lois McNay (2000), who suggests that reflexivity arises from a lack of fit between habitus and social field. Thus, those who move regularly between social fields (and to some extent are excluded in this process) are likely to be reflexive in the sense that they have insights into a diversity of ways that knowledge, identity and authority are constructed. If detraditionalisation is understood in terms of a new relationship between authority and identity (Heelas et al, 1996), then reflexivity is the mechanism through which this relationship is mediated.

But more than acting as a mechanism of personal and social change, it has also been suggested that reflexivity is an axis of new forms of inequality. Lash, for example, talks in terms of 'reflexivity winners and losers' (Lash, 1994). Here we must distinguish two things – first, that reflexivity may be produced unevenly (ie only certain people and institutions are inspecting previously unthought categories), and second, that only certain kinds of reflexivity are recognised (Adkins, 2002a). This brings to the fore questions of authority – how and by whom particular performances are authorised as reflexive while others are not (Lovell, 2000; Adkins,2002b; Skeggs 2002). Rather than thinking in terms of the reflexive individual, we need to think about the meaning of reflexive performances in relation to particular social fields. It is here that the conceptual framework of Bourdieu is invaluable.

Identity, subjectivity and possibility

Bourdieu talks in terms of each social field having a range of pre-reflexive assumptions or doxa. Those power relations that conserve this status quo are termed 'orthodoxy' and those which subvert it are termed 'heresy', giving rise to heterodoxy (Bourdieu, 1977: 159). In considering the part (if any) played by reflexivity in the detraditionalisation of gender it is important to understand the extent to which individuals, in this case young people, intervene within wider power relations on the basis of their interrogation of taken-for-granted categories. But reflexivity cannot simply be the property of individuals or social fields; rather, it needs to be understood as produced in and by individuals in relation to changing social possibilities. If we elaborate on Harriet Bjerrum Nielsen and Monica Rudberg's (1994) contention that within any historical moment there will be a lack of fit or 'contemporaneity' between gender identity and subjectivity, it may be possible for us to understand the production of reflexivity as both indelibly individual and indexically situated. What then happens as a result of the insight that is produced by this lack of fit is another matter.

The case histories explore the relationship between gender identity (the kind of man or woman the young people want to be), gender subjectivity (their sense of 'me') and the material and social possibilities available to them. Each young person is uniquely situated in relation to the configuration of these three dimensions. For example, pursuing the gender identity of a successful and independent black woman demands that Sherleen acts in ways that are both consistent and inconsistent with her social location. This imagined identity is not simply at odds with her gender subjectivity but is wrapped up with an awareness of the frustrated ambitions of the women of her family, giving rise to an ironic interplay between her experiences of female solidarity and independence, and notions of dependence on and care for others. Sherleen neither desires nor presumes to fulfil her ambitions without her family's support, and thus notions of loyalty and belonging are central to her narrative.

It is not possible to prise apart the three dimensions of gender identity, subjectivity, and social and material possibilities as the model implicitly invites us to do. What is more productive, I suggest, is to see how Sherleen enacts her reflexivity and critical insights. Certain areas of her life appear to be out of the frame of critical reflection – in particular, the educational project itself and the burden of the intergenerational life project. Sherleen puts much critical energy into decoding the educational system, tensions between popularity and success, and the production of privilege. Yet hers is a bounded reflexivity, in her determined pursuit of success she does not (yet) challenge the authority that holds within the different social fields that she operates within. Rather than inciting heresy within the educational field, she seeks to make implicit rules explicit, so that as an outsider she may succeed within the rules of the game. As Heidi Mirza argues, 'what appears on the surface to be compliance and willingness to conform to systems and structures of educational meritocracy, [can] be redefined as strategic or as evidence of a covert social movement for change' (1997: 269).

This contrasts dramatically with Karin, for whom rebellion is a biographical motif. Her accounts are oriented towards the identification and disavowal of authority. This is most obvious in relation to education (although she does what is necessary in order not to fail), and in the way she orients herself towards the gender politics that frame her leisure activities. What is striking about Karin's account is the way in which her heresies give rise to a response that could be characterised as a defence of orthodoxy by the dominant agents within the field (Bourdieu, 1977: 191; May, 1996: 130). I suggest that the trouble that arises for Karin within her friendship groups and her subsequent struggles to control her reputation are responses to her transgression of codes of acceptably feminine behaviour. Yet we can also see a more subtle version of the same dynamic in her eventual acceptance of educational authority and the revision of her ambitions in line with the individualised learning demanded by the college environment.

Again, it is worth thinking of Karin within the three-dimensional model of identity, subjectivity and possibility. As for Sherleen, social mobility provides an important subtext for her story and brings with it dissonance between a gender subjectivity produced within a working-class family and a gender identity that is colonising a middle-class future. The social and material possibilities that constitute the backdrop for this drama are expansive in that Karin deliberately seeks out new (and relatively public) arenas through which to project her identity. But before we locate Karin on the vanguard of detraditionalisation we should also note that these investments are paralleled by the evacuation of other potential arenas of identity work, such as the neighbourhood and the family. If we compare Sherleen and Karin in terms of reflexivity, we might suggest that the source of their reflexivity is similar (a lack of fit between gender identity, subjectivity and possibility), yet the relative public or private character of the expression of such reflexivity is significant – not least in terms of the extent to which they are disciplined for their actions. Moreover, their social locations are crucial in framing their reflexive dispositions and thus explaining an engagement in explicit rebellion by one and in self-improvement by the other.

Although Karin is critical of almost everything, her relationship with her mother appears to be exempt from reflexive interrogation in such a way as to suggest the significance of emotional investments. Sherleen's relationship with her mother displays similar kinds of moral density and contradiction. In both cases their attempts to explore and question these relationships appear to give rise to displacements, mediated through relationships with men and expressed in intergenerational terms. One way of explaining this ambiguity is through the observation that women are simultaneously both objects and subjects within the gender order, being the bearers of gender identity for others (their families and partners) as well as agents of their own. Dorothy Smith (1990: 198) describes this in terms of the 'double subject', where women are simultaneously constituted as a 'subject-in-discourse' (appearing passive and awaiting definition) and a 'subject-at-work' (active, competent and situated). Terry Lovell writes about the same duality employing theoretical tools derived from Bourdieu, describing women both as objects – 'repositories of capital for someone else' (2000: 22) – and as 'capital-accumulating subjects' in their own right (2000: 22).

Tensions arising from this duality can be seen to characterise the accounts of both young women, particularly in relation to their obligations towards their families. If we want to think in terms of reflexivity it becomes important to think about whether and how this duality may restrict and complicate the extent to which gender identity may be seen to be the property of the young person and open to negotiation. For both young women, the biographical impasses identified in the first part of this chapter may be understood as shaped in part by these intergenerational family dynamics, and the unfinished work and desires of earlier generations (Scott and Scott, 2001).

Turning to the cases of the two young men, it is important to ask whether a similar duality can be seen to be in operation. On the one hand, it is clear that elements of their gender subjectivities and identities are rooted within the culture of their families. For example, the most powerful elements of hetero–normativity identified by Devon relate to his experience of family life. He is acutely aware of the ways in which he may have disappointed his father, and judges the normality of his own life in relation to familiar domestic practices. Likewise, Stan draws heavily on family resources and narratives in the process of exploring alternative masculine identities. Both are critical of their fathers (as are Karin and Sherleen) and supportive of their mothers. However, as I will discuss later, it may be the case that these identifications with family bring with them fewer obligations than for the two young women.

Sexuality and social class distinguish these two young men's projects of self in obvious ways, which are consequential for the production of reflexivity. In early interviews there is a sense in which Devon is forced into a reflexive stance by the impossibility of occupying the gender and class habitus of his father. The disjunction between his gender subjectivity and identity lies primarily in the absence of social and cultural possibilities for him to be an 'out' gay man within his community of origin. On the one hand, this is something that is outside his control as he begins to negotiate the pathologised subject position of the pervert. Yet Devon disassociates himself from his father's 'failed' masculinity, constructed in terms of his ability to support his family. By his last interview there is a sense in which Devon has succeeded in recolonising aspects of the working-class masculinity that he had previously evacuated, through his experience as a competent worker.

It is interesting, then, to explore the uses to which Devon puts the reflexivity that is produced in response to his experiences of exclusion. Initially he operates almost entirely within a hetero-normative world, the exceptions to this being the lesbian and gay youth club and his forays into the commercial gay scene. Over time he is able to build up a parallel universe in which he can operate as an insider. The relocation of both work and home within a gay universe may be better described in terms of an escape from rather than a transcendence of hetero-normativity. If we remember, Devon turned down an offer to be 'out' in a straight workplace. In particular he is careful not to challenge the authority of the straight workplace, expressing his agency in terms of withdrawal (walking out) or the private enjoyment of dissonance.

Devon's response to the experience of exclusion has consistently been to pursue inclusion. Making gender trouble is not his style. In some ways we could see his case history as resembling that of Sherleen, both of whom employ the considerable insights produced by their outsider status in order to forge progressive and safe trajectories into the future. The costs involved are already high, without seeking out battles that they may not be able to win or even survive. Although this strategy has some resemblance to the notions of 'passing' that have so interested those concerned with the performance and parody of identity (Butler, 1990; Lovell, 2000), both young people maintain a strong allegiance to core dimensions of their identities as gay or black and working class. It is not clear that either Devon or Sherleen want their reflexivity to be recognised by a wider audience (with the important exception of the interviewer), seeing it as a necessary resource rather than a personal style.

Stan is very different in this respect. In dropping out of school he engages in extensive criticism of a form of corporate masculinity. If we accept that Stan is positioned within a particular social and historical moment in which the reproduction of white middle-class privilege is far from assured, we can understand his experiments in gender identity as part of a defence of class privilege. So, although Stan is critical of the deferred gratification and rational disembodiment demanded by pursuit of a professional future, he does not question the hetero-normative assumptions of marriage and a gendered division of labour that underpin it. What is most interesting about Stan's case is the lack of an assured alternative to corporate masculinity. Thus, we see him move between a range of masculine gender identities, including the playboy, the traditional artisan and the charismatic leader.

In many ways Stan provides an apt illustration of the middle-class individualised risk biography described by Beck and others (for youth versions see Du Bois-Reymond, 1998). But although the openness of Stan's biographies gives rise to considerable biographical work, anxiety and what Giddens would see as reflexivity (life planning and risk assessment), it does not, at this point, give rise to any sustained critical engagement with the politics of gender. Although he wants to be a new kind of man, he also expects to be his own man – the breadwinner and a traditional husband and father. In this sense we can think of him as being detraditionalised without being detraditional, similarly to the way that it is possible to be queered without being queer (Mock, 2003), and different while being conformist (Miles, 2000). It is a distinction that brings us back to Lisa Adkins' discussion of the kinds of reflexivity that are rewarded within contemporary cultural economies. Stan presents a reflexive gender identity that explicitly signals the kind of man he want to be – sophisticated, mobile, ironic, spontaneous. This is a gender identity that is consistent with the social and cultural possibilities of his middle-class milieu. Yet it is a stylised identity that is relatively disconnected from a gender subjectivity predicated on traditional and relatively uninspected assumptions of privilege.

Tradition?

Tradition is a seductive term, speaking both to the temporal order (relationships between phenomena over time) and the structural order (relationships between phenomena across social and physical space) (Thompson, 1996). There is a danger in confusing the objects of tradition for the relationships which they denote. The process of detraditionalisation does not concern the disappearance of particular acts or practices; rather, it concerns the loss of authority in relation to these phenomena (Rose, 1996). For example, it is not that people are no longer marrying, it is just that marriage no longer means what it once did. If detraditionalisation is primarily about changes in the constitution and operation of authority, then it makes sense that our attention shifts from what young people do towards how they are received, recognised and authorised (Thomson, 2000).

This book is an empirical exemplar of what such debates may mean in the context of young people's lives. The question, then, is less one of whether these individuals are sufficiently reflexive, iconoclastic or heretical, and more one of who and what are the audiences for these performances? How are judgements made? Can judgements be disputed and what does solidarity mean in this context? This is the politics of recognition and resources described so well by Ken Plummer (1995), who suggests that, for a new story to be successful, we must be able to imagine and articulate it. To do this we need to be able to form identities that enable us to become storytellers. For a story to be told, it must be heard, and the vital fourth criterion is the existence of communities of support who will form the audience for the story.

A focus on the detraditionalisation of gender also brings with it a moral subtext in which certain practices are coded as progressive and others as defensive or even retrogressive. It is a moral subtext that characterises many contemporary debates in the arena of identity. For example, debates rage over what it is that distinguishes identities that are sufficiently 'queer', 'parodic' or 'detraditionalised' from those dismissed as 'essentialist', 'immanent' and thus politically regressive or ineffectual. These case histories show that there is no simple distinction between tradition and innovation, especially when we look at young lives. Teenage identities are, by definition, 'improvised', and flux and contradiction are expected and indulged.

Lois McNay has argued that one of the consequences of an overly spatialised understanding of identity is the idea that disruption can only come from outside the norm. By documenting the active dimensions of subject formation that McNay encourages, it is possible to see 'how the inculcation of norms is always partially transcended in the process of living through of those norms' (2003: 143). One of the lessons of this research is that tradition is a situated concept, implicated in classed, sexualised and racialised cultures. What may look like innovation may in fact be the transposition of tradition into a new historical and social context. What looks like tradition may in fact be forging new ground (Comaroff and Comaroff, 1992). In the same way that we need to be careful to observe distinctions between being and doing reflexivity, we need to distinguish between the absence of tradition and being *detraditionalised*, in the form of a style that may be cultivated and performed.

In reviewing these young people's cases through the lens of reflexivity I have not wanted to place them within a hierarchy of more or less 'detraditionalised' gender identities, but it is difficult to escape doing so, as notions of progress and decline are so implicated in theories of late modernity and in feminist perspectives on gender identity (McLeod and Thomson, 2009). Placing these four case histories into conversation has demanded that I ask rather different questions of the data, along the lines of 'how do they do it?' and 'what might the consequences be?' These are questions that are suited to the generative framework that 'must be conceptualised in order to explain how, when faced with complexity and difference, individuals may respond in unexpected and innovative ways that may hinder, reinforce or catalyse social change' (McNay, 2003: 141).

Unfolding lives

Most research on young people collects data in relation to policy-relevant subject areas, comparing young people in the ways in which they encounter education, work, family life and leisure. Such approaches tend to find some individuals wanting while others successfully occupy the subject positions made available within this arena. The danger is that such an approach leads to a deficit model in which some are seen to make less of an investment than others. This form of problematisation can be offset by a recognition of the very different resources that young people have to draw on, thereby forging a relationship between resources and resourcefulness, and this is something that my colleagues and I have sought to do in the wider study of which these data form a part (for example Thomson et al, 2002; Henderson et al, 2007).

The kind of in-depth case histories that are showcased in this book have a part to play in understanding youth transitions. By forging a holistic model of the fields of existence for an individual, in which investments can be understood in response to competence and recognition, I hope to have found a way of representing an equality of potential between individuals. How time, energy and investments are then divided up is a matter of biography and circumstance. All are equally resourceful. The task is not to *explain* how the young person is both the product and maker of their social location; rather, it is to *understand* how their resourcefulness plays out, and what the consequences are. This is a subtle but important distinction in a policy and research agenda in which the understandings of inequality are increasingly individualised through notions of risk and resilience. A concern with recognition has the potential to reorient attention from the individual young person towards the institutions, groups and regimes of knowledge that frame their practice.

This book has also been a demonstration of a method-in-practice, documenting a way of analysing and representing qualitative longitudinal data. In situating this approach in relation to biographical and life-history methods, I also hope to forge links between methodological literatures. While life-history research has been concerned with temporality, most of this work generates retrospective understandings. The introduction of a prospective view to life history marks an important new development. Qualitative longitudinal research has enormous potential for the generation of useful and policy/practice-relevant knowledge. It does this by foregrounding complexity, drawing attention to the importance of narrative coherence, timing and consequentiality. Yet, in revealing it also obscures, privileging self-narratives over the kinds of collective improvisations that are made visible through ethnography. Yet longitudinal approaches have the potential to facilitate a 'long view' which is humanising of research subjects, encouraging understanding and recognition of the integrity of young lives. In this respect, longitudinal methods have the potential to disrupt the search for biographical typologies that characterises much youth research. Whether policy makers are prepared to wait for results, or are content with the privileging of depth over breadth is another matter. What does seem to be the case is that practitioners respond well to this kind of material, recognising that which many already know, but which has been squeezed out of the new managerialism and 'what works' cultures of many of the services working with young people (Thomson, 2003).

The case history data sets

Sherleen

Research wave	Date of interview	Age at interview	Time elapse
Focus group	1997	12	
Interview 1	May 1998	13	
Interview 2 (lifeline)	July 1999	14	14 months
Interview 3 (memory book)	April 2000	15	8 months
Interview 4 (lifeline)	March 2001	16	11 months
Interview 5*	December 2002	17	20 months

Stan

Research wave	Date of interview	Age at interview	Time elapse
Focus group	November 1997	16	
Interview 1 (lifeline)	June 1999	18	20 months
Interview 2 (memory book)	April 2000	19	10 months
Interview 3 (lifeline)	February 2001	20	10 months

Devon

Research wave	Date of interview	Age at interview	Time elapse
Focus group	July 1997	17	
Interview 1** (lifeline)	January 1999	18	18 months
Interview 2 (memory book)	March 2000	19	14 months
Interview 3 (lifeline)	November 2001	21	20 months
Interview 4*	February 2003	23	15 months

Karin

Research wave	Date of interview	Age at interview	Time elapse
Focus group	January 1998	14	
Pair interview	May 1998	14	4 months
Interview 1 (lifeline)	August 1999	16	14 months
Interview 2 (memory book)	March 2000	17	8.5 months
Interview 3 (lifeline)	May 2001	18	14 months
Interview 4	March 2003	19	21 months

Notes: * Interviews conducted after the case histories were written, and considered in Chapter Eight.

** Interview 1 took place over two dates one week apart. The first interview focused primarily on the main interview schedule and the second on the lifeline exercise.

References

Aapola, S., Gonick, M. and Harris, A. (2001) 'Between girl power and reviving Ophelia: girls, femininity and agency', paper presented at 'A new girl order: young women and the future of feminist enquiry', Kings College London, 14–16 November.

Aapola, S., Gonick, M. and Harris, A.(2004) *Young femininity: girlhood, power and social change*, Houndmills and New York: Palgrave.

Adkins, L. (1998) 'Feminist theory and economic change', in S. Jackson and J. Jones (eds) *Contemporary feminist theories*, Edinburgh: Edinburgh University Press, pp 34–49.

Adkins, L. (2002a) *Revisions: gender and sexuality in late modernity*, Buckingham: Open University Press.

Adkins, L. (2002b) 'Reflexivity and the politics of qualitative research: who speaks for whom, why, how and when?', in T. May (ed) *Qualitative research in action*, London: Sage, pp 332–48.

Adkins, L. (2003) 'Reflexivity: freedom or habit of gender', *Theory, Culture and Society*, vol 20, no 6, pp 21–42.

Adkins, L. (2005) 'Social capital: the anatomy of a troubled concept', *Feminist Theory*, vol 6, no 2, pp 195–211.

Alexander, C. (2000) *The Asian gang*, Oxford: Berg.

Archer, M. (2007) *Making our way in the world: human reflexivity and social mobility*, Cambridge: Cambridge University Press.

Attias-Donfut, C. and Wolff, F. (2001) 'La dimension subjective de la mobilité sociale', *Population*, vol 56, no 6, pp 919–58.

Back, L. (1996) *New ethnicities and urban culture: racism and multiculture in young lives*, London: UCL Press.

Bauman, Z. (1996) 'From pilgrim to tourist – or a short history of identity', in S. Hall and P. du Gay (eds) *Questions of cultural identity*, London: Sage, pp 18–36.

Bauman, Z. (2000) *Liquid modernity*, Cambridge: Polity Press.

Bauman, Z. and Tester, K. (2001) *Conversations with Zygmunt Bauman*, Cambridge: Polity Press.

Baumberger, J. and Richards, A. (2000) *Manifesta: young women, feminism and the future*, New York: Farrar, Strauss and Giroux.

Bech, H. (1999) 'Commentaries on Seidman, Meeks and Traschen: "Beyond the closet"', *Sexualities*, vol 2, no 1, pp 343–9.

Beck, U. (1992) *Risk society: towards a new modernity*, London: Sage.

Beck, U. and Beck-Gernsheim, E. (1995) *The normal chaos of love*, Cambridge: Polity Press.

Bell, D. (1995) 'Pleasure and danger: the paradoxical spaces of sexual citizenship', *Political Geography*, 14 (2):139-53.

Bertaux, D. (1981) 'From the life-history approach to the transformation of sociological practice', in Bertaux, D. (ed) *Biography and society: the life history approach in the social sciences*, London: Sage, pp 29–45.

Bertaux, D. and Bertaux-Wiame, I. (1997/2003), 'Heritage and its lineage: a case history of transmission and social mobility over five generations', in D. Bertaux and P.Thompson (eds) *Pathways to social class: a qualitative approach to social mobility*, Oxford: Clarendon Press, pp 62–97.

Bertaux, D. and Delacroix, C. (2000) 'Case histories of families and social processes: enriching sociology', in P. Chamberlayne, J. Bornat and T.Wengraf (eds) *The turn to biographical methods in the social sciences: comparative issues and examples*, London: Routledge, pp 71–89.

Bertaux, D. and Thompson, P. (eds) (1997) *Pathways to social class: a qualitative approach to social mobility*, Oxford: Clarendon Press.

Bjerrum Nielsen, H. (1996) 'The magic writing pad – on gender and identity', *Young: Journal of Nordic Youth Research*, vol 4, no 3, pp 2–18.

Bjerrum Nielsen, H. and Rudberg, M. (1994) *Psychological gender and modernity*, Oslo: Scandinavian University Press.

Bjerrum Nieslen, H. and Rudberg, M. (2000) 'Gender, love and education in three generations: the way out and up', *The European Journal of Women's Studies*, vol 7, no 4, pp 423–53.

Blasius, M. (1995) *Gay and lesbian politics: sexuality and the emergence of a new ethics*, Philadelphia: Temple University Press.

Bourdieu, P. (1977) *Outline of a theory of practice*, Cambridge: Cambridge University Press.

Bourdieu, P. (1986) *Distinction: a social critique of the judgement of taste*, London: Routledge.

Bourdieu, P. (1999) 'Understanding', in P. Bourdieu et al *The weight of the world: social suffering in contemporary society*, Cambridge: Polity Press, pp 607–26.

Brannen, J. and Nilsen, A. (2002) 'Young people's time perspectives: from youth to adulthood', *Sociology*, vol 36, no 3, pp 513–37.

Brannen, J., Lewis, A. Nilsen, A. and Smithson, J. (eds) (2002) *Young Europeans, work and family: futures in transition*, London: Routledge.

Bruner, J. (1986) *Actual minds, possible worlds*, Cambridge, MA: Harvard University Press.

Bruner, J. (1987) 'Life as narrative', *Social Research*, vol 54, no 1, pp 11–52.

Butler, J. (1990) *Gender trouble: feminism and the subversion of identity*, London: Routledge.

Butt, T. and Langdridge, D. (2003) 'The construction of self: the public reach into the private sphere', *Sociology*, vol 37 no 3, pp 477–93.

Bynner, J. (2001) 'British youth transitions in comparative context', *Journal of Youth Studies*, vol 4, no 1, pp 5–24.

Byrne, B. (2003) 'Reciting the self: narrative representations of the self in qualitative interviews', *Feminist Theory*, vol 4, no 1, pp 29–49.

Chamberlayne, P., Bornat, J. and Wengraf, T. (eds) (2000) *The turn to biographical methods in the social sciences: comparative issues and examples*, London: Routledge.

Chisholm, L., Buchner, P., Kruger. H. and Brown, P. (eds) (1990) *Childhood, youth and social change: a comparative perspective*, London: Falmer.

Clifford, J. and Marcus, G. (1986) *Writing culture: the poetics and politics of ethnography*, Berkeley, CA: University of California Press.

Coffey, A. (2002) 'Ethnography and self: reflections and representations', in T. May (ed) *Qualitative research in action*, London: Sage.

Cohen, P. (1972) 'Subcultural conflict and working-class community', in *Working Papers in Cultural Studies*, vol 2, Spring, pp 5–52, reprinted in abridged form in S. Hall, D. Hobson, A. Lowe and P. Willis (eds) (1980) *Culture, media, language*, London: Hutchinson.

Cohen, P. and Ainley, P. (2000) 'In the court of the blind? Youth and cultural studies in Britain', *Journal of Youth Studies*, vol 3, no 1, pp 79–95.

Comaroff, J. and Comaroff, J. (1992) *Ethnography and the historical imagination*, Boulder, CO: Westview Press.

Connell, R.W. (1987) *Gender and power*, Cambridge: Polity Press.

Connell, R.W. (1995) *Masculinities*, Cambridge: Polity Press.

Connolly, P. (1998) *Racism, gender identities and young children*, London: Routledge

Corden, A. and Millar, J. (2007) 'Time and change: a review of the qualitative longitudinal research literature for social policy', *Social Policy and Society*, vol 6, no 4, pp 583–92.

Crompton, R. (1992) '"Where did all the bright girls go?" Women and higher education and employment since 1964', in N. Abercrombie and A. Warde (eds) *Social change in contemporary Britain*, Cambridge: Polity Press, pp 57–9.

Crompton, R. (1997) *Women and work in modern Britain*, Oxford: Oxford University Press.

Davies, C.A. (2008) *Reflexive ethnography: a guide to researching selves and others* (2nd edn), London: Routledge.

Du Bois-Reymond, M. (1998) '"I don't want to commit myself yet": young people's life concepts', *Journal of Youth Studies*, vol 1, no 1, pp 63–79.

Dwyer, P. and Wyn, J. (2003) *Youth, education and risk: facing the future*, London: Routledge.

Dwyer, P., Smith, G., Tyler, D. and Wyn, J. (2003) *Life-patterns, career outcomes and adult choices*, Research Report 23, Youth Research Centre, University of Melbourne.

Egerton, M. and Savage, M. (2000) 'Age stratification and class formation: a longitudinal study of the social mobility of young men and women, 1971–1991', *Work, Employment and Society*, vol 14, no 1, pp 3–49.

Elliott, J., Holland, J. and Thomson, R. (2007) 'Qualitative and quantitative longitudinal research', in L. Bickman, J. Brannen and P. Alasuutari (eds) *Handbook of social research methods*, London/Thousand Oaks: Sage, pp 228–48.

Fahey, T. (1995) 'Privacy and the family: conceptual and empirical reflections', *Sociology*, vol 29, no 4, pp 687–703.

Ferri, E. and Smith, K. (2003) 'Partnership and parenthood', in E. Ferri, J. Bynner and M. Wadsworth (eds) *Changing Britain, changing lives: three generations at the turn of the century*, London: Institute of Education, pp 133–47.

Finnegan, R. (1997) 'Storying the self: personal narrative and identity', in H. MacKay (ed) *Consumption and everyday life*, London: Sage, pp 65–112.

Foucault, M. (1994) 'The ethic of care for the self as a practice of freedom: an interview with Michel Foucault on January 20, 1984', in J. Bernauer and D. Rasmussen (eds) *The final Foucault*, Cambridge MA: MIT Press, pp 1–20.

Frith, H. (2001) 'Young women, feminism and the future: dialogues and discoveries', *Feminism and Psychology*, vol 11, no 2, pp 147–51.

Frosh, S., Phoenix, A. and Pattman, R. (2002) *Young masculinities*, Basingstoke: Palgrave.

Fuller, M. (1982) 'Young, female and black', in E. Cashmore and B. Troyna (eds) *Black youth in crisis*, London: George Allen and Unwin, pp 142–58.

Furlong, A. and Cartmel, F. (1997/2006) *Young people and social change: individualization and risk in late modernity*, Buckingham: Open University Press.

Geertz, C. (1973) *The interpretation of cultures*, New York: Basic Books.

Giddens, A. (1991) *Modernity and self identity: self and society in the late modern age*, Cambridge: Polity Press.

Giddens, A. (1992) *The transformation of intimacy: sexuality, love and eroticism in modern societies*, Cambridge: Polity Press.

Giddens, A. (1994) 'Living in a post-traditional society', in U. Beck, A. Giddens and S. Lash (eds) *Reflexive modernization: politics, tradition and aesthetics in the modern social order*, Cambridge: Polity Press, pp 56–109.

Giele, J. and Elder, G. (eds) (1998) *Methods of life course research: qualitative and quantitative approaches*, London: Sage.

Gordon, D. and Kay, K. (1993) 'Look back/talk back', in P. Church Gibson and R. Gibson (eds) *Dirty looks: women, pornography, power*, London: British Film Institute, pp 90–100.

Halberstam, J. (1998) *Female masculinity*, London: Routledge.

Hall, K. (1995) 'There's a time to act British and a time to act Indian: the politics of identity among British-Sikh teenagers', in S. Stephens (ed) *Children and the politics of culture*, Chichester: Princeton University Press, pp 243–64.

Hannerz, U. (1996) *Transnational connections: cultures, people, places*, London: Routledge.

Heaphy, B. (2007) *Late modernity and social change: reconstructing social and personal life*, London: Routledge.

Hearn, J. and Morgan, D. (1990) *Men, masculinity and social theory*, London: Unwin Hyman.

Heath, S. and Cleaver, E. (2003) *Young, free and single: twenty-somethings and household change*, Basingstoke: Palgrave.

Heelas, P. (1996) 'On things not being worse and the ethic of humanity', in P. Heelas, S. Lash and P. Morris (eds) *Detraditionalization*, Oxford: Blackwell, pp 200–22.

Heelas, P., Lash, S. and Morris, P. (eds) (1996) *Detraditionalization*, Oxford: Blackwell.

Henderson, S. (2005) 'Sticks and smoke: growing up with a sense of the city in the countryside', *Young: Nordic Journal of Youth Research*, vol 13, no 4, pp 3–20.

Henderson, S., Holland, J. and Thomson, R. (2006) 'Making the long view: perspectives on context from a qualitative longitudinal (QL) study', *Methodological Innovations Online*, vol 1, no 2.

Henderson, S., Taylor, R. and Thomson, R. (2003) 'In touch: young people, communication and technologies', *Information, Communication and Society*, vol 5, no 4, pp 494–512.

Henderson, S., Holland, J., McGrellis, S., Sharpe, S. and Thomson, R. (2007) *Inventing adulthoods: a biographical approach to youth transitions*, London: Sage.

Hennessy, R. (1995) 'Queer visibility in commodity culture', in L. Nicholson and S. Seidman (eds) *Postmodernism: beyond identity politics*, Cambridge: Cambridge University Press, pp 142–85.

Holdsworth, C. (2004) 'Family support and the transition out of parental home in Britain, Spain and Norway', *Sociology*, vol 38, no 5, pp 909–26.

Holdsworth, C. and Morgan, D.H.J. (2005) *Transitions in context: leaving home, independence and adulthood*, Open University Press at McGraw Hill, Maidenhead.

Holland, J. and Thomson, R. (2009) 'Gaining a perspective on choice and fate: revisiting critical moments', *European Societies*, vol 11, no 3, pp 1–19.

Holland, J., Ramazanoglu, C. and Sharpe, S. (1993) *Wimp or gladiator: contradictions in acquiring masculine sexuality*, WRAP paper 9, London: The Tufnell Press.

Holland, J., Ramazanoglu, C., Sharpe, S. and Thomson, R. (1998, 2nd edn 2004) *The male in the head: young people, heterosexuality and power*, London: The Tufnell Press.

Hollands, R. (1995) *Friday night, Saturday night: youth cultural identification in the post industrial city*, Newcastle upon Tyne: University of Newcastle upon Tyne.

Hollway, W. (1984) 'Gender difference and the production of subjectivity', in J. Henriques, W. Hollway, C. Urwin, C. Venn and V. Walkerdine (eds) *Changing the subject: psychology, social regulation and subjectivity*, London: Methuen, pp 227–63.

Hollway, W. and Jefferson, T. (2000) 'Biography, anxiety and the experience of locality', in P. Chamberlayne, J. Bornat and T. Wengraf (eds) *The turn to biographical methods in the social sciences: comparative issues and examples*, London: Routledge, pp 167–80.

Hollway, W. and Jefferson, T. (2001) *Doing qualitative research differently*, London: Sage.

hooks, b. (1981) *Ain't I a woman: Black women and feminism*, Boston: South End Press.

Hubbard, P. (2001) 'Sex zones: intimacy, citizenship and public space', *Sexualities*, vol 4, no 1, pp 51–71.

Irwin, S. (2003) 'Interdependencies, values and the reshaping of difference: gender and generation at the birth of twentieth century modernity', *British Journal of Sociology*, vol 1, no 54, pp 565–84.

Irwin, S. and Bottero, W. (2000) 'Market returns? Gender and theories of change in employment relations', *The British Journal of Sociology*, vol 51, no 2, pp 261–80.

Jackson, S. (1999) *Heterosexuality in question*, London: Sage.

Jamieson, L. (1998) *Intimacy: personal relationships in modern societies*, Cambridge: Polity Press.

Jamieson, L. (1999) 'Intimacy transformed? A critical look at the "pure relationship"', *Sociology*, vol 33, no 3, pp 477–94.

Jamieson, L. (2000) 'Migration, place and class: youth in a rural area', *Sociological Review*, vol 48, no 2, pp 203–23.

Jones, G. (1999) 'Trail-blazers and path-followers: social reproduction and geographical mobility in youth', in S. Arber and C. Attias-Dufont (eds) *Changing generational contracts*, London: Routledge, pp 154–73.

Jones, G. and Martin, C. (1999) 'The young consumer at home: dependence, resistance and autonomy', in J. Hearn and S. Roseneil (eds) *Consuming cultures: power and resistance*, London: Macmillan, pp 17–41.

Jones, G., O'Sullivan, A. and Rouse, J. (2006) 'Young adults, partners and parents: individual agency and problems of support', *Journal of Youth Studies*, vol 9, no 4, pp 375–92.

Kehily, M.J. (2007) *Understanding youth: perspectives, identities and practices*, London: Sage.

Kiernan, K. (1997) 'Becoming a young parent: a longitudinal study of associated factors', *British Journal of Sociology*, vol 48, no 3, pp 406–8.

Kemper, R. and Peterson Royce, A. (eds) (2002) *Chronicling cultures: long term field research in anthropology*, Walnut Creek, CA: Altamira Press.

Kuhn, A. (2002) *Family secrets: acts of memory and imagination*, London: Verso.

Lasch, C. (1980) *The cult of narcissism*, London: The Abacus Press.

Lash, S. (1994) 'Reflexivity and its doubles: structure, aesthetics, community', in U. Beck, A. Giddens and S. Lash (eds) *Reflexive modernization: politics, tradition and aesthetics in the modern social order*, Cambridge: Polity Press, pp 110–73.

Law, J. (2004) *After method: mess in social science research*. London: Routledge.

Lawler, S. (2000) *Mothering the self: mothers, daughters, subjects*, London: Routledge.

Lawler, S. (2002) 'Narrative in social research', in T. May (ed) *Qualitative research in action*, London: Sage, pp 242–58.

Lawler, S. (2008) *Identity: sociological perspectives*, Cambridge: Polity Press.

Leonard, D. and Delphy, C. (1992) *Familiar exploitation: a new analysis of marriage in contemporary western societies*, Cambridge: Polity Press.

Lovell, T. (2000) 'Thinking feminism with and against Bourdieu', *Feminist Theory*, vol 1, no 1, pp 11–32.

Lovell, T. (2003) 'Resisting with authority: historical specificity, agency and the performative self', *Theory, Culture and Society*, vol 20, no 1, pp 1–17.

Lucey, H. and Reay, D. (2000) 'Social class and the psyche', *Soundings: A Journal of Politics and Culture*, vol 15, May, pp 139–54.

Lury, C. (1998) *Prosthetic culture: photography, memory and identity*, London: Routledge.

McDonald, K. (1999) *Struggles for subjectivity: identity, action and youth experience*, Cambridge: Cambridge University Press.

McDowell, L. (1997) *Capital culture: gender at work in the city*, Oxford: Blackwell.

McGrellis, S. (2005a) 'Pure and bitter spaces: gender, identity and territory in Northern Irish youth transitions', *Gender and Education*, vol 17, no 5, pp 515–29.

McGrellis, S. (2005b) 'Pushing the boundaries in Northern Ireland: young people, violence and sectarianism', *Contemporary Politics*, vol 11, no 1, pp 53–71.

McLeod, J. (2000a) 'Metaphors of the self: searching for young people's identity through interviews', in J. McLeod and K. Malone (eds) *Researching youth*, Hobart: Australian Clearing House for Youth Studies, pp 45–58.

McLeod, J. (2000b) 'Subjectivity and schooling in a longitudinal study of secondary students', *British Journal of Sociology of Education*, vol 21, no 4, pp 501–21.

McLeod, J. (2003) 'Why we interview now – reflexivity and perspective in a longitudinal study', *International Journal of Social Research Methodology*, vol 6, no 3, pp 201–12.

McLeod, J. and Thomson, R. (2009) *Researching social change: qualitative approaches*, London: Sage.

McLeod, J. and Yates, L. (2006) *Making modern lives: subjectivity, schooling and social change*. Albany, NY: State University of New York Press.

MacNamee, S., Valentine, G., Skelton, C. and Butler, R. (2003) 'Negotiating difference: lesbian and gay transitions to adulthood', in G. Allan and G. Jones (eds) *Social relations and the lifecourse*, Basingstoke: Palgrave, pp 120–34.

McNay, L. (1992) *Foucault and feminism: power, gender and self*, Cambridge: Polity Press.

McNay, L. (1999) 'Gender, habitus and the field: Pierre Bourdieu and the limits of reflexivity', *Theory, Culture and Society*, vol 16, no 1, pp 95–117.

McNay, L. (2000) *Gender and agency: reconfiguring the subject in feminist and social theory*, Cambridge: Polity Press.

McNay, L. (2003) 'Agency, anticipation and indeterminancy in feminist theory', *Feminist Theory*, vol 4, no 2, pp 139–48.

McRobbie, A. (2001) 'Good girls, bad girls, female success and the new meritocracy', keynote address, 'A new girl order: young women and the future of feminist enquiry', Kings College London, 14–16 November.

McRobbie, A. (2004) 'Notes on postfeminism and popular culture: Bridget Jones and the new gender regime', in A. Harris (ed) *All about the girl: culture, power and identity*, London: Routledge, pp 3–14.

Mannheim, K. (1952) 'The problem of generations', in P. Kecskemeti (ed) *Essays on the sociology of knowledge*, London: Routledge & Kegan Paul, pp 276–323.

Martin, L.H., Gutman, H. and Hutton, P. (1988) *Technologies of the self: a seminar with Michel Foucualt*, London: Tavistock.

Massey, D. (1993) 'Power geometry and a progressive sense of space', in J. Bird, B. Curtis, G. Putnam, G. Robertson and L. Tickner (eds) *Mapping the futures: local cultures, global change*, London: Routledge, pp 60–70.

Massey, D. (1994) *Space, place and gender*, Cambridge: Polity Press.

Massey, D. (1998) 'The spatial construction of youth cultures', in T. Skelton and G. Valentine (eds) *Cool places: geographies of youth culture*, London: Routledge, pp 122–30.

Mauthner, M. (2002) *Sistering: power and change in female relationships*, Basingstoke: Palgrave.

Mauthner, N. and Doucet, A. (2003) 'Reflexive accounts and accounts of reflexivity in qualitative data analysis', *Sociology*, vol 37, no 3, pp 413–31.

Mauthner, N., Parry, O. and Backett-Milburn, K. (1998) 'The data are out there, or are they? Implications for archiving and revisiting qualitative data', *Sociology*, vol 32, no 4, pp 733–45.

May, T. (1996) *Situating social theory*, Buckingham: Open University Press.

Maynard, M. (1989) 'The re-shaping of sociology? Trends in the study of gender', *Sociology*, vol 24, no 2, pp 269–90.

Maynard, M. (1995) 'Beyond the big three: the development of feminist theory into the 1990s', *Women's History Review*, vol 4, no 3, pp 259–81.

Miles, S. (2000) *Youth lifestyles in a changing world*, Buckingham: Open University Press.

Miller, R. (2000) *Researching life stories and family histories*, London: Sage.

Mirza, H.S. (1992) *Young, female and black*, London: Routledge.

Mirza, H.S. (1997) 'Black women in education: a collective movement for social change', in Mirza, H.S. (ed) *Black British feminism: a reader*, London: Routledge, pp 269–77.

Mirza, H. (2008) *Race, gender and educational desire: why black women succeed and fail*, Abingdon: Routledge.

Misztal, B. (2000) *Informality: social theory and contemporary practice*, London: Routledge

Mock, R. (2003) 'Heteroqueer ladies: some performative transactions between gay men and heterosexual women', *Feminist Review*, vol 75, no 1, pp 20–37.

Modood, T. and Acland, T. (1998) *Race and higher education*, London: Policy Studies Institute.

Morgan, D. (2002) 'Men, masculinities and the lifecourse', paper presented at 'Gender and the life course: different methodological approach', MANDEC, Manchester, 11 January.

Nardi, P. (ed) (1999) *Men's friendships*, London: Sage.

Nayak, A. and Kehily, M.J. (2007) *Gender, youth and culture: young masculinities and femininities*, Basingstoke: Palgrave.

Neale, B. and Flowerdew, J. (2003) 'Time, texture and childhood: the contours of longitudinal qualitative research', *International Journal of Social Research Methodology*, vol 6, no 3, pp 189–200.

Nicholas, S., Povey, D., Walker, A. and Kershaw, C. (2005) *Crime in England and Wales, Home Office Statistical Bulletin 2004/5*, London: Research Development and Statistical Directorate.

Nixon, S. (1996) *Hard looks: masculinities, spectatorship and contemporary consumption*, London: UCL Press.

Oakley, A. (1996) 'Gender matters: man the hunter', in H. Roberts and D. Sachdev (eds) *Young people's social attitudes: having their say, the views of 12–19 year olds*, London: Barnardos, pp 23–43.

O'Donnell, M. and Sharpe, S. (2000) *Uncertain masculinities: youth, ethnicity and class in contemporary Britain*, London: Routledge.

Pateman, C. (1988) *The sexual contract*, Cambridge: Polity Press.

Pilkington, H. and Johnson, R. (2003) 'Peripheral youth: relations of identity and power in global/ local context', *European Journal of Cultural Studies*, vol 6, no 3, pp 259–83.

Platt, L. (2005) *Migration and social mobility: the life chances of Britain's ethnic minority population*, Bristol: The Policy Press, for Joseph Rowntree Foundation.

Plummer, K. (1995) *Telling sexual stories: power, change and social worlds*, London: Routledge.

Plummer, K. (2001) *Documents of life 2: an invitation to a critical humanism*, London: Sage.

Plumridge, L. and Thomson, R. (2003) 'Longitudinal qualitative studies and the reflexive self', *International Journal of Social Research Methodology*, vol 6, no 3, pp 213–22.

Polkinghorne, D.E. (1995) 'Narrative configuration in qualitative analysis', in A. Hatch and R. Wisniewski (eds) *Life history and narrative*, Qualitative Studies Series 1, London: Falmer, pp 5–23.

Pollard, A. with Filer, A. (1996) *The social world of children's learning: case studies of pupils from four to seven*, London: Cassell.

Pollard, A. and Filer, A. (1999) *The social world of pupil career: strategic biographies through primary school*, London: Cassell.

Rabinow, P. (ed) (1984) *The Foucault reader*, London: Penguin.

Rahman, M. and Witz, A. (2003) 'What really matters? The elusive quality of the material in feminist thought', *Feminist Theory*, vol 4, no 3, pp 243–61.

Reay, D. (2002) 'Shaun's story: troubling discourses of white working class masculinities', *Gender and Education*, vol 14, no 3, pp 221–34.

Reay, D. and Lucey, H. (2000) '"I don't really like it here but I don't want to be anywhere else": children and inner city council estates', *Antipode*, vol 34, no 4, pp 410–28.

Reissman, C. (1987) 'When gender is not enough: women interviewing women', *Gender and Society*, vol 1, no 2, pp 172–207.

Reiter, H. (2000) 'Past, present, future – biographical time-structuring of disadvantaged young people at the threshold to employment', Paper presented at NYRIS 7, 7–10 June, Helsinki.

Reynolds, R. (1999) 'Postmodernizing the closet', *Sexualities*, vol 2, no 1, pp 346–9.

Reynolds, T. (1997) '(Mis)representing the black (super)woman', in H.S. Mirza (ed) *Black British feminism: a reader*, London: Routledge, pp 97–112.

Ribbens McCarthy, J. (2006) *Young people's experiences of loss and bereavement: towards an interdisciplinary approach*, Buckingham: Open University Press.

Ribbens McCarthy, J. and Edwards, R. (2001) 'Illuminating meanings of "the private", in sociological thought: a response to Joe Bailey', *Sociology*, vol 35, no 3, pp 765–77.

Ribbens McCarthy, J. and Edwards, R. (2002) 'The individual in public and private: the significance of mothers and children', in A. Carling, S. Duncan and R. Edwards (eds) *Analysing families: morality and rationality in policy and practice*, London: Routledge, pp 199–217.

Roberts, B. (2002) *Biographical research*, Buckingham: Open University Press.

Rose, N. (1996) 'Authority and the genealogy of subjectivity', in P. Heelas, S. Lash, and P. Morris (eds) *Detraditionalization*, Oxford: Blackwell, pp 294-327.

Rose, N. (1999) *Governing the soul: the shaping of the private self*, London: Free Association Books.

Roseneil, S. (2000) 'Queer frameworks and queer tendencies: towards an understanding of postmodern transformations of sexuality', *Sociological Research Online*, vol 5, no 3.

Rosenthal, G. (1993) 'Reconstruction of life stories: principles of selection in generating stories for narrative biographical interviews', in R. Josselson and A. Lieblich (eds) *The narrative study of lives 1*, London: Sage, pp 59–92.

Rosenthal, G. (ed) (1998) *The Holocaust in three generations: families of victims and perpetrators of the Nazi regime*, London: Cassell.

Rutherford, J. (1998) 'A place called home', in J. Rutherford (ed) *Identity: community, culture and difference*, London: Lawrence and Wishart, pp 9–23.

Rutherford, J. (2000) 'The art of life', in J. Rutherford (ed) *The art of life: on living, love and death*, London: Lawrence and Wishart.

Rutter, M. and Smith, D.J. (1995) *Psychosocial disorders in young people: time trends and their causes*, London: Wiley.

Saldana, J. (2003) *Longitudinal qualitative research: analyzing change through time*, Walnut Creek, CA: Altamira Press.

Sartre, J.-P. (1968) *Search for a method*, New York: Vintage.

Schutz, A. (1982) *Life forms and meaning structure*, trans H. Wagner, London: Routledge and Kegan Paul.

Scott, S. and Scott, S. (2001) 'Our mother's daughters: autobiographical inheritance through stories of gender and class', in T. Cosslet, C. Lury and P. Summerfield (eds) *Feminism and autobiography: texts, theories and methods*, London: Routledge, pp 128–40.

Segal, L. (1990) *Slow motion: changing masculinities, changing men*, London: Virago Press.

Segal, L. (1999) *Why feminism? Gender, psychology, politics*, Cambridge: Polity Press.

Seidman, S., Meeks, C. and Taschen, F. (1999) 'Beyond the closet? The changing social meaning of homosexuality in the United States', *Sexualities*, vol 2, no 1, pp 9–34.

Sennett, R. (1986) *The fall of public man*, London: Faber.

Sheller, M. and Urry, J. (2003) 'Mobile transformations of "public" and "private" life', *Theory, Culture and Society*, vol 20, no 3, pp 107–26.

Silverman, D. (1993) *Interpreting qualitative data: methods for analyzing talk, text and interaction*, London: Sage.

Skeggs, B. (1997) *Formations of class and gender: becoming respectable*, London: Sage.

Skeggs, B. (2002) 'Techniques for telling the reflexive self', in T. May (ed) *Qualitative research in action*, London: Sage, pp 349–74.

Skeggs, B. (2004) *Class, self, culture*, London: Routledge.

Smith, D. (1990) *Texts, facts and femininity: exploring the relations of ruling*, London: Routledge.

Spellman, E. (1990) *Inessential woman: problems of exclusion in feminist thought*, London: Women's Press.

Stanley, L. (1992) *The auto/biographical I: theory and practice of feminist auto/biography*, Manchester: Manchester University Press.

Steedman, C. (2000) 'Enforced narratives: stories of another self', in T. Cosslet, C. Lury and P. Summerfield (eds) *Feminism and autobiography: texts, theories and methods*, London: Routledge, pp 25–39.

Stephenson, S. (2000) 'Narrative', in G. Browning, A. Halcli and F. Webster (eds) *Understanding contemporary society: theories of the present*, London: Sage, pp 112–26.

Taussig, M. (1993) *Mimesis and alterity: a particular history of the senses*, London: Routledge.

Temple, B. (1996) 'Time travels: time, oral histories and British-Polish identities', *Time and Society*, vol 5, no 1, pp 85–6.

Thompson, B. (1996) 'Tradition and self in a mediated world', in P. Heelas, S. Lash and P. Morris (eds) *Detraditionalization*, Oxford: Blackwell, pp 89–107.

Thompson, P. (1981) 'Life histories and the analysis of social change', in D. Bertaux (ed) *Biography and society: the life history approach in the social sciences*, London: Sage, pp 289–306.

Thomson, R. (2000) 'Authority', in J. Rutherford (ed) *The art of life: on living, love and death*, London: Lawrence and Wishart, pp 152–63.

Thomson, R. (2003) 'Joined up lives: children and young people in the 21st century', Paper presented at Spotlight Working seminar organised by the National Children's Bureau, Children's Development Unit, NCVO, London, 12 November.

Thomson, R. (2007) 'The qualitative longitudinal case history: practical, methodological and ethical reflections', *Social Policy and Society*, vol 6, no 4, pp 571–82.

Thomson, R. and Holland, J. (2002) 'Imagined adulthood: resources, plans and contradictions', *Gender and Education*, vol 14, no 4, pp 337–50.

Thomson, R. and Holland, J. (2003a) 'Making the most of what you've got: resources, values and inequalities in young people's transitions to adulthood', *Educational Review*, vol 55, no 1, pp 33–46.

Thomson, R. and Holland, J. (2003b) 'Hindsight, foresight and insight: the challenges of longitudinal qualitative research', *International Journal of Social Research Methodology*, vol 6, no 3, pp 233–44.

Thomson, R. and Holland, J. (2005) 'Thanks for the memory: memory books as a methodological resource in biographical research', *Qualitative Research*, vol 5, no 2, pp 201–91.

Thomson, R. and Taylor, R. (2005) 'Between cosmopolitanism and the locals: mobility as a resource in the transition to adulthood', *Young: Nordic Journal of Youth Studies*, vol 13, no 4, pp 327–42

Thomson, R., Plumridge, L. and Holland, J. (2003) 'Longitudinal qualitative research: a developing methodology', *International Journal of Social Research Methodology*, vol 6, no 3, pp 185–8.

Thomson, R., Bell, R., Holland, J., Henderson, S., McGrellis, S. and Sharpe, S. (2002) 'Critical moments: choice, chance and opportunity in young people's narratives of transition', *Sociology*, vol 36, no 2, pp 335–54.

Thomson, R., Holland, J., McGrellis, S., Bell, R., Henderson, S. and Sharpe, S. (2004) 'Inventing adulthood: a biographical approach to understanding youth citizenship', *Sociological Review*, vol 52, no 2, pp 218–93.

Tronto, J. (2003) 'Time's place', *Feminist Theory*, vol 4, no 2, pp 119–38.

Urry, J. (1995) *Consuming places*, London: Routledge.

Urry, J. (2000) *Sociology beyond societies*, London: Routledge.

Van Every, J. (1995) *Heterosexual women changing the family: refusing to be a wife*, London: Taylor and Francis.

Walby, S. (1997) *Gender transformations*, London: Routledge.

Walker, R. and Leisering, L. (1998) 'New tools towards a dynamic science of modern society', in L. Leisering and R. Walker (eds) *The dynamics of modern society*, Cambridge: Polity Press.

Walkerdine,V. (1995) 'Subject to change without notice: psychology, postmodernity and the popular', in S. Pile and N.Thrift (eds) *Mapping the subject: geographies of cultural transformation*, London: Routledge, pp 282–301.

Walkerdine, V., Lucey, H. and Melody, J. (2001) *Growing up girl: psychosocial explorations of gender and class*, Basingstoke: Palgrave.

Walkerdine, V., Lucey, H. and Melody, J. (2002) 'Subjectivity and qualitative method', in T. May (ed) *Qualitative research in action*, London: Sage, pp 179–96.

Weeks, J. (1995) *Invented moralities: sexual values in an age of uncertainty*, Cambridge: Polity Press.

Weeks, J. (1996) 'The idea of a sexual community', *Soundings: A Journal of Politics and Culture*, vol 2, Spring, pp 71–84.

Weeks, J. (2007) *The world we have won: the remaking of erotic and intimate lives*. London: Routledge.

Weeks, J., Heaphy, B. and Donovan, C. (2001) *Same sex intimacies: families of choice and other life experiments*, London: Routledge.

West, P. and Sweeting, H. (1996) 'Nae job, nae future: young people and health in a context of unemployment', *Health and Social Care in the Community*, vol 4, no 1, pp 50–62.

Weston, K. (1991) *Families we choose: lesbians, gays, kinship*, New York: Columbia University Press.

Whelehan, I. (1995) *Modern feminist thought: from second wave to post-feminism*, Edinburgh: Edinburgh University Press.

Wilkinson, H. and Mulgan, G. (1995) *Freedom's children: work, relationships and politics for 18–34 year olds in Britain today*, London: Demos.

Williams, S. (1995) 'Theorising class, health and lifestyles: can Bourdieu help us?', *Sociology of Health and Illness*, vol 17, no 5, pp 577–604.

Wilson, E. (1993) 'Is transgression transgressive?', in J. Bristow and A.Wilson (eds) *Activating theory: lesbian, gay, bisexual politics*, London: Lawrence and Wishart, pp 107–17.

Index

A

Aapola, S. 42
academic feminism and gender inequality
    32-5
Adkins, L. 15, 33-4, 166, 176
adult status
    and couple relationship 86
    and parenthood 8, 42, 94, 97
aesthetic technology of self 161*tab*, 164
'aesthetics of existence' 23-4
agency 2, 14, 41, 130, 171
    and experimentation 156, 157
    and resistance 37
androgyny 40-1
Archer, M. 16, 153
'autobiographical society' 16
autonomy of youth 4

B

Bauman, Z. 163
Bech, H. 39
Beck, U. 29-30, 32, 33, 40, 41, 83
Beck-Gernsheim, E. 29, 30, 83
belonging 7-8, 9, 87
    case histories
        Devon 94, 143, 147-8
        Sherleen 156, 162, 173
Bertaux, D. 13, 20-1, 24, 26, 151
biographical challenges 8-10
biographical impasses 155, 156, 157, 158, 174
    and 'magical solutions' 155, 159
biographical methods 13-17, 178
    and conversation approach 154, 169, 177
biographical motifs 155, 159-60
Bjerrum Nielsen, H. 86
    gender identity and subjectivity 34, 36, 55,
        117, 163, 172
    'magic writing pad' 15, 141, 159
Bottero, W. 35
boundary drawing 37
    case histories
        Devon 89, 92, 94, 99, 102, 107-8, 142, 145,
            158, 167, 171
        Sherleen 50, 51, 52, 64
        Stan 78, 80, 88, 98
Bourdieu, P. 25, 26, 153, 165
    habitus 15, 155
    on interviews 17, 22
    and reflexivity 171-6
    social fields 24, 31, 160
Brannen, J. 43, 156
Bruner, J. 17, 21, 26
Butler, J. 37

Butt, T. 166
Byrne, B. 16-17

C

care system: Devon (case study) 90
Cartmel, F. 41
case histories 2, 10
    data sets 181
    method-in-practice and longitudinal case
        histories 13-27, 178
    see also Devon; Karin; Sherleen; Stan
challenges in youth transitions 9
choice biographies 9, 40, 171
Cohen, P. 159
confidence
    case histories
        Devon 100, 103-4, 105, 106, 142-3, 157-8
        Sherleen 48, 62
Connell, R.W. 21, 30, 38, 68, 87, 88
consumption 4
    Stan (case study) 73-6, 78, 79-80
    and technology of self 161, 164
conversation and unfolding biographies 154-
    69, 177
'corporate masculinity' 68, 71, 86, 87, 164,
    175-6
cosmopolitanism: Stan (case study) 168
couple relationships 8, 32
    case histories
        Devon 148-9
        Karin 126, 127, 157
        Sherleen 135
        Stan 78, 80-1, 83-6, 88, 156
    see also intimacy/intimate relationships
Crompton, R. 39

D

debt: Stan (case study) 79, 156
Delacroix, C. 20-1, 24, 151
dependency
    gender and 'co-resourced household' 35
    of young people on family 4, 8, 9, 88, 156,
        168
        extended dependency 5, 42, 136-7
        need to leave family home 86, 162
        return to family home 97
        and transport 7, 74
    see also independent living
detraditionalisation of gender 29-30, 33, 35-7,
    176-7
    and young people 2, 39-43, 138-9, 171
        and reflexivity 171, 172, 174, 176, 177
Devon (case study) 89-109, 134, 157-8, 171
    case history data set 181

family life 90-5, 107-8, 143-6, 147-8, 149-50, 174-5
gender order and mediums for living 161-2
exclusion and spatial horizons 166-7
and technologies of self 161, 163, 164-5
intimate relationships 93, 106-7, 148-50
and play 99-100, 102-8, 146-7
sexual identity 90-1, 93-4, 95, 146-7
and erotic technology of self 161, 164-5
gay scene and sexual relations 102-8, 148-50
and reflexivity 175
and work environment 97-101
and work 89, 95-101, 141-2
disembedding/re-embedding: Devon (case study) 108-9
disinvestment/disidentification 160, 165-6
division of labour
gender and social change 29, 30, 42
Stan's relationship 84, 85
Donovan, C. 39
'doubleness' in women's lives 30, 40, 174
drinking and young people's well-being 4, 7
driving and independence 74
drug-taking and young people's well-being 7
Du Bois-Reymond, M. 40

E

Economic and Social Research Council
Children 5–16: Growing up in the 21st century 18
Youth, citizenship and social change programme 18
education
and case histories
Karin 111-18, 130
Sherleen 46-9, 52-4, 60, 66, 134-5, 137-8, 163-4, 173
Stan 68, 69, 70, 71-2
educational achievement and careers 45-9
expansion of higher education 4
as field of existence 161
and identity 48, 50, 57
informal school culture 49-52
Inventing Adulthoods findings 5-6
minority ethnic groups 4, 5, 10
see also higher education
Egerton, M. 39-40
erotic technology of self 161
ethnic groups *see* minority ethnic groups
exclusion: Devon (case study) 166-7
experimentation and agency 2, 8
case histories
Karin 125, 127, 130, 157, 164
Sherleen 47, 50, 163
Stan 10, 81, 156, 157, 168, 176

F

Fahey, T. 31

family and family life
case histories
Devon 90-5, 107-8, 143-6, 147-8, 149-50, 174-5
Karin 116-17, 127-9, 130, 174
Sherleen 52-62, 64, 65, 136-9, 140, 155, 162, 167-8, 174
Stan 68, 69, 81-6, 87, 162, 174-5
and fields of existence 161, 162, 163
gender and 'co-resourced household' 35
and gender identities 174
as resource and support 4, 8, 140
see also dependency: of young people on family; home; parenthood; parents
'fateful biographical moment' 78, 159
feminism
and couple relationships 83
and gender and social change 30, 31-5
academic feminism and gender inequality 32-5
and masculinity 38-9
and mobility 166
and young people 41-3
'fields of existence' 23-4, 160, 161-3, 169, 178
financial dependency 4
financial independence/security 74, 82-3, 94
Finnegan, R. 26
Foucault, M. 23-4, 63, 153, 160, 163, 165
friendships
and gay lifestyle 92, 103-4, 106, 107
and informal school culture 50-1
and intimate relationships 84, 121-7
and segregation in Northern Ireland 111-12
and youth cultures in Northern Ireland 112, 118-21, 123, 124
Fuller, M. 46
Furlong, A. 41

G

gang culture 6
gay young people *see* lesbian and gay young people
Geertz, C. 21
gender
female friendships 121-7
gender order and mediums for living 160-8, 169
and informal school culture 49-50
and social change 29-44
and detraditionalisation 33, 39-43
sociological interpretations 29-39
and young people 39-43
see also detraditionalisation of gender; gender identities; gender subjectivity
gender identities 2, 36-7
case histories
Devon 90-1, 93-4, 95, 146-7, 164-5, 175
Sherleen 55, 57-62, 66, 173
Stan 68, 71, 86, 87, 88, 156, 164, 175-6
and education 48, 50, 57

and gender subjectivity 15, 34, 36, 55, 57,
    117, 147, 163
    and reflexivity 172-6
    'good girl'/'bad girl' subject positions 41-2,
    125-6
    see also masculinity
gender subjectivity 34, 36
    case histories
        Devon 147, 175
        Karin 117, 173-4
        Sherleen 55, 57, 173
    and home 163
    and reflexivity 172-6
geographical mobility 87, 166, 167
    see also social mobility; travel
Giddens, A. 38, 39, 40, 41, 78, 83, 176
    and gender and social change 30, 31
    and 'reflexive project of self' 15-16, 153, 155,
    158-9
'girl power' discourse 42
girls
    educational achievement 5
        Sherleen case study 46-9, 52-4, 60, 66, 134,
        163-4
    'good girl'/'bad girl' subject positions 41-2,
    125-6

H

habitus 15, 155, 172
Hall, K. 24
Hannerz, U. 168
health *see* well-being
Heaphy, B. 38, 39
Hearn, J. 38
heterodoxy and reflexivity 172-6
higher education
    attitudes in case histories
        Sherleen 46-7, 134
        Stan's motivational crisis 68, 69, 70-1
    expansion 4, 5-6
Hollway, W. 26
home
    and belonging: Devon (case study) 94, 143,
    147-8
    establishing home life and adult status 8, 86
    as field of existence 162-3
    see also family and family life
homosexuality *see* lesbian and gay young
    people
Hubbard, P. 95

I

identification *see* investments/identifications
identity
    case histories
        Karin and education and style 116
        Sherleen and martial arts 60, 61, 62-5, 163
        and Stan's religious conversion 78-9
    and research methods 15-17, 19-22
    see also gender identities; sexual identity
incursion 157

independent living
    case histories
        Devon 90-1, 92, 96, 143
        Sherleen 139
        Stan 86
individualisation
    gender and social change 29, 30, 33-4, 35, 66
    and young people 2, 130
    and social class 40-1
inequality
    gender inequality 29-30, 31-2, 33
    men and gender equality 38
information and communication technology
    3-4
innovation and tradition 2, 11, 36, 43, 111,
    171, 177
intergenerational change 10, 66, 87, 146, 174
    Sherleen's family 137-9, 167-8
    and social mobility 116-17, 167-8
internet 3
'interview society' 16
interviews and narrative style 16-17, 22
intimacy/intimate relationships
    case histories
        Devon 93, 106-7, 148-50
        Karin 117-18, 121-2, 123-7, 128-9
        Sherleen 50-2, 55-62, 134-5
        Stan 77-8, 79, 80-1, 83-6, 88
    and family background 8
    and friendships
        female friendships 121-7
        male friendships 84
    and gender and social change 30, 31
    and lesbian and gay practices 39
    and young people 40
    see also home
Inventing Adulthoods study 1-11
    areas covered 5-8
    method-in-practice 17-27
investments/identifications 160, 161, 165-6
Irwin, S. 35

J

Jamieson, L. 31-2, 41, 83
Jefferson, T. 26

K

Karin (case study) 111-30, 157, 158, 171
    case history data set 181
    education 111-18, 130
    family life 116-17, 127-9, 130, 174
    gender identity and reflexivity 173-4
    gender order and mediums for living 161
        and aesthetic technology of self 164
        and spatial and social horizons 167
    intimate relationships 117-18, 121-2, 123-7,
    128-9
    play 118-27, 130

L

labour market: demise of youth labour market 4, 6
Langdridge, D. 166
Lasch, C. 31
Lash, S. 108, 172
Lawler, S. 16, 20, 133
lesbian and gay young people
　case histories
　　Devon 89–109, 148–50
　　Karin and bisexuality 125–6, 126–7
　detraditionalisation and gender 39
　and educational achievement 5
life chances 4
　and education 47
life stories 16–17
　and life histories 20–1
life-history research 13–14, 20–1, 22–3, 178
　see also biographical methods
living arrangements
　case histories
　　Devon 90–1, 92, 96, 143
　　Sherleen 139, 162
　　Stan 86, 162
　and home as field of existence 162–3
　see also dependency; independent living
local
　and mobility 7–8
　Sherleen (case study) 139–41, 167–8
longitudinal research 2, 178–9
　and biographical methods 14–15
　case history data sets 181
　method-in-practice for constructing case histories 13–27, 178
　　conversation approach 154–69
　　creating case histories and secondary analysis 17–22
　　and identity in process 19–22
　　stages of analysis 22–7
　　temporal dimension 2, 13–14, 133–4, 150–1, 154, 155–60
　　validity and data 25–7
Lovell, T. 36, 156, 174
Lucey, H. 41–2, 166
Lury, C. 120

M

McDonald, K. 120
McGrellis, S. 111
McLeod, J. 15, 24, 133
McNay, L. 31, 32, 166, 177
　and Foucault 23, 163
　gender identities 36–7
　and reflexivity 102, 108, 172
　resilience of gender inequality 33
McRobbie, A. 41, 42
'magic writing pad' 15, 141, 159
'magical solutions' 155, 159
Mannheim, K. 3, 9
marriage: case study views 56, 57, 85

martial arts and identity: Sherleen (case study) 60, 61, 62–5, 163
masculinity
　and feminist theory 38–9
　life-history research 21
　masculine identities and case histories
　　Devon 96, 147, 175
　　Stan 68, 71, 86, 87, 88, 156, 164, 175–6
Massey, D. 151, 166
Mauthner, N. 19
mediums for living and gender order 160–8, 169
Melody, J. 41–2
men
　and gender equality 38
　and gender inequality 30
　see also masculinity
mental health problems 5
middle classes
　and deferred parenthood 39, 82
　downward social mobility 10, 168
　and higher education 4, 5
　and work
　　'corporate masculinity' 68, 71, 86, 87, 175–6
　　part-time work 6
Miller, R. 13, 14, 25
mimetic faculty 158
minority ethnic groups
　gender and education 4, 5, 10
　Sherleen case study 46–9, 52–4, 60, 66, 134
Mirza, H. 46, 173
Misztal, B. 31
mobile phone use 3
mobility
　and belonging 7–8
　geographical mobility 87, 166
　see also social mobility
Morgan, D. 16, 38
motivational problems: Stan (case study) 67–73, 88
Mulgan, G. 40–1

N

narrative analysis approach 26
narrative style and life stories 17, 22–3
neighbourhood and young people's well-being 6
New Labour and 'good girl' subject 41
Nielsen, H. Bjerrum *see* Bjerrum Nielsen, H.
Nilsen, A. 156
normal and choice biographies 9, 40, 171

O

Oakley, A. 41
orthodoxy and reflexivity 172–6

P

parenthood
　and adult status 8, 42, 94, 97

case study views 56, 57, 81, 82, 93, 97, 127, 128
middle classes and deferred parenthood 39, 82
parents
  case study relations with parents
    Devon 90, 91-2, 107, 143-6, 149-50, 166, 174-5
    Karin 116-17, 127, 128-9, 166, 174
    Sherleen 54-5, 57-62, 64, 65, 136-7, 174
    Stan 81-3, 174-5
    see also family and family life
Parks, R. 37
particular: focus on 3
Pateman, C. 32
pedagogical technology of self: Sherleen 161, 163-4
performativity and gender 37, 38-9
personal relationships *see* intimacy/intimate relationships
Piper, M. 42
play
  case histories
    Devon 99-100, 102-8, 146-7
    Karin 118-27, 130
  see also consumption
Plummer, K. 14, 16, 17, 21, 22-3, 177
Polkinghorne, D.E. 26
popular culture and confessional form 16
post-structuralist theory and gender and social change 36-7
power relations and reflexivity 172-6
private/public spheres and gender 31
'project of action' approach 15
psychological disorders 7
public/private spheres and gender 31

Q
'qualitative longitudinal method' 14-15

R
Reay, D. 166, 171-2
rebellion and Karin's story 157, 173
reflexivity 171-6, 177
  'reflexive project of self' 15-16, 153, 154, 155, 158-9
  reflexive resources 22
Reissman, C. 16
relationships *see* intimacy/intimate relationships
religious belief
  Karin 129
  Stan's conversion 76-8
research study *see* Inventing Adulthoods study
resistant practices
  education and authority 113-15, 116, 130
  and gender 37
responsibility: Devon (case study) 94-5, 142-3, 165
retraditionalisation and gender 33-4, 39
risk society and gender 29

Roberts, B. 13
Rose, N. 31, 36
Rosenthal, G. 13
Rudberg, M. 34, 36, 55, 86, 117, 163, 172
Rutherford, J. 15

S
Saldana, J. 24
Sartre, J.-P. 21
'saturation' in research 14, 21
  case history data 22, 25
Savage, M. 39-40
Schutz, A. 15-16
secondary analysis of data 19-20
Segal, L. 32-3, 38
self
  'reflexive project of self' 15-16, 153, 154, 155, 158-9
  and Stan (case study) 67, 73
  technologies of self 23-4, 154, 160, 161*tab*, 163-8
self-improvement and minority ethnic groups 52-4
Sennett, R. 31
serendipity 14
serendipity and unfolding lives 2, 11, 14, 150, 155-6, 161
sexual identity
  Devon (case study) 90-1, 93-4, 95, 146-7, 175
    gay scene and sexual relations 102-8, 148-50
    and technology of self 161, 164-5
    and workplace 97-101
    and fields of existence 162
  Karin (case study) and bisexuality 125-6, 126-7
sexual relations
  case histories
    Devon 104-8, 148-50
    Karin 121-2, 124-7
    Stan 83-4
  gender and social change 31-2, 51
  see also intimacy/intimate relationships; sexual identity
'shape shifters' 156
Sharpe, S. 45, 67
Sherleen (case study) 45-66, 134-41, 155-6, 158, 171
  case history data set 181
  education 45-52, 57, 60, 66, 134, 137-8, 163-4, 173
  family life 52-62, 64, 65, 136-9, 140, 155, 162, 167-8, 174
  gender identity 55, 57-62, 66
  and reflexivity 173, 174
  gender order and mediums for living 161, 162
    and pedagogical technology of self 163-4
    and spatial and social mobility 167-8
  intimate relationships 50-2, 55-62, 134-5

martial arts and identity 60, 61, 62–5, 163
Silverman, D. 16
Skeggs, B. 165, 166
Smith, D. 174
social change *see* gender: and social change
social class and youth transitions 4, 39–40
 higher education 5–6
 and individualisation 40–1
 work 6
 see also middle classes; working classes
social fields 24, 31, 160
 and reflexivity 172
social horizons 160, 161, 163
social mobility 7–8, 42, 87, 166
 and gender identity 173–4
 and spatial and social horizons 167–8, 171
 downward social mobility 10, 168
 working classes and higher education 5, 112,
 116–17
spatial dimensions 151, 157
 gender order and mediums for living 160–8,
 169
 gender and social change 36
spatial horizons 160, 161
spending *see* consumption
Stan (case study) 67–88, 134, 156, 158, 171
 case history data set 181
 consumption and having fun 73–6, 78, 79–
 80, 164
 family life 68, 69, 81–6, 87, 162, 174–5
 gender identity and reflexivity 175–6
 gender order and mediums for living 161
 spatial and social horizons 168
 and technologies of self 161*tab*, 163
 intimate relationships 77–8, 79, 80–1, 83–6,
 88
 religious conversion 76–8
 work and motivation 67–73, 88
Stanley, L. 21, 141
Steedman, C. 90
story-telling 16–17, 177
structural factors and agency 14, 41, 154, 166
subjectivity 15–16, 153
 see also gender subjectivity

T

Taussig, M. 158
technological change 3–4
technologies of self 23–4, 154, 160, 161, 163–8
temporal processes and biographical methods
 2, 13–14, 133–4, 150–1, 154, 155–60
 and reflexive project of self 15–16
Terkel, S. 22
theoretical basis of research method 23–5
 gender and social change 29–34
 and reflexivity 172–3, 174
'thick' account of research 25
Thompson, E.P. 35
Thompson, P. 13–14, 26
Thomson, R. 159
time *see* temporal processes

tradition 176–7
 see also detraditionalisation of gender
transgressive practices and gender 37, 157
transport and dependency 7, 74
travel abroad 7
 and case histories
 Karin 112, 117, 127, 157
 Stan 69–70, 75–6, 81, 84, 87, 156, 168
Tronto, J. 156

U

uncertainty and psychological disorders 7
unemployment: Devon (case study) 95, 96, 97
'unfolding theory' 154
university *see* higher education
Urry, J. 15

V

violence: culture of violence 6, 7
voluntary work: Devon (case study) 97–8, 143

W

Walkerdine, V. 25, 41–2, 87, 165
Weeks, J. 31, 39, 55, 95
well-being: Inventing Adulthoods findings 6–7
Wilkinson, H. 40–1
work *see* working lives
work experience 6
working classes
 Devon and masculine identity 96, 147, 175
 and higher education 4, 5, 112
 mobility and belonging 7, 8
 and shrinking labour market 4, 6
working lives
 case histories
 Devon 89, 95–101, 141–2
 Stan 67–73
 educational achievement and careers 46–9,
 52–4
 gender and social change 29, 30, 33–4, 39–40
 Inventing Adulthoods findings 6
 later transition to 6
 working-class desire to enter labour market
 6
 see also voluntary work

Y

Young People's Social Attitudes Survey 41
youth cultures 9
 in Northern Ireland 112, 118–21, 123, 124
Youth Transitions and Social Change study
 18, 19
Youth Values study 18, 19